MIXING

MIXING

Race, Higher Education,
and the Case of Clyde Kennard

Sherita L. Johnson, Cheryl D. Jenkins,
Loren Saxton Coleman, and Rebecca A. Tuuri

UNIVERSITY PRESS OF MISSISSIPPI / JACKSON

The University Press of Mississippi is the scholarly publishing agency of the Mississippi Institutions of Higher Learning: Alcorn State University, Delta State University, Jackson State University, Mississippi State University, Mississippi University for Women, Mississippi Valley State University, University of Mississippi, and University of Southern Mississippi.

www.upress.state.ms.us

The University Press of Mississippi is a member of the Association of University Presses.

Any discriminatory or derogatory language or hate speech regarding race, ethnicity, religion, sex, gender, class, national origin, age, or disability that has been retained or appears in elided form is in no way an endorsement of the use of such language outside a scholarly context.

Copyright © 2026 by University Press of Mississippi
All rights reserved
Manufactured in the United States of America
∞

Publisher: University Press of Mississippi, Jackson, USA
Authorised GPSR Safety Representative: Easy Access System Europe - Mustamäe tee 50, 10621 Tallinn, Estonia, gpsr.requests@easproject.com

Library of Congress Control Number: 2025042219

Hardback ISBN 978-1-4968-5985-3
Paperback ISBN 978-1-4968-5984-6
Epub single ISBN 978-1-4968-5986-0
Epub institutional ISBN 978-1-4968-5987-7
PDF single ISBN 978-1-4968-5988-4
PDF institutional ISBN 978-1-4968-5989-1

British Library Cataloging-in-Publication Data available

CONTENTS

Acknowledgments VII
Introduction IX

CHAPTER 1.
"A Little Man Who Has Done a Lot of Big Things":
Clyde Kennard in the Civil Rights Movement and *Jet* Magazine 3
    Sherita L. Johnson, Cheryl D. Jenkins, Loren Saxton Coleman, and Rebecca A. Tuuri

CHAPTER 2.
Letters to the Editor: Clyde Kennard's Public Appeals
for Justice and Equality 25
    Sherita L. Johnson

CHAPTER 3.
The Student Printz and Archival Recovery of a Segregated Past 49
    Loren Saxton Coleman and Cheryl D. Jenkins

CHAPTER 4.
"Making Sure His Legacy Did Not Die with Him":
Black Student Activism and the Memory of Clyde Kennard 67
    Rebecca A. Tuuri

EPILOGUE.
Honoring Clyde Kennard 91

Appendixes 109
Notes 121
Index 157

ACKNOWLEDGMENTS

We would like to acknowledge the following individuals, organizations, and other resources for all the institutional, communal, and fiscal support we received in the production of this work:

- USM's College of Arts and Letters, for initial funding of a seed grant to create the Freedom50 Research Group in 2015
- The Mississippi Humanities Council, for awarding a Racial Equity Grant that funded the documentary film as a basis for this book
- The Sixth Street Museum District, Latoya Norman, and Vanessa Molden, for partnering with us to create safe spaces to present public lectures, film screenings, and dialogues about race and reconciliation
- Residents of the Kelly Settlement, north of Hattiesburg, who shared their memories of Clyde Kennard: Gloria Jean Pack, Alvin Eaton, and Ralph Lindsey. Also, special thanks to Ellie Dahmer; her son, Dennis Dahmer; and her daughter, Betty Dahmer.
- USM's Archives and Special Collections, for providing open access to campus publications: *The Student Printz*, *The Unheard Word*, and *The Southerner* yearbook
- Kathleen Feeney, University archivist, Special Collections Research Center, University of Chicago Library, for providing assistance documenting Clyde Kennard's attendance at the university
- Riva Brown, for her work with *The Student Printz* and *The Unheard Word*; also, her collaborative spirit, committed to preserving Clyde Kennard's legacy, while a student activist at USM and now as a colleague at large
- Eddie Holloway, for being a guiding light, supporting all our projects about Clyde Kennard (lectures, a documentary film, and now this book) and sharing oral histories to preserve Hattiesburg's Black history

USM alumni Raylawni Branch, Gwendolyn Elaine Armstrong, Jacqueline Leggett Hayes, Melvin Miller, Charles McArthur, Charlie Jones, Anthony Harris, Alvin Williams, Deborah Gambrell, Isaac Bishop, Robert Taylor, Marcus Cathey, LaKeisha Bryant, Tangee Carter, and Curtis Austin, for sharing their recollections and keeping the memory of Clyde Kennard alive on campus

The University Press of Mississippi editors, especially Emily Bandy, and our anonymous reviewers, for helpful feedback and support.

In full measure, we humbly dedicate *Mixing* to those who truly inspired us the most:

Henry Bethley, whose memory is preserved in all the work we have done to honor Clyde Kennard on USM's campus and within the broader community

Clyde Kennard, whose legacy we strive continually to preserve without compromise

INTRODUCTION

> [I]n all things competitive, merit [must] be used as a measuring stick rather than race . . . [F]or [people] to work together best, they must be trained together in their youth. . . . In school, one learns to appreciate and respect the abilities of the other.
> —CLYDE KENNARD, LETTER TO THE EDITOR,
> "MIXING," *HATTIESBURG AMERICAN*, DECEMBER 6, 1958

Unpretentious and soft-spoken, Clyde Kennard was not the kind of man you would expect to talk about race unabashedly. But as the first Black undergraduate to try to integrate a public college or university in Mississippi, he had an earnest desire to complete his education, and his story has had a lasting impact on the state and nation. Kennard believed that "when merit replaces race as a factor in character evaluation, the most heckling social problem of modern times will have been solved."[1] This is the "integrationist's creed" at the heart of Kennard's appeal for racial equality and social justice. While generations have benefitted from his courage, few, if any, know of Clyde Kennard's determination to succeed against insurmountable odds, including being framed and convicted twice; sentenced to seven years in prison for the felony crime of stealing twenty-five dollars' worth of chicken feed; and subsequently denied medical treatment for cancer while serving jail time for his conviction. Kennard died from advanced complications from cancer at age thirty-six on July 4, 1963.

Shortly before his own murder in June 1963, Mississippi civil rights leader Medgar Evers believed Clyde Kennard's case to be one of the most tragic of the civil rights era. This was echoed years later by renowned civil rights historian John Dittmer, who called Kennard's case the "saddest story of the whole movement" in an interview with investigative journalist Jerry Mitchell. A version of Dittmer's quote was used as the title of Timothy Minchin and John Salmond's pivotal article about Kennard's case. Now

Devery S. Anderson's in-depth biography, *A Slow, Calculated Lynching: The Story of Clyde Kennard*, echoes that idea. Kennard's treatment as he sought to integrate Mississippi Southern College in the 1950s was indeed a travesty and must be acknowledged as such. However, this edited collection seeks to not only illuminate the injustice of what happened to Kennard but also highlight his remarkable life and legacy, especially as seen through his writing and the activism he inspired for generations.[2]

Clyde Kennard was born in Forrest County on June 12, 1927, spent his first three years of life near Hattiesburg, and then spent the next ten in Utica, Mississippi. Kennard's father died shortly after the family had arrived in Utica, but Clyde moved back to the Hattiesburg area with his mother, stepfather, and siblings around 1940. Shortly after his return to Forrest County, he went to live briefly with his sister in Chicago, only to return to Forrest County by 1943.[3] Before completing high school, he entered the military in September 1945 and continued to serve through the Korean War (with a brief stint outside of the military in 1949 and 1950). While he served, he worked in de-Nazification classes, where he taught German youth about American democracy. Because of the timing of his service, Kennard received a World War II Victory award but never served in combat in World War II. He was honorably discharged and earned a Korean Service Medal with one Bronze Star Medal (for service to the United Nations) and a Good Conduct Medal. After securing his GED at the age of twenty-three, he attended Fayetteville State Teachers College from 1950 through 1952 and then the University of Chicago from 1953 until he returned home in the summer of 1955 to help his mother with his family's chicken farm after his stepfather had a debilitating stroke.[4]

While back in Hattiesburg, Kennard wanted to complete his education even if it meant integrating the all-white Mississippi Southern College (MSC).[5] He claimed to work alone, without the help of the NAACP, of which he was youth director for the local Forrest County chapter. He insisted that he just wanted an education and believed that William D. McCain, then president of MSC, would be compelled to do the right thing and admit Kennard when he applied.[6] Around this time, while visiting the home of local NAACP leader Vernon Dahmer, Dahmer's wife, Ellie, asked Kennard why he was continuing to put his life and livelihood at risk in his effort to desegregate the college; he pointed down at Dahmer's young daughter, Betty, and said that he was doing it for her.[7]

Kennard first began his attempts to enroll at Southern in November 1955 but was denied the next month because he did not have five recommendations from alumni (who were all white). He tried again in early winter 1956 to have the alumni recommendation requirement waived but was told by President McCain that he would need to be cleared by the higher education board in Jackson and was ultimately denied a waiver.[8] Two and a half years later, in fall 1958, Kennard let McCain know again of his desire to attend Southern. Once again, McCain enforced the technical requirements that were difficult to fill. Applicants still needed five recommendations from alumni who had known the student for more than two years and would attest to their moral character.[9] Meanwhile, Kennard wrote an eloquent editorial in the *Hattiesburg American*, the first of a series he penned during his entire ordeal, about his desire to enter the college.

Some in the community seemed to support Kennard's attempts to enroll at Southern. Journalist P. D. East was a white supporter of Kennard's attempt. He claimed that some Southern students also supported Kennard's bid to join the college.[10] Mississippi's spy organization, the Mississippi State Sovereignty Commission, interviewed white employers of Kennard who spoke positively about his character. Rabbi Charles Mantinband was a friend of Kennard, but many more whites wanted him gone. According to the Sovereignty Commission, Dudley Conner, a lawyer in town and founder of the local Citizens Council, claimed that he could find the means to remove Kennard. In December 1958, John Reiter, the first chief of security at MSC, had been approached by individuals who proposed that dynamite be put in Kennard's car so that it would explode and kill him when he started the car. Others commented that liquor could be planted in the car (which is exactly what happened after Kennard was on campus in September 1959) to violate local statutes of prohibition. Both members and nonmembers of the Citizens Council tried to keep Kennard from trying to enroll at MSC through social and economic pressure.[11]

Behind the scenes, the Sovereignty Commission (with help from Governor J. P. Coleman and President McCain) scrambled to encourage Black local leaders, including Rev. R. W. Woullard, N. R. Burger, C. E. Roy, and others in the community to sway Kennard from his attempts. While these local leaders agreed to try to speak with Kennard, they also tried to pressure the Sovereignty Commission to build a junior college in the area that would serve Black students. Recognizing their small but significant bargaining power in this situation, they tried to do something beneficial for the Black community if Kennard could not go to MSC. That pressure worked once. Kennard decided not to continue to try to enroll in early winter 1959, as he had indicated in 1958.[12]

Still, no one could stop Kennard from eventually pursuing his goal. He tried again in early fall 1959. Once again, McCain tried to dissuade him, but Kennard said that he would continue with his effort. There seemed to be nothing negative that could justify blocking him. Even administrators within Southern acknowledged that he was a man of high integrity and "was not offensive in any way."[13] This time, he was denied admission because he seemingly altered his medical papers and was not in good academic standing at the University of Chicago. As Kennard returned to his car after his meeting, Constables Lee Daniels and Charlie Ward arrested him for possession of whiskey and reckless driving. Although Sovereignty Commission papers suggest that the commission and state police had nothing to do with the framing, and it was likely a product of the constables themselves with a tipoff from someone at MSC, they did not stop the bogus charges and conviction from proceeding. Likewise, District Attorney Daniel W. Dabbs continued to support the case, even though he was "shocked at the way the arrest took place" since it looked like the liquor was planted from Kennard's car. This did not stop the local justice of the peace, T. C. Hobby, setting Kennard's bond at $600 and ultimately finding him guilty.[14]

John Reiter, MSC's head of security, had apparently been shown a warrant for arrest based on lunacy before Kennard came to campus. He was "elated" that Kennard had been arrested and claimed that he was not aware of the reckless driving or illegal possession of whiskey charge.[15] Regardless of the details, it is clear from Mississippi Sovereignty Commission records that officials at Mississippi Southern College complied with and possibly aided in Kennard's first framing.[16]

Despite this false arrest, Clyde Kennard did not back down. He immediately appealed the conviction. He also wrote two more editorials that were published in the *Hattiesburg American* in late September 1959 (a few days before his conviction) and February 1960 (a few months afterward). As Minchin and Salmond have pointed out, the Sovereignty Commission recognized that Kennard had secured funding for the appeal of his conviction, and he had claimed that he might file a suit in federal court to enter MSC. White authorities worried that it would be difficult to find justification to deny Kennard admission again.[17]

When this misdemeanor conviction did not stop Kennard, he was framed for stealing five bags of chicken feed valued at twenty-five dollars in September 1960. Johnny Lee Roberts, a teenager, claimed that Kennard had instructed him to steal the chicken feed. An all-white jury found Kennard guilty, and Judge Stanton Hall sentenced him to seven years at Parchman penitentiary, while Roberts only received five-years' probation.

Since Kennard had now been convicted of a felony, he could no longer be admitted to any college or university in Mississippi.[18]

Civil rights groups, including the NAACP and SNCC, along with other local organizations around Mississippi, fought to have Kennard released from Parchman. They first highlighted his bogus conviction and later, after publicizing in fall 1962 that he had developed a severe stomach condition, fought against his unjust treatment in being forced to stay at Parchman while he was so ill. Growing pressure from SNCC-led letter-writing campaigns and Black activists and celebrities (including Dick Gregory), along with a visit by *Jet* magazine reporter Larry Still in January 1963 and pressure from R. Jess Brown, Kennard's lawyer, persuaded Governor Ross Barnett to release Kennard for medical treatment. By the time Kennard was released from prison, his cancer was far advanced. He died tragically on July 4, 1963.[19]

While Clyde Kennard's case is a travesty of justice, we examine his writings about segregation / school integration, evidence of student activism in journalism, and the generational legacy of Black students at the University of Southern Mississippi (USM), which Mississippi Southern College became in 1962, to understand better the complexity of his martyrdom. By revealing the conversations about race (both from Kennard and later university students) that were happening (or not) between white and Black members of the university and the local Hattiesburg community, we come to understand the tensions, limitations, and possibilities of dialogue as a path to change. We also move beyond seeing Clyde Kennard as only a victim and instead see him as an agent who helped achieve Black empowerment, social justice, and (possibly) racial reconciliation.

Our work contributes to growing volumes of interdisciplinary civil rights studies. Scholars are only beginning to examine the historical legacies of slavery and segregation on higher education in America. Craig Steven Wilder's *Ebony and Ivy: Race, Slavery, and the Troubled History of America's Universities* (2014) attracted wide appeal beyond academia by excavating archival records of human bondage that helped to finance Ivy league schools. Since its publication, numerous universities have launched research initiatives about slavery—Brown, Harvard, Yale, Princeton, Georgetown, Rutgers, and, most recently, the University of Mississippi—but few turn to a more recent past to consider school segregation's lingering taint. If so, studies of *Brown v. Board of Education* generally turn to legal trials or individual memoirs of students traumatized by the experience of elementary and secondary school desegregation. In higher education, countless works have presented the case of James Meredith's integration of the University of Mississippi, for instance, given the broad media attraction it drew. While both historical perspectives yield revealing stories of the civil rights movement, *Mixing* seeks to bring critical awareness to the culture of segregation as presented by archival documents, oral histories, and print media that privilege the perspective of ordinary individuals. Thus, our work looks at the movement from the ground up, focusing on the local scene that bolstered a national outcry for justice and equality.

Mixing consists of an introduction, four chapters, an epilogue, and an appendix. With the exception of chapter 1, each chapter looks at the Clyde Kennard case from one disciplinary angle of inquiry—probing archives for news media, oral histories, and institutional records—to recover materials that might lead to a fuller understanding of the man and the times in which he tried to survive. Ultimately, using such materials, each scholar examines the construction of race in narratives that document progressive struggles for equality and justice.

That generations of African Americans (and other minorities) have studied and worked at what is now the University of Southern Mississippi is indeed a testament to Clyde Kennard's sacrifice. Our experience, as the Freedom50 Research Group, demonstrates interdisciplinary (and interracial) collaborations over an extended period since we have a mutual interest in studying progressive actions to achieve social justice, especially in Mississippi with its history of segregation.[20] We therefore consider the extent to which measurable milestones appear decades later as traceable to the case of Clyde Kennard. Understanding Kennard's integrationist philosophy, the role of print media to document social history and to advocate for change, and student activism on a college campus helps us to recognize the (in)visible signs of cultural change that have occurred at a local site marked by historical trauma. This book therefore accounts for the ways memory and narratives are formed by and about a place and how individuals and an institution in the present negotiate spaces of historical significance.

The collectively written chapter 1, "'A Little Man Who Has Done a Lot of Big Things': Clyde Kennard in the Civil Rights Movement and *Jet* Magazine," examines coverage of Kennard in *Jet* (apx. 1959–1997), considering its efforts to document the typical experiences of African Americans in the struggle for civil rights. Essential to understanding the broader movement in a local setting, this publication brings attention to Kennard's case for a national audience. We therefore present the archival recovery of Kennard by considering his stature as an activist who is forgotten and/or ignored in standard civil rights histories, weigh the significance of how this publication documents Kennard's case in light of its coverage of other major events (e.g., the murder of Emmett Till) in the movement, and analyze the crafting of narratives in print culture that use Black bodies as texts to incite change.

In chapter 2, "Letters to the Editor: Clyde Kennard's Public Appeals for Justice and Equality," Sherita L. Johnson analyzes Kennard's series of letters published in the *Hattiesburg American*, a local newspaper that he used as a platform to enlighten the public about "the race problem" and the solutions of integration. Using Kennard's own words, this chapter examines his role as an activist-intellectual in the protest tradition of African American literature and culture. Kennard grapples with the constructions of "race" (as a social and political concept) and power relations that determine the progress of African Americans. That he felt compelled to launch a public campaign for integration, however, was based solely on his personal circumstances. The series of letters Kennard wrote to the editor as published in the *Hattiesburg American* makes a clear case for social change and racial progress. He presents a pragmatic analysis of a segregated society and conveys it with an intellectual poise, grounded by historical and philosophical allusions as well as logical reasoning. In these open letters that inform the public about the discriminatory practices of a state college, Clyde Kennard is *not* a victim, though his public image is later framed by others as such. We must instead consider how Kennard uses writing as a form of activism, to assert his civil rights, promote social justice, and advocate racial equity in higher education.

In chapter 3, "*The Student Printz* and Archival Recovery of a Segregated Past," Loren Saxton Coleman and Cheryl D. Jenkins illuminate how newspapers help make sense of the intricacies of the nexus of social, political, and economic structures necessary to build and sustain community. As cultural artifacts, they provide evidence of the complexities of culture and the changing patterns of social and cultural life. Student newspapers traditionally are recognized as agents of change and can be examined to help understand the formation and constantly evolving university community, particularly during the era of segregation and immediately following the implementation of desegregation at many universities in the South. The student press in this era often served as the channel for information and perspective regarding race, segregation, desegregation, and student activism on college campuses. The distinct narratives found in student newspapers have historically positioned these papers to serve as both "university ambassador" and "social crusader," especially when the papers highlighted these particularly complex issues during the late 1950s and 1960s following the historic *Brown v. Board of Education* case in 1954.

This chapter examines how student media at the University of Southern Mississippi has historically covered issues of race on its campus and specifically how the issues of segregation and desegregation affected students at this public institution. Established in 1927, *The Student Printz* is the university's official student newspaper. Coleman and Jenkins explore student perspectives on race from 1955 through 2015 in this chapter, with specific emphasis on the Clyde Kennard case in 1955, 1958, and the early 1990s. For more context and historical perspective, the chapter also explores the content of *The Unheard Word*, an alternative publication distributed on campus from October 1990 to March 1993. It presents the perspective of African American students not presented in the official "voice" of the student press. *The Unheard Word* was created by Riva Brown, who was also the first Black editor of *The Student Printz*.

In chapter 4, "'Making Sure His Legacy Did Not Die with Him': Black Student Activism and the Memory of Clyde Kennard," Rebecca A. Tuuri examines the legacy of Kennard as seen through the first generations of African American students on the University of Southern Mississippi campus (USM) after the university's integration in 1965. Despite the enduring racism at USM, several individuals chose to attend as the university's first generation of African American students. Few had activist reasons for attending—most attended because it was affordable and local; like Kennard, many still needed to take care of family members while attending college. Once on campus, however, the students learned (and shared information) about Kennard, his unsuccessful attempts to integrate Mississippi Southern College, his framing, and his tragic death.

Long before the Mississippi State Sovereignty papers were open to the public or the university acknowledged Kennard's impact, Black students on campus kept his memory alive. Even students who were not openly active in civil rights work viewed Kennard as a role model, recognized the tragedy of his example, and pushed for students to remember him. Such students at USM linked his attempt to their continuation of integration on the campus. The students also used his bold insistence on equal access as a model for Black pride. Despite the massive literature on the pre-1965 civil rights movement in the South and autobiographies and biographies of key figures, only a few scholars have examined the collective experiences of the first generations of Black students at predominantly white institutions of higher education in the South after integration. The bulk of literature on the history of the Black campus movement has focused on the North and West in the late 1960s and 1970s. This chapter adds to the body of literature on Southern colleges and universities, where Black college students were doing some of the most dangerous and challenging civil rights work of the era.

Finally, in the collectively written epilogue, "Honoring Clyde Kennard," we show how our work is a continuation of prior efforts to bring attention to the case of Clyde Kennard. The measure of progress is evident in phases of student activism, community support, and campus leadership. The University of Southern Mississippi has taken steps to atone for its role in the injustice that Clyde Kennard experienced while trying to receive an education. We recognize, therefore, more recent work to commemorate Kennard, including the establishment of the Kennard Scholars Program in 2014; the erecting of a historical marker as part of the Mississippi Freedom Trail on campus in 2018; granting Kennard an honorary degree, posthumously, also in 2018; and the naming for Kennard a section of Highway 49 that runs parallel to USM's campus in 2021. We also reflect on our work as the Freedom50 Research Group that has helped reignite much of the interest in Kennard on campus. Finally, we conclude our study by acknowledging that Clyde Kennard's sacrifice for and contributions to institutes of higher learning in the United States, a progressive Mississippi, and the national conscience is immeasurable.

MIXING

CHAPTER 1

"A LITTLE MAN WHO HAS DONE A LOT OF BIG THINGS"

Clyde Kennard in the Civil Rights Movement and *Jet* Magazine

SHERITA L. JOHNSON, CHERYL D. JENKINS, LOREN SAXTON COLEMAN, AND REBECCA A. TUURI

Small in stature, mild-mannered, and philosophical, Clyde Kennard was not a revolutionary who led the civil rights movement in protest marches or delivered fiery speeches before throngs of people, but in the pages of *Jet*, he was sanctified. Reports describe Kennard as a courageous, tenacious, teetotalist scholar and US Army veteran. His military career was deemed exceptional for a young Black man, and his heroic attempts at integration consecrated him. How Kennard appears in the media, however, does not match the magnitude of the man's stature in US civil rights history. Unsung, Kennard was the first undergraduate student to try to integrate a public Mississippi college or university, and others, including James Meredith, later followed his historic lead.[1] Readers of the magazine were introduced to Kennard shortly after his third attempt to integrate Mississippi Southern College in the fall of 1959, then for the next four decades, they were reminded of his tragic life as part of *Jet*'s mission to "inform, educate and entertain readers . . . [while] pleading the cause of Blacks and serving as an advocate in the struggle for freedom and justice."[2]

The coverage of Kennard in *Jet* has a unique tone compared to the often-limited coverage in what was considered to be mainstream media during this same period. For one, the small digest-sized publication had quickly established itself as the preeminent source of news relevant to Black life and culture. As a magazine source, it could stress specific and subjective topics and current issues, which were of general interest, compared to newspapers, which traditionally offered brief and objective reports. During this period, the publication also stood as a testament to the power of Black magazines as a news and information source and as a distinctive political tool in the Black community.

Our focus on *Jet* brings due attention to the development of Black print culture in the United States and the broader impact of its reporting on civil rights struggles, especially at a local level.[3] Black newspapers and magazines have a long history traceable to the early nineteenth century. *Jet*'s coverage of civil rights struggles in the twentieth century has as its foundation abolitionist newspapers created by African Americans such as *Freedom's Journal* (1827–1829) and *The Colored American* (1837–1842). Also, Frederick Douglass's *The North Star* (1847–1851) and, later, the *Frederick Douglass Paper* (1851–1860) became the most widely circulated Black newspapers that featured especially the colored conventions movement, political organizing by African Americans throughout the nineteenth century.[4] The trajectory from these Black newspapers extends to *The Colored American Magazine*, appearing around the turn of the twentieth century as the most immediate predecessor to *Jet*. "From 1900 to 1909, during a period of intensifying racial violence and Black disfranchisement in the United States, *The Colored American Magazine* served a vital role in promoting the development of African American literature, protesting injustice, and contesting dominant representations of African American culture and history."[5] Within this sociohistorical context, we examine primary materials—original copies of *Jet* now digitized and available to the public—as ephemeral objects that jolt collective memories of a time, a place(s), and a people as their experiences were documented in the magazine. We want our investigation to generate dialogue with others working in the burgeoning field of Black print culture studies. Therefore, our interdisciplinary collaboration on this chapter (and the entire project) is a necessary and deliberate methodology for (re)evaluating an extraordinary Black man's life as chronicled in print, preserved in cultural memory, and, unfortunately, neglected in civil rights history.

In this chapter, we examine coverage of Clyde Kennard in *Jet* from 1959 to 1997, considering its efforts to document the typical experiences of African Americans in the struggle for civil rights. Essential to understanding the broader movement in a local setting, this publication brings attention to Kennard's case for a national audience. Therefore, we recognize the significance of archival recovery in telling "the Clyde

Kennard story" by reconstructing in real time chronological events and by investigating media constructs of a historical actor. We weigh the significance of how *Jet* documents Kennard's case in light of its coverage of other major events in the movement, reconsider how historians have overlooked Kennard and *Jet*'s coverage of his case, and analyze the crafting of narratives in Black print culture that use Black bodies as texts to incite change to understand just how Clyde Kennard was indeed "a little man who has done a lot of big things."[6]

IN BLACK AND WHITE: PRINT MEDIA, THE CIVIL RIGHTS MOVEMENT, AND *JET* MAGAZINE

The tradition of Black magazines is consistent with the goals of the Black press and the role that Black newspapers played during the "best-known period of civil rights action in the US." Between 1953 and 1970, Black Americans became involved in direct disruptive action often in the form of boycotts, sit-ins, and mass marches. While to some, it seemed like these organized protests came out of nowhere, scholars have historicized these disruptive tactics in cultural traditions and organizations within Black communities. In particular, organizations such as Black newspapers played an integral role during the civil rights movement. The Black press served as a source of information and means to disseminate information critical to direct action.[7]

The Black press played a particularly important role across the Deep South. State censorship and white mob violence made it difficult in places like Mississippi for Black alternative news sources to emerge and thrive. Several Black newspapers, such as *The Advocate*, *Mississippi Enterprise*, and *The Delta Leader*, received monetary support from white businesses. As a result, their coverage of the civil rights movement was censored and limited. Yet, readers criticized these accommodationist papers and demanded more from their alternative sources. And thus, more "freedom papers" emerged in Mississippi to help fill the information gap.[8] Some of these papers were led by women, such as Colia Liddell, who edited the NAACP's *North Jackson Action* and Susie B. Ruffin, who edited the *Mississippi Freedom Democratic Party Newsletter*. These freedom papers provided a broader, humanized, and unbought perspective of civil rights coverage. And this coverage helped create the foundations for antiracist thought and challenged the mainly stereotypical and biased coverage of majority press in the Deep South.[9]

Despite regional policing of print media, national Black newspapers, such as *The Chicago Defender* and *The Pittsburgh Courier*, included news about Southern locales, with correspondents in the South. National papers were sometimes sold in Southern towns and cities. In addition, the newspapers often circulated, despite white resistance. As historian William Sturkey has pointed out, Pullman porters (and other Black travelers) often brought these newspapers with them as they traveled around the South. Local Black Hattiesburgers longed for *The Chicago Defender* and would pass the paper around to one another. Black newspapers were deemed so dangerous by white authorities in Hattiesburg that local police tried to limit their sales in 1943. Some Black leaders would distribute not only Black newspapers but also magazines such as *Jet* and *Ebony* as well.[10]

Jet was founded by John H. Johnson in 1951 in the same tradition of his other magazines, the *Negro Digest* and *Ebony*.[11] Many critics dismiss *Jet*, a weekly publication, for its focus on celebrity news, yet its representation of Black people, especially famous ones, still played an important economic, social, and political role in Black communities nationwide. By 1955, the magazine had a circulation of 478,666 subscriptions. For Johnson, he and his business model valued the Black consumer and reader in ways that mainstream magazines did not.[12] *Jet* published short articles and featured photographs of celebrities and ordinary African Americans that challenged mainstream media's degrading portrayals of Black life. *Jet* readers saw beauty in Black life, with its coverage of Black marriages, music, and models.[13] One regular feature of the magazine simply published what "People Are Talking About." Johnson's success in magazines was responsible for both the emphasis on Black entertainers and entrepreneurs and its coverage on civil rights issues, such as Emmett Till's murder and botched trial.

As historian Lance Hill has said, "*Jet* was the most widely read black weekly digest in America and the principal source of black news and opinions for much of the black working class. Standard reading fare in barbershops and beauty salons—the communication centers of the black community—*Jet* reached deep into the rural South."[14] Simeon Booker, *Jet*'s Washington bureau chief for over fifty years, has rightfully called the publication the "Bible" for news about the civil rights movement. "'If it wasn't in *Jet*,' they'd say, 'it didn't happen.' And if it did happen, *Jet* . . . would tell you the truth about it."[15]

As with *Jet* magazine, the circulation of Black print media helped to propel the movement when most of the national press had paid relatively little attention to civil rights issues until *Brown v. Board of Education*, according to award-winning journalist Jack Nelson. Most of the majority press showed no interest in covering such a volatile issue in the South and were content to ignore civil rights until the school decision touched off social unrest and resistance to desegregation by whites. While part of the majority press uncovered and reported injustices, much of the Southern press "dug in its heels and fought any change to the 'Southern way of life.'"[16]

The one-sided mainstream press often neglected local Black life, relying on stereotypes to report on civil rights struggles. As Sturkey reminds us, "Many mainstream papers in the Jim Crow South didn't mention African Americans unless they were arrested or killed."[17] Stories about civil rights were often decontextualized and reported using a conflict frame that often made the Black community/person the villain, eliminating any accountability or responsibility from white state political leaders and organizations. For example, after Emmett Till's murder in 1955, mainstream Mississippi newspapers conveyed "editorial outrage." The newspaper coverage did not report on the violent impulses of white people but instead, the supposedly extremist, Communist, South-hating agenda of the NAACP. Similarly, other Mississippi newspaper articles about the abduction and murder conveyed skepticism and doubt. That some articles even misspelled Emmett's name and his mother's, despite the Till story's high profile, signifies little care or concern for the accuracy of details and deprioritizes the significance of Emmett's life.

Till's murder served as a turning point, not just for the civil rights movement, but also for the relevance and significance of *Jet*. Mamie Bradley, Till's mother, decided to have an open casket funeral in Chicago, to show the world the brutality and disregard for Black life evidenced in her son's mutilated body. In doing so, the funeral attracted thousands of people, including reporters from across the nation.[18] *Jet*'s staffer, David Jackson, was one of the photographers at the funeral. His photograph of Emmett Till's "wildly disfigured and indiscernible face" was featured in *Jet*'s mid-September issue. That issue sold out, and for the first time, *Jet* printed additional copies. The photographs from Till's funeral in *Jet* are often credited for causing outrage, moving people from across the nation to travel South and join the struggle for civil rights.

Additionally, an account by former Detroit congressman Charles Diggs in the PBS documentary *Eyes on the Prize*, called the *Jet* photographs "probably one of the greatest media products in the last 40 or 50 years, because that picture stimulated a lot of anger on the part of blacks all over the country." Chris Metress, editor of *The Lynching of Emmett Till*, a book that includes contemporary news accounts of the killing and trial, explains the racial divide in its reporting and the lasting impact of its media coverage:

"You get testimony from white people coming of age at the time about how the case affected them, but you don't get them testifying, like countless blacks, that the *Jet* photo had this transformative effect on them, altering the way they felt about themselves and their vulnerabilities and the dangers they would be facing in the civil rights movement. Because white people didn't read *Jet*."[19]

Many Black youths in the Deep South who would go on to become civil rights activists just a few years later were profoundly moved by the pictures from *Jet*. Joyce Ladner, quite appropriately, has called them the "Emmett Till Generation." They included herself, her sister Dorie Ladner, and Cleveland Sellers, among many others.[20]

In addition to the magazine's photographs of Emmett Till, *Jet* also published eleven stories about his death and trial, more than any other magazine between 1955 and 1956.[21] These stories contextualized Till's murder, noting that he was the third Black youth killed in Mississippi in four months. Although the articles were largely editorial in nature, they still called out the discrimination of the justice system in their reporting of the informality of the proceedings.[22] Just as Mia Anderson posits, to the extent that mainstream magazines *Life* and *Look* provided national and world news to mainstream America, Black media sought to deliver news relevant to the African American community. In this sense, the African American magazine performs an important role for Blacks and for US journalism as a whole.[23] Moreover, as the Black press in general had become as much a commercial venture as its mainstream counterparts, the more humanizing narrative scope of advertisement-heavy publications such as *Ebony* and *Jet* magazines were heralded as suitable journalistic depictions of Black life in America.

Cheryl Thompson-Morton, Black media initiative director for the Center for Community Media (CUNY), states that since its origins in 1827, the Black press has centered the humanity of people who were often dehumanized by society and especially within mainstream media.[24] This humanizing element is quite prevalent in the many narratives about civil rights figures in the Black press, especially in *Jet*'s telling of the Clyde Kennard story. For example, several of the headlines in the features and news briefs about Kennard refer to him as a "Korean War Vet," "Ex-GI," as a "student" or by his full name. His sister even refers to him as "Clyde" in a January 1963 article, recalling him as if he were already familiar to readers. These descriptors differ from those found in some of the mainstream news accounts that reported on Kennard's attempts to enroll at the all-white college. In most of the early coverage, particularly the local and student newspaper accounts, Kennard is referred to simply as a "Negro," or a "Hattiesburg Negro," not unlike how Black people were identified in white newspapers in the late nineteenth century.[25] In most of the mainstream news accounts about Kennard's troubles, the issue was chalked up as a general news item that seemed to elicit little concern from major players in the community's social or political circles. This point comes with limited scope as coverage of Kennard's case has most often been found in historical scholarly publications that chronicle the lives of martyrs of the civil rights era. This makes sense considering Kennard was an active member of the NAACP and was considered a dear friend to some of the more well-known civil rights leaders in Mississippi, including Medgar Evers (from Jackson) and Vernon Dahmer (from Hattiesburg). Comparatively speaking, little work has centered on the coverage and narrative of Kennard's more humanistic traits that encompass his activism and social conscience.

In their foundational work "The Saddest Story of the Whole Movement," Timothy J. Minchin and John A. Salmond note that not until the campaign to clear Clyde Kennard's name began in the late twentieth century did many accounts of his story begin to highlight "the important and largely unrecognized role he played in America's civil rights struggle." As they point out, a near-complete erasure of his fullness occurs in telling "the Clyde Kennard story," yet he was "a genuine civil rights pioneer who put his life on the line in an effort to desegregate higher education in Mississippi" because he paved the way for other Black Mississippians to attend college.[26] Yet his early efforts to enroll at Mississippi Southern College were largely kept out of mainstream papers.[27] While *Jet* was not the first publication to highlight Kennard's case after his bogus arrests in September 1959 and 1960, it was pivotal to flesh out his story, build support for him, and secure his release from Parchman penitentiary for medical treatment.

Jet first picked up coverage on Kennard after his 1959 arrest. Though the news article was only a brief paragraph and appeared over two weeks after his arrest, its anonymous writer was careful to end the excerpt with Kennard's own words emphasizing that he was innocent and did not drink.[28] As discussed later in this chapter, subsequent articles in *Jet* touted Kennard's accomplishments, especially as a veteran, scholar, and activist. Most importantly, *Jet* humanized Kennard by using his first name and highlighting his own words. While other mainstream national and regional papers reported the arrest before *Jet* did, these mainstream sources unsurprisingly gave no hint that the arrest was fraudulent.[29]

As Kennard appealed his first conviction and then as he was arrested for stealing chicken feed in September 1960, news of his second arrest and conviction again flooded national media. When Medgar Evers, the state NAACP leader, spoke out against Kennard's unjust felony conviction and sentence of seven years in Parchman penitentiary, national Black news sources, including *Jet* and *The Chicago Defender*, reported on Evers's sentence of thirty days in jail and $100 fine for contempt of court. While the Black press periodically reported on the progress of Kennard's efforts to appeal his felony conviction and Evers's efforts to appeal his contempt conviction, news coverage on Kennard dwindled in 1961 and early 1962 until James Meredith led his highly publicized effort to integrate the University of Mississippi. This case drew widespread attention, especially by September 1962, when it pitted the governor of Mississippi, Ross Barnett, against President John F. Kennedy. Barnett's resistance emboldened other whites. On September 29, 1962, after President Kennedy sent federal troops to help ensure Meredith's admission, a white mob gathered on the university's campus and attacked soldiers and journalists. One Oxford worker and a French journalist were killed in the ensuing violence.

Even before the highly publicized violence associated with Meredith's admission, the Black press pointed out that Clyde Kennard's integration attempt preceded Meredith's and that he should not be forgotten. In late July 1962, a newly founded Black Mississippi newspaper, *The Mississippi Free Press*, raised the parallel between Kennard and Meredith when it commissioned a seven-part series, the most in-depth coverage to date, to describe Kennard's case to the public. The seven articles, written by twenty-year-old white northerner Ronald A. Hollander, covered Kennard's efforts to attend Mississippi; his first arrest, for stealing whiskey and reckless driving; and his second framing and arrest, conviction, and sentencing for stealing chicken feed. Hollander had first been introduced to Clyde Kennard's story by Bob Moses, field secretary of the Student Nonviolent Coordinating Committee (SNCC). He then was commissioned by the Everses to write this story.[30] In November, in *The Reporter*, a national mainstream magazine, Hollander summarized his articles on Kennard in a shorter essay. He then followed up with a letter to the editor in *The Reporter* in early December including an update that Kennard had been blocked from receiving medical attention in Jackson in September, and prison authorities had told his mother that he would not be allowed to receive further care.[31] While both the *Mississippi Free Press* and *The Reporter* were beginning to publicize the story of Kennard, these publications did not reach the same widespread Black audience as did *Jet*.

Meanwhile, local and national civil rights workers were mobilizing to free Kennard from jail. In early December 1962, students at Tougaloo, led by student activist Dorie Ladner, began a petition to John F. Kennedy and Attorney General Robert Kennedy to release Kennard.[32] The *Mississippi Free Press* printed the petition, encouraged readers to fill it with signatures, and mail it to President Kennedy. Readers were then supposed to write to Ladner to report on how many petitions readers had sent.[33] SNCC also encouraged its members and supporters to engage in the letter-writing campaign.[34] At the end of the year, as *Mississippi Free Press* editors reflected on the newspaper's eventful first year, they pointed to the high-profile events surrounding integration at the University of Mississippi, but the newspaper admonished readers to participate in the campaign to "Remember Clyde Kennard."[35]

As in the case of *Jet*'s reporting on Emmett Till's murder, the magazine spotlighted the state-sanctioned violence against Black people. *Jet* investigative reporter Larry Still was the first to announce, on January 24, 1963, that Kennard had cancer.[36] But even before this article's publication, Still played an important role in providing an eye-witness account of Kennard's frail state. Kennard had sent a letter to his sister Sarah Tarpley letting her know that he was being denied treatment for an intestinal condition, after undergoing surgery in the spring of 1962. Now he was hemorrhaging blood but being denied treatment, despite a Jackson doctor's prognosis that he had a less than 20 percent chance of surviving over five years.[37]

Comedian Dick Gregory paid for Tarpley to fly down to Mississippi, to visit her brother in Parchman, along with her mother and Forrest County NAACP president J. C. Fairley, on January 20, 1963. According to Taylor Branch, in his book *Pillar of Fire*, the group claimed to be guests who wanted to take a family portrait. Although Still had tried to bring in a large flash camera that he suspected would be confiscated, he also brought in a small camera taped to his ankle. As Branch points out, this was a dangerous mission for all involved. However, once the team of three made it out alive, "*Jet*'s photographs of the emaciated prisoner contradicted Mississippi's official position that Kennard was a healthy but undeserving thief of chicken feed."[38] What the group saw shocked them. According to Still, Kennard was thin and was clearly under "dire physical strain due to lack of treatment." When Kennard saw his mother and sister, he could not hold back his tears. He told them that he felt like crying at everything and lately "just [didn't] have any more wind" and that he could "hardly move about." After this visit, Kennard's mother and sister were rightfully convinced that the prison was trying to kill him by denying him treatment.[39]

After returning from the visit, the team shared their information with attorney R. Jess Brown, who filed a petition with the Mississippi State

Supreme Court for Kennard to be hospitalized and declared immediately eligible for parole. *Jet* also saw copies of the medical report and helped share them with the US Civil Rights Commission, which then investigated the case further. This visit by Still and Kennard's family and friends to Parchman was crucial to pushing Governor Barnett first to move Kennard from Parchman to the University of Mississippi Hospital in Jackson on Thursday, January 24, and then to suspend his sentence indefinitely on Monday, January 28.[40]

Still's writing about Kennard's case also helped humanize and publicize his story nationally. He had been covering civil rights topics as a reporter for *Jet* since at least 1959, when he covered news about Arkansas's decision that year to racially separate donated blood.[41] He went on to cover the 1961 Freedom Rides, James Meredith's integration efforts at the University of Mississippi in 1962, and the Selma to Montgomery March.[42] Dorie Ladner recalled his work reporting on the civil rights movement in Mississippi and said that Still and other members of the Black press were a lifeline to the outside for civil rights activists in Mississippi.[43] Countless other activists, including Martin Luther King Jr., Bob Moses, and Charlie Cobb, also recalled meeting Still during civil rights work in the Deep South.[44] Still not only covered major events of the civil rights movement but also was sympathetic to the movement for Black Power in the 1960s and portrayed it fairly, unlike most news outlets at the time. Historian Lance Hill names Still as one of the reporters from *Jet* who covered the work of the mid-1960s Black self-defense group the Deacons for Defense. They were "sympathetic to militant groups that were counterposed to the NAACP and other mainstream organizations" because they reflected the pride and sentiments of ordinary Black Americans.[45]

Although Still's reporting on Kennard was published later than other news outlets, he prioritized a Black perspective that highlighted family and community. In his articles, he pointed to the longstanding devotion and strength of Kennard's mother and sister, who never stopped trying to secure Kennard's release. Consciously pushing back against the racist Jim Crow system that drew a distinction between "white ladies" and "black females" and denied Black women courtesy titles, Still identified Kennard's mother as "Mrs. Smith" and his sister as "Mrs. Tarpley." To personalize his stories further, he also quoted Kennard's letters and words that addressed them in more familiar ways, such as "Mama" and "Sarah."[46]

Still also highlighted the tremendous support of the Black locals surrounding Kennard. He wrote about students at Tougaloo College, as discussed earlier, who supported Kennard with a petition to free him. He also pointed out that families in Hattiesburg and the Mississippi NAACP had begun the Clyde Kennard Fund for donations to the family, and the Order of the Eastern Star had also aided his sister, Sarah Tarpley, a worthy matron for all her efforts. Two Black businessmen in Jackson, Cornelius Turner and Dr. William E. Miller, had been paying off the mortgage on Kennard's property since he was sent to jail, and Hattiesburg leaders were collecting supplies and money for Kennard's mother.[47] Still even quoted Kennard from his January 20, 1963, visit, relaying Kennard's encouraging assessment that if there was one good thing to come out of his incarceration, "it will show the world that we [African Americans, locally and nationally] all know how to work together."[48]

THE HISTORICAL MEMORY OF CLYDE KENNARD

The earliest historical works to discuss Clyde Kennard came from activists themselves. In his 1966 autobiography, *Three Years in Mississippi*, James Meredith cites both Kennard and Clennon King, who had tried to integrate the University of Mississippi in 1958, as his predecessors. However, Meredith had vowed also "to engage in this war without becoming a casualty" like them by ensuring that he kept his attempt to enroll at the University of Mississippi in the public eye.[49] A year later, in 1967, Myrlie Evers covered Kennard's story extensively in her memoir, *For Us, the Living*.[50]

Professional and documentary historians were slower to acknowledge Kennard's story. The highly publicized 1987 documentary series *Eyes on the Prize* overlooked Kennard's story.[51] Around this same time, Taylor Branch's Pulitzer Prize–winning, one-thousand-page tome *Parting the Waters: America in the King Years, 1954–63*, spent only four sentences on Kennard's arrests.[52] Branch's source was Evers's *For Us, the Living*. Black autobiography, like the Black press, thus has been the most reliable source covering the Clyde Kennard story from the start.

Only after the historiographical turn to studying the local sphere in civil rights history did historians begin to focus on the movement in Mississippi, and Kennard's story emerged from Meredith's shadow, though Kennard has continued to be portrayed primarily as a victim. John Dittmer was the first historian to spend a significant part of his book on the topic of Kennard in *Local People* in 1994. Dittmer also was the first historian to name *Jet* as significant in publicizing Kennard's story, though he did not cite any articles from the publication. Like previous historians, Dittmer used Evers's *For Us, the Living*, but he also included Hollander's article in *The*

Reporter, articles from the *Jackson Daily News*, and interviews. Unlike other historians, Dittmer used the newly public State Sovereignty Commission records to show even more clearly how the state had conspired to ensure that Kennard would never be allowed to attend MSC. Dittmer also drew upon a 1964 interview between John Howard Griffin and Bradford Daniel to emphasize Kennard's victimhood.[53] The following year, Charles Payne's *I've Got the Light of Freedom* briefly discussed the details of Kennard's case as well. His sources were SNCC papers, Evers's *For Us, the Living*, interviews with SNCC activists and Forrest County natives Joyce and Dorie Ladner, and Dick Gregory's autobiography.[54]

Though Taylor Branch's first book about the early civil rights movement did not cover Kennard's story in depth, a decade later, his sequel, *Pillar of Fire*, went even further in both spotlighting Kennard's story and using *Jet* as a source. Branch centered the story of Kennard and the Dahmer family (though *Pillar* was supposed to begin in the year 1963). Aided by testimony of those closest to Kennard, Branch emphasized how Forrest County civil rights leader Vernon Dahmer had been so moved by the injustices that Kennard faced that he defied state and national NAACP leaders who resisted working with rival civil rights groups such as SNCC. According to Branch, Dahmer welcomed SNCC leader Bob Moses, whom other local leaders viewed as troublesome and ineffective. Branch claims, "Moses retained a foothold [in Mississippi] only because of one hardheaded farmer. Vernon Dahmer, obsessed by the sufferings of his friend Clyde Kennard, responded to a kindred grit in Moses." Dahmer was a major force in welcoming SNCC to town when he brought activists Hollis Watkins and Curtis Hayes to his home in fall 1962.[55]

Newer works about Kennard have drawn upon the now-digitized Sovereignty Commission papers, which were first publicly available through the Mississippi Department of Archives and History in 1998. Yasuhiro Katagiri covered the Sovereignty Commission's framing of Kennard in his 2001 *The Mississippi State Sovereignty Commission*.[56] And, as previously discussed, Minchin and Salmond in 2009 wrote "'The Saddest Story of the Whole Movement': The Clyde Kennard Case and the Search for Racial Reconciliation in Mississippi, 1955–2007." These scholars were the first two to focus on Kennard's case in depth. Minchin and Salmond's article does an excellent job not only drawing upon media and Sovereignty Commission records but also consulting multiple oral histories of locals who offered first-hand descriptions of Kennard. However, the article still emphasized the tragedy of Kennard's case. Patricia Boyett's 2016 *Right to Revolt* and William Sturkey's 2019 *Hattiesburg: An American City in Black and White* both cover Kennard's story in depth as part of larger local studies about the civil rights movement and the Jim Crow era, respectively.[57] Finally, a couple of very recent full-length biographies of Kennard have continued nonetheless to profile him as a victim. In 2018, Scottish author Derek R. King wrote about Kennard's attempts to integrate MSC using mainly Sovereignty Commission records.[58] Devery Anderson has published a more personalized account in *A Slow, Calculated Lynching: The Story of Clyde Kennard*. He draws extensively on sources from *Jet* but does not emphasize the importance of the publication in helping to free Kennard from jail. Anderson, however, does interview dozens of people from Kennard's community to expand upon both his life and the long exoneration efforts of locals and national activists to clear his felony conviction.[59]

It is worth emphasizing that early histories documenting Clyde Kennard's case breezed over *Jet*'s pivotal role in telling his story in full. By doing so, they neglected to engage fully with the role that Kennard's family and community played in helping to secure his release. Also, in ignoring the most prominent national Black magazine, historians initially overlooked the narrative about Kennard that was most well known among Black Americans. And, in not also looking to Kennard himself, unfortunately, even recent biographers do not capture the essence of the man, his character, and his consciousness. What *Jet* magazine offers, then, that we must consider are not just fragmented memories of Kennard in the civil rights movement, but more so embodied narratives preserved for posterity.

RECONSTRUCTING CLYDE KENNARD

The tortured, mutilated body of Emmett Till, as featured in *Jet* and discussed earlier, *is* the image that launched the modern civil rights movement. Readers could not turn away from photographs of the corpse of the fourteen-year-old Black boy murdered by two Southern white men for "whistling" at a white woman in 1955.[60] The image of Till's body is etched into the memory of a nation.[61] As novelist and essayist John Edgar Wideman recalls a recurrent nightmare, a fiend that chases him has a face "too terrifying for the dream to reveal."[62] However, having been the same age as Till when he was killed, Wideman believes that it is Till's face—"crushed, chewed, mutilated, his gray face swollen, water dripping from holes punched in his skull. Warm, gray water on that August day in 1955 when they dragged his corpse from the Tallahatchie"—that haunts him still.[63] The horrid details of his vision are all too realistic even if his nightmares predate the first time Wideman remembers seeing Till's body in the magazine: "I certainly hadn't been searching for Emmett Till's picture in *Jet*. It found me. A blurred, grayish something resembling an aerial snapshot of a landscape cratered by bombs or ravaged by natural disaster. As soon as I realized the thing in the photo was a dead black boy's face, I jerked my eyes away. But not quickly enough."[64] As prologue, the body of Emmett Till prepared *Jet* readers to witness the atrocities of the movement, making the story of Clyde Kennard less shocking but more dramatic.

Kennard's integration attempt initially is a news brief that eventually becomes a featured story in *Jet*. Though it is not sensationalized as Till's spectacle, we see the crafting of a tragic narrative to introduce Kennard to readers becoming familiar with Mississippi's brand of racism.[65] In the October 1, 1959, issue of *Jet*, the urgent reporting obscures details about Kennard described as a "30 year-old Negro farmer and former University of Chicago student."[66] He was thirty-two years old and had experienced much more than the brief reveals; it had been Kennard's third attempt to enroll at MSC, after which he was arrested on false accusations of driving reckless and illegal alcohol possession. The next story, appearing on October 8, 1959, fleshes out more with a portrait of Kennard in his military uniform and describes him as being "five-foot, five-inch, 145 pounds ... a little man who has done a lot of big things."[67]

With his military experience and education, Kennard becomes larger than life in *Jet*. His story is of Black achievement—rather than Black defiance, Black innocence as with Emmett Till's—leading to Black death: "As a sergeant in the 82nd Airborne Div., paratrooper Kennard plummeted from the skies on 36 occasions. As an infantryman in Korea, he won two Bronze Stars for gallantry in ground combat, is part of the history of men who fought and died in the Korean snows of Old Baldy Mountain."[68] Readers experience the thrill of combat and victory as Kennard the Korean War veteran also becomes a metaphorical foot soldier of the movement. In the fight for justice, Kennard's maturity counterbalances Till's youth to expose the high-stakes denial of full citizenship and human rights in a segregated society. If, as John Edgar Wideman reasons, "[i]t's no accident that Emmett Till's dead face appears inhuman" since "the point of inflicting the agony of his last moments, killing and mutilating him, is to prove he's not human," the violence therefore was justifiable under segregation.[69] *Jet* humanizes Kennard to show proof otherwise in cases of racial terrorism.

The dimensional perspectives of his character are revealed in a complex profile of Kennard the scholar, the soldier, and the integrationist. The subjective reporting brings attention to the subtleties of his life as a young

Black man with a far greater purpose than that which becomes of him. During his three years enrolled at the University of Chicago as a political science major, as we are assured, Kennard "maintained a B average," and he had career plans "to work for the State Department."[70] Later, as reported after his arrest and imprisonment at Parchman, even as he was recovering from cancer surgery, Kennard remained optimistic about completing his education, possibly returning to the University of Chicago or enrolling at Howard University to study constitutional law.[71] We come to understand that his "bold actions" to try integrating an all-white institution seem most likely motivated by his military experience. "It's the same feeling you get when you are about to jump from a plane," he tells us.[72] The image of Kennard in his army uniform therefore holds readers' interests even more. Likely taken around the time of his enlistment, Kennard wears a standard-issue olive-drab, serge, wool coat, with a khaki-colored necktie and cotton khaki shirt in contrast to the darker hue of the winter service uniform, complete with an olive-drab, serge, wool service cap.[73] Looking deeply into the photograph, Kennard's faraway gaze draws readers closer. Curiously, the magazine constructs Black masculinity with sensual aesthetics of gallantry and possessive fervor. Kennard is a handsome "bachelor" who "still 'loves Mississippi'" as much as it denies him. The sexual taboo of racial transgressions—the state here figured as a white space threatened by his Blackness—resonates in Kennard's sense of belonging in (rather than an attraction to) a place like the Jim Crow South. Readers may anticipate the outcome, remembering Till's disfigured face, a nightmarish "thing," but, however, they can remain hopeful with Kennard's dignified portrait; he seems poised for the integration battles ahead in trying to return home.

The embodied discourse of breaking news subverts the criminalization of Clyde Kennard even as his case is reported in *Jet*.[74] The coverage of Kennard's case no longer appears, for instance, under the "Education" section but rather in the "Crime" section after he's convicted on November 14, 1960, by an all-white jury of stealing chicken feed, charges which he disputed. He was sentenced to the maximum seven years at Parchman penitentiary. In reports on Kennard in *Jet* after his conviction, he is less often described as a farmer, scholar, or veteran. The details of his legal case are reprinted though to justify his struggles in the court of public opinion. By 1961, Kennard's integration story has been widely publicized nationally, appearing in the *Pittsburgh Courier* and other outlets of the Black press, and *Jet* continues its lead in drawing attention to the unjust case rather than the victim. Kennard's attorney, R. Jess Brown, is brought more to the foreground by filing petitions to exonerate his client from theft and charges of voting violations and by filing appeals in federal courts.[75] Also, others create a national campaign to free Kennard from prison: members of the Student Nonviolent Coordinating Committee (SNCC), students from Tougaloo College, members of the NAACP, Robert F. Kennedy, and most notably, comedian-activist Dick Gregory. Once again, as *Jet* begins reporting early in 1963, Kennard is identified by name (rather than just "a Mississippi man"), as a "Negro student sentenced to . . . Parchman Prison farm" and as an "ex-GI, convicted of buying . . . stolen chicken feed," which brings renewed focus to the injustice of a corrupt legal system that is biased against all African American citizens.[76] Reprints of Kennard's military photo also punctuate the narrative of patriotism and protest.

When *Jet* published feature stories of Clyde Kennard in January 1963, readers were reintroduced to someone quite familiar. He was still serving his jail sentence at Parchman farm as highly publicized by the magazine; the cause célèbre was backed by a national campaign for his release. However, his case had become overshadowed by James Meredith's integration of the University of Mississippi in October 1962.[77] Larry Still thus carefully sketches Kennard's life as that of a devoted son of Leona Smith, a widower, and a doting brother raised mostly by his elder sister, Sarah Rose Tarpley. A full-spread family album makes the investigative reporting even more intimate. The enlarged military photograph of Kennard is counterbalanced by photographs of his uniformed brothers—Albert and Melvin, veterans of the army and navy, respectively. The Clyde Kennard story becomes a universal, patriotic narrative about a military family with a heroic son, who made a sacrifice for the advancement of the civil rights movement just as he'd done for freedom serving his country on the battlefields of Germany and Korea.

With wounds inflicted by systemic racism and from combat, Kennard was a disabled veteran suffering from a "bleeding cancer" as disclosed by the reporter. Inadequate medical care, exploitative labor practices, and other punitive abuses while at Parchman all contributed to his physical decline.[78] Much of what we learn in the report apparently comes from letters written by Kennard to his sister and perhaps also her own testimony as she was likely interviewed by Still as the family representative. We are granted intimate access to a Black family coping with a fatal illness as well as the mental trauma of racism. Excerpts of Kennard's letters sent to his mother and sister suggest hushed conversations: "I supposed Mom mentioned to you that I'll have to have another operation. It is about the same place as the other one. I have seen a doctor, but haven't gotten the X-rays yet. If I have to have it, I think the sooner the better. Some blood is leaving me, but not as much as the other time."[79] Kennard's body is presented here for a public examination in a manner that hearkens back to Emmett Till's autopsy and open-casket funeral photos in the pages of *Jet*. Kennard's significant loss of blood conjures a fragility that we might imagine as a near-death experience.[80] This is different from the image of Kennard in his army uniform, but the cancer patient remains a fighter.

Kennard appears to languish while he is also resilient in *Jet*'s reporting. Repeatedly, he is compared to James Meredith, drawing iconic parallels for readers to contemplate the severity of Kennard's punishment for not achieving what Meredith eventually did with military force. Kennard is represented again by his attorney, whose commentary fills gaps in the narrative without Kennard's own testimony, attorney Brown referring to him as "poor boy." What's most unusual in Still's report is how he reframes Kennard's story as that of a savvy businessman and not just as a "chicken farmer," which connotes a rural backwardness. Such stereotyping might appeal to a reading public envisioning the South as America's exceptional problem. Beyond viewing Kennard simply as a tragic victim of Jim Crow policing, we learn how he "invested" in the farm with earnings from his military service. The farm was a reasonable business venture that could have led to generational wealth for a Black family in the rural South, a legacy too often denied.[81]

The strength of the family's bond is tested throughout the ordeal, and there is much to learn about their survival as they rallied around Kennard. Without direct access to him, the "Clyde Kennard story" is too often told by outsiders. Friends may remember him fondly as someone who didn't "even drink soda pop," certainly not alcohol, as he was accused. It's meaningful to recover such sentiments that outline his personality. As discussed earlier, *Jet* goes further though than most outlets to present Kennard in his textured fullness. Such is the case, for example, when his sister Sarah Rose speaks about her brother after she visits him in the state penitentiary during January 1963:

> This is the first time I have been able to see him. Every penny I could get has been going to pay on debts for Clyde and the family.[82]
>
> I remember [*Jet*] magazine carried stories about Clyde long before anyone else. Those articles ... were the only things that kept us going because we knew that he would not be forgotten.
> This is what hurts ... [t]hat Clyde should be sent to jail for stealing. Everyone knows that we were brought up as a Christian family and

did not believe in taking anything that did not belong to us . . . I don't know what made Johnny [Roberts] say that about Clyde.[83]

By calling him simply "Clyde," she presents a subtle narrative viewpoint that amends that which the public thinks it already knows about Kennard. Hers is a third-person perspective yet a very revealing, personal one that brings readers closer to the truth of her brother's being. Kennard the falsely accused, a victim of social injustice, was also a provider for his family (debts accrued only while imprisoned were paid on his behalf to prevent foreclosure on the farm) and a person with a good moral character in a very close-knit community (as "everyone knows"). Like the mother of Emmett Till before her, Sarah Rose Tarpley wanted *Jet* readers to "see him," her brother, so Kennard "would not be forgotten."

Prior to his release from prison for medical care in Chicago and his recovery, Kennard is given a platform to address readers directly. The images of Kennard as a soldier finally align with his testimony of survival against all odds. His first words, addressed to his mother and sister, are uttered through tears of joy, offset by the responses of a grieving mother and defiant sister: "I'm getting to be such a cry baby lately, it seems like everything that happens to me, I start crying . . . and I just don't have any more wind. I can hardly move about."[84]

In *Jet*'s reporting, Kennard appears weakened but not despondent. "'Don't worry Mama,' Kennard tries to assure her, 'You know cancer takes its toll, but I believe if I get the right treatment, I'll be all right.'" A medical report documents significant weight loss and procedures, which draws our attention more to the disabled body of the cancer fighter. He has lost about forty pounds, had fourteen blood transfusions, and undergone two operations to treat intestinal tumors. Equally compelling is how the reporter manipulates readers' gaze in the narrative to reveal the wounds of his treatment as evidence of the abuse he suffered: "He unbuttoned his striped prison pants and pulled up his heavy parka hood to show the visitors the scars of [the] two operations performed at the University of Mississippi Hospital to relieve a malignant tumor."[85] Here, the textual replaces the visual, a reversal of the Till exposé, and readers may examine Kennard's body momentarily as narrative shifts from different viewpoints describing his condition. His attorney declares his client is "serving a death sentence" without proper medical care, and the medical report confirms "the patient's extremely poor prognosis" in recommending parole. Typical of *Jet*'s reporting on the Kennard's case, though, images compel readers to empathize as an immediate response to the injustice he experienced. The uniformed soldier, prisoner, and cancer patient all vie for readers' attention in the photographic narrative with a series of three images: Kennard's military portrait, a hazy view through bars of the prison hospital, and a photo of an inmate serving "hard bread." The reporting constructs the subject in images and text oddly juxtaposed to incite bold actions.[86]

But it is Clyde Kennard, himself, who inspires with his swan song. He shows gratitude for all his supporters, especially in working to save the family's farm: "One good thing that has come out of my being here is that it will show the world we all know how to work together."[87] He is candid about the talks he had with William McCain, MSC's president, and Governor J. P. Coleman during the enrollment attempts at the all-white school: "We made no deals" to prevent his enrollment. Kennard did agree however to delay it until after elections, which made it a "political issue."[88] He insists that his "concern was not to do anything that would close the school"; instead, he wanted "to enroll in school myself."[89] Unapologetically, Kennard vows he would try to do it all again, attempt to attend the university despite the challenges he had faced: "I did not do it for publicity. . . . But, if I thought it could serve a purpose . . . If I could learn something, I'd do it again."[90] In using the platform *Jet* provides, Kennard advocates also for prison reform: "This prison right here is a problem . . . [I]t provides food and supplies for thousands of white families in the area and most of the labor is Negro. We are helping to create the state's greatest resource and our people do not share any of it, . . . If a suit was filed to integrate [Parchman prison] it might be more important than integrating a school." Kennard then turns his focus back to his own generational legacy and land ownership; he pleads to his mother and sister to "never sell or rent or lease" their property "unless we share in the future profits." Kennard's concern is not just for his family but also his beloved community, African Americans in general. In his final words to his family, and, ultimately, to the magazine's readers, he says he wants them to "always remember . . . never, never accept anything on a segregated basis . . . never."[91] The impassioned speech, as presented in *Jet*, brings Kennard the revolutionary into focus enough to underscore what is often misunderstood now about the man and construed as tragic myth—his quiet strength.

Unfortunately, Clyde Kennard's testimony is absent from much of the coverage in *Jet* following his release from Parchman. Readers learn of a "series of quick-moving developments" in the timeline of his suspended sentence and hospitalization in Chicago as a result of *Jet*'s relentless campaign. Reports briefly mention his abdominal surgery and recovery while staying with his sister, Sarah Rose. By spring 1963, the Clyde Kennard story has reached its climax in *Jet*'s coverage over the years. In April, as he had done when interviewed from the prison cell, Kennard does appear exhausted by his struggles, but he remained determined to create a more just society. Reporting about his condition is more urgent and empathetic. His "frail body" as prop for the melodrama, a "slim, full faced" Kennard, "speaking in a soft, Dixie-tinged voice," explains his desire to return home to Mississippi. He vows "to devote the rest of my life to improving conditions for my people and my state" despite having been diagnosed with only a few years to live. "Maybe [doctors] will come up with something to keep me going for a long time," Kennard explains, "But, I'm going to work on the things I have been talking about just as if I will live 1,000 years."[92] To save his farm, help his family and community, this is the incomplete mission of a soldier, humbled by the battles he has endured, wounded both in Germany and on the home front. Missing from the feature report though is the image of Kennard in his uniform that had been essential in the magazine's reporting. The body of a Black soldier discarded on the home front in the struggle for equal rights is a poignant narrative that underlies the Kennard coverage in *Jet*. That the trope of disability appears consistently in the reporting reveals the tragic consequences of military service without receiving medical benefits.[93] One quick shot of Kennard in pajamas and robe sitting with friends Dorie Ladner, Dr. Andrew Thomas, and his sister Sarah is the last we see of him alive. However, it is not the last time we *hear* from Kennard in the pages of the magazine.

In a seamless ventriloquist act, Kennard's voice resonates in the magazine even in death. His body is constructed carefully by *Jet*'s reporting for almost four years, and Kennard's lingering presence is palpable in the weeks just before and immediately after the veteran died on July 4, 1963. We receive reports of the cancer patient in absentia of an NAACP dinner earlier in June, when he "spoke to the crowd from his Billings hospital bed."[94] It is a matter of timing that the magazine takes advantage to announce later that the veteran died on Independence Day, ironically, a week after receiving a lifetime membership from the NAACP and while Myrlie Evers received the Spingarn Medal awarded posthumously to her husband, Medgar, murdered (June 12) just weeks before Kennard slips into a coma.[95] But Kennard sends a "final message to all mankind," as reported by Larry Still in the July 25, 1963, issue of *Jet*. Still's feature story allows others to speak for Kennard in sincere tributes. The ritual brings the body and spirit of the man before the public for a final performance in words and images. Attending the funeral (foreshadowing his own death in 1966), local NAACP leader Vernon Dahmer Sr. believed that Kennard was "more like Christ than any man [he had] ever heard of since biblical times." Clyde and Medgar, linked in memoriam, because they "believed in the same freedom" and "deliberately murdered," Kennard's former attorney R. Jess Brown testifies. Charles Evers, older brother of the slain activist, vows to continue the fight, as does the minister, who goads the congregation to do the same. Kennard, the fallen soldier, inspires even more the revolution that he helped to launch with his simple acts of civil disobedience.[96]

Clyde Kennard's death and burial as a civil rights martyr is a twice-told tale crafted in the pages of *Jet* magazine. Coverage of Kennard's funeral brings his tragic life to climax in the magazine's reporting over the previous five years. Rare images of his funeral, close-ups of Kennard's family mourning, provide the realism of visual media that substantiates the printed record to create an archive of civil rights history.[97] Journalists and photographers covering Kennard's case over the years bore a great responsibility to document a collective memory.[98] Those in the Black press were at the vanguard exposing Southern atrocities to the nation. *Jet*'s radical stance in publishing explicit content about political rallies, arrests of activists, murders of Black leaders, court trials, and funerals was possible only in the North; the Southern Black press was under much more scrutiny from white supremacists, who controlled and/or threatened local publications.[99] Looking at Clyde Kennard in *Jet*, what we see and come to understand about his martyrdom is how and why the magazine erects a memorial to him with images featured in the months leading up to his death.[100] When Mamie Till partnered with *Jet* in 1955 (and also other outlets in the Black press during the months of the murder trial) to "make the whole world see" how her son had been tortured, the public took a good look at his mangled body to understand lynching better as an extreme act of terror, and ironically, in the archives of lynching photographs, Till's casket photos shift the focus from the victim to the perpetrators of unimaginable racial violence. Again, as prologue, Till's public memorial prepared readers for Kennard's demise. His emaciated body exposed often enough coalesce empathic readers' response with political action to dismantle systemic racism in higher education, policing / criminal justice, and healthcare.[101]

As we move in phases of *Jet*'s coverage, we discover Clyde Kennard's afterlife to see how the changes he incites are long-term goals achieved as chronicled by the magazine. He receives brief mentions in continual coverage of the civil rights movement, though ironically as the "forgotten man." *Jet* features of comedian and activist Dick Gregory a year later include only slight references to his work on behalf of Kennard. Gregory "spent a small fortune trying to save the life of Mississippi cancer victim Clyde

Kennard," while Gregory's father was dying of cancer too. By 1964, readers would have been quite familiar with the story of Kennard as reported in *Jet*. And, therefore, even a slight mention of his name may have triggered memories of Kennard's life and death as covered extensively in the magazine. If not, readers were reminded of Kennard after the murder of Vernon Dahmer in 1966. Two pictures of the deceased are published with the January 27 news brief: one of Dahmer hospitalized after the arson attack on his home and the other image of Kennard, with his sister Sarah, arriving in Chicago for medical care. As with Medgar Evers, Clyde Kennard appears in memoriam with Vernon Dahmer in *Jet*'s archive of civil rights history. His contribution to the magazine is immeasurable considering also how anniversary issues of the publication consistently emphasize the investigative reporting of Kennard's imprisonment and release which clarifies *Jet*'s mandate for giving "voice" to Black America. This achievement was touted again in 1993 with a culminating feature about the ceremonial dedication of a building partially named in honor of Kennard on the University of Southern Mississippi's campus (formerly Mississippi Southern College).[102] Pictured uniformed as both a soldier and a convalescent, Clyde Kennard lives on in the school's institutional memory, as represented by the diversity of its campus population, and within that of the local community that lays claim to his body resting in peace.

CONCLUSION

Indeed, *Jet* played a major role in documenting the Clyde Kennard story, as a source that is oft cited but not carefully examined. Yet, its reporting is invaluable to historical accounts about the civil rights movement that may not be as detailed about local events. Reading the archival records of such an important periodical, what emerges from such cultural narratives to shift our attention from the tragic victim to his textual body is a story best told by the man himself. Examined in the next chapter is Clyde Kennard's embodied discourse shifting attention more to his "voice."

CHAPTER 2

LETTERS TO THE EDITOR

Clyde Kennard's Public Appeals for Justice and Equality

SHERITA L. JOHNSON

> It is interesting to me that subjects which are most widely discussed are those which seem to be least understood by the public whom these discussions are designed to inform.
> —CLYDE KENNARD, "MIXING," *HATTIESBURG AMERICAN* (1958)

The case of Clyde Kennard's multiple attempts to integrate Mississippi Southern College is often remembered as "the saddest story" of the modern civil rights movement.[1] It has compelling elements of a tragic, Southern gothic: the twisted plot of a heroic character, isolated and marginalized, up against antagonistic, "evil" forces; the death of the emaciated protagonist effectuated by circumstances beyond his control, unrelenting racial terror; a haunting setting—the segregated South, or Mississippi in particular—that exposes a bitter reality experienced by many African Americans under Jim Crow. All such elements make for a horrific melodrama indeed. But that is not the Clyde Kennard story as we understand it. To (re)tell this story, historians and journalists have collected oral accounts from witnesses and gathered documents from law officials, politicians, college administrators, and state agencies. Few of these accounts also include Kennard's own testimony (for instance, the admission requests he wrote to President William D. McCain and Aubrey Lucas, administrators at Mississippi Southern College).[2] Looking to the subject himself as a primary source then is where I turn to find a critical perspective of his life and times, shifting attention more to his embodied narrative, not seeing Kennard only as a victim of circumstance, but, instead, listening to his voice of reason. Written in the form of open letters, the essays on race problems and school integration Clyde Kennard wrote that were published in the *Hattiesburg American* prove most useful in telling *his story*.

Each appearing unobtrusively within the normal thread of news coverage and advertisements, Kennard's essays were published under the Letter to Editor column: "Mixing" (Friday, December 6, 1958), "The Race Question" (Friday, September 25, 1959), and "School Mix" (Tuesday, January 26, 1960).[3] Charles Green Andrews ("Andy") Harmon had been the editor of the Hattiesburg paper since 1932, but it's clear that he's not the addressee for Kennard's letters.[4] Andy Harmon was among the majority white editors of Southern newspapers that covered race relations and school desegregation as a lead story following the 1954 landmark US Supreme Court ruling in *Brown v. Board of Education*. These editors typically presented only the segregationist, white perspective of the race problem in also representing the views of the newspapers' white subscribers and readership.[5] In firm opposition to the ruling, for instance, Harmon tried to incite mob retaliation with his editorial published in the *Hattiesburg American* on August 2, 1954: "If all the people of Mississippi want to retain racial segregation in the public schools[,] they can do it simply by standing together," proclaimed the editor, who went on to declare that "no power on earth can compel more than a million people to do something that is against the law of God and nature."[6] In a move that appears contradictory to his editorial stance, Andy Harmon later published Kennard's epistolary essays, which were clearly intended also for a broad audience.[7] That Kennard began writing them three years after his first enrollment attempt and while his case was circulating in newspapers statewide, the target audience likely would have included state and school officials.[8] Also, with the State Sovereignty Commission monitoring his every move, Kennard decidedly chose the *Hattiesburg American* to garner widespread support from an uninformed public of white readers.[9] He takes the opportunity thus to assuage racial tension in a strikingly intimate tone. The first of the series establishes his premise to discuss integration as he makes an argument both personal and public about the race problem in each of the epistolary essays. As a form of literary activism, Kennard's message is informative and persuasive, written in response to civil rights struggles locally, especially his initial enrollment attempt at Mississippi Southern College (MSC).[10]

Archival recovery of Kennard's epistolary essays is essential to understanding his public campaign and the preservation of cultural memory when Black lives are terrorized, especially during the freedom struggles in his lifetime. As in the previous chapter where we examine the pages of *Jet* magazine, Kennard's letters serve as an ephemeral record of his experiences as a civil rights pioneer. Well preserved in periodical archives, these letters are a public record of racial segregation and of the local movement for civil rights. That his writings appear in a publication with a predominately white audience during the movement is unexpected, when most often Southern newspapers such as the *Hattiesburg American* published reports of black criminality not of black intelligence.[11] In my analysis of civil rights print culture, I consider the production and circulation of Kennard's epistolary essays within the activist tradition of African American literature and as traceable to a much older biblical tradition. Formal letters of instruction, for instance, as written by the apostle Paul to Christians in the ancient world, are structured as spiritual narratives especially for a public audience to fortify its moral conscience (e.g., as Paul addresses the Romans, Corinthians, Galatians, Ephesians, Philippians, Colossians, and Thessalonians). Paul's messages sent hundreds of years ago resonate for Christians still today, and, likewise, Kennard's epistles carry his message of moral fortitude into the twenty-first century resounding just as movements for social justice continues.[12]

Paying attention to the form and function of Clyde Kennard's letters, we can look to ancient letter writing, recognizing rhetorical features, intellectual reasoning, and traits of his religious faith. Studies of the writings of the apostle Paul are vast, accumulating centuries of scholarship, but what can be gleaned from such work to understand Kennard's letters is the nature of letter writing itself, the act of appealing to audiences both distant and intimately; to answer questions by addressing a mounting crisis; to assure the public of an equitable conflict resolution grounded by truth and providing justice for all.[13] The essential paradox of Paul's letters, for example, to churches in Rome (where he had not visited) and in Corinth (where he had been absent) is just how his ideas inspire right changes in society and individual consciousness. These intimate conversations Paul had with far-spread congregates sought to unite them in one body in Christ (1 Corinthians 12:12–27). In this same spirit, Clyde Kennard appealed to readers of the *Hattiesburg American* by opening his letters as conversations. Announcing to readers the subject of "mixing" as the headline, the first letter opens with a direct address simply to "Editor, *The American*" as

Kennard immediately gestures to a public debate about integration and segregation as subjects "least understood" though "widely discussed." Using personal pronouns, *me* and *I*, repeatedly brings Kennard into focus (as his own case is central to the debates), but he broadens the scope to the collective *our* and *us*, which equalizes his readers as one body of citizens: "*In our state* the officials spend much of their time and perhaps *much of our money* trying to convince the integrationists, and reassure the segregationists, that the policy of perpetual segregation is the *wisest course for us to pursue*, in spite of the tremendous cost of duplication" (emphasis added). Considering how Paul wrote to clarify divine law, Kennard's epistles allow for social interaction, which defies the laws of segregation. Thinking about the "epistolary situation" in which we find Kennard engaging in conversations with a majority white audience is quite compelling: "It denotes the entire historical background in which writer and addressee are united. In the strictest sense, it denotes the specific problems existing between and uniting the sender and the recipient in a unique and exclusive relationship. The letter then is the specific means through which these specific problems are being dealt with."[14] Mindful of committing a misdemeanor even rhetorically, Kennard concludes his letters with peace and grace, a Pauline formula, to ensure the message is sanctioned by truth and love (Galatians 6:17–18; Ephesians 6:23–24) and not maligned by malice and hatred:

> I had rather meet my God with this [integrationist] creed than with any other yet devised by human society.[15]

> ... I like to quote from the great Indian leader, Mahatma Gandhi, in his discourse on the existence of God. He says: "In the midst of death, life persists; in the midst of untruth, truth persists; in the midst of darkness light persists." So, let it be, in our case.[16]

Only the last letter does not end with a spiritual reference but a call for federal action, which "makes [Kennard's] heart heavy," to consider it as his last resort of conflict resolution.[17] To think of Kennard writing then in a protest tradition, we can turn to epistolography as a common form of literary activism used by African Americans for generations.

Kennard's epistolary essays express his sincere belief in freedom, democracy, and a common humanity like those written by other African Americans. Traceable even to America's birth, such abolitionist or civil rights epistles righteously proclaim liberal principles of equality and constitutional decrees of justice. We find Phillis Wheatley writing, for example, in 1774 to

Samson Occom, a Mohegan tribal leader and Presbyterian minister, lending her voice to condemn the enslavement of Africans in America and throughout the diaspora. Wheatley acknowledges Occom's "Vindication of their natural Rights" as an ally to the cause of freedom while she condemns slave owners for their avarice. She writes "to convince [slave-holding colonists] of the strange Absurdity of their Conduct whose Words and Actions are so diametrically opposite" (foreshadowing the Declaration of Independence from British tyranny in 1776).[18] Wheatley's letter was printed in newspapers to appeal to a broader audience inclusive of Occom, and with this open-letter format, she makes the personal and political argument of liberation for the oppressed. So too does Benjamin Banneker in his letter to Thomas Jefferson in 1791, in which Banneker refutes Jefferson's scientific reasoning of Black inferiority in *Notes on the State of Virginia*.[19]

Later in 1848, Frederick Douglass provides yet another template of the abolitionist / civil rights epistle. In "To My Old Master, Thomas Auld," published in *The North Star*, Douglass, as editor himself, uses the open letter to create a public forum appealing to readers unfamiliar with the abuse suffered by himself and others who remained enslaved.[20] In his letter, Douglass makes a public appeal for justice on behalf of other enslaved Blacks, especially his own family members, by emphasizing a common humanity: "Not a few there are in our country, who, while they have no scruples against robbing the laborer of the hard earned results of his patient industry, will be shocked by the extremely indelicate manner of bringing [Thomas Auld's] name before the public. . . . I will frankly state the ground upon which I justify myself in this instance, . . . All will agree that a man guilty of theft, robbery, or murder, has forfeited the right to concealment and private life; that the community have a right to subject such persons to the most complete exposure."[21] Though slavery was still legal, Douglass challenges the system and stakeholders like his former master in the court of public opinion. Douglass indicts the slaveholder as a criminal and effectively harnessed the power of the press to draw attention to the immorality of slavery by making his appeal personal.

We learn about his experiences as a slave on a Maryland plantation and as a witness to the treatment of other slaves (e.g., violent punishment, selling and distribution of chattel property, etc.). Eventually, as he explains to Auld as having an intimate conversation with a friend, Douglass opens up about his family life. He boasts of having "as comfortable a dwelling as [Auld's] own" and, with his wife (Anna Murray Douglass), being able to educate his four children. He is a proud father and protector, though he also remembers "the chain, the gag, the bloody whip, the death-like gloom overshadowing the broken spirt of the fettered bondman, the appalling liability of his being torn away from wife and children and sold like a beast in the market."²² Sentiment is a rhetorical style that Douglass favors in his writings about slavery; he uses it to break unjustifiable barriers by bringing together the public—enslaved and free, whites and Blacks, Northerners and Southerners—into one human race. As a fugitive, Douglass used his escape and his activism in the abolitionist movement to illustrate the perils of his journey to freedom. The public therefore comes to understand the race problem in the life of an individual to effect change for thousands of others.

Continuing in this tradition, Clyde Kennard appeals to a local audience of white citizens in Hattiesburg to get them to understand how his experience is typical for most other African Americans trying to survive segregation. His approach is not as radical as that of Frederick Douglass; Kennard does not draw on sentiment as much to condemn his oppressors (as Douglass does in positioning Auld as representative of slaveholders). Kennard makes a logical appeal, however, to pierce a racist conscience. Consider, for instance, how Kennard had much respect for the law, but he expresses doubt in the merits of a segregated society based on *unjust laws*. "If there is one quality of Americans which would set them apart from almost any other peoples, it is the history of their struggle for liberty and justice under the law . . . [T]his nation was conceived in liberty and dedicated to the proposition that all men are created equal."²³ The constitutionality of school integration was fortified later by the ruling of *Brown v. Board of Education*, upon which Kennard builds his analysis of "mixing" in higher education and in general society. He tries to reason with public opposition: "Segregationists whose convictions are based on reason rather than passion might agree that the most honorable and actually the only path to our goal, would be to allow integration at some level."²⁴ Thwarted in making his final appeal, Kennard concedes, "If [Mississippi] should lead out with only the smallest amount of integration [by allowing him to enroll in MSC], it would never have to worry about Federal intervention."²⁵ Kennard anticipates the tactics that would lead eventually to James Meredith's admission to the University of Mississippi years later. But Kennard acquiesces, in his letters at least, because "the thought of presenting this request [for forced enrollment] before a Federal Court for consideration, with all the publicity and misrepresentation which that would bring about, makes [his] heart heavy."²⁶ The fact that Kennard risks addressing the problems of integration in such a public forum (with a series of editorials) is a radical move that did endanger his life. And, as I will discuss later, Kennard's epistolary essays extend the nineteenth-century tradition into the twentieth century, preceding even those written by Dr. Martin Luther King Jr., thereby providing rich contextualization for such pivotal treatises.[27]

Using Clyde Kennard's own writing, this chapter examines his role as an activist-intellectual in the tradition of African American protest literature and political history. He is positioned as an alert individual in a specific time and place (and therefore affected by such conditions) creating and responding to progress in a once static society.[28] Kennard grapples with the construction of "race" in political discourses and interrogates power relations that determine the progress of African Americans and of the nation at large.[29] That he felt compelled to launch a public campaign for integration, however, was based solely on personal circumstances. The letters Kennard wrote to the editor as published in the *Hattiesburg American* make a clear case for social change and racial progress. In these open letters that inform the public about the discriminatory practices of a state college, Clyde Kennard is *not* a victim, though his public image is mostly framed by others as such.

It is important to note that, like the apostle Paul, Kennard's subjectivity as constructed in the letters might appear to differ from the historical self, the person behind the letter. Oral accounts of Kennard being "mild-mannered" and "soft-spoken," for instance, might suggest then that he was not a radical rhetorician as he appears in the letters. That he did not lead an actual protest to integrate MSC but stands by his "integrationist creed" in the letters might further confound readers. Yet, Paul, too, had critics (especially at the church in Corinth) who did not believe that his writing was authentic: "For some say, 'His letters are weighty and forceful, but in person he is unimpressive and his speaking amounts to nothing'" (II Corinthians 10:10). In defense of his ministry, Paul responds not with force to such criticism but with reason: "Such people should realize that what we are in our letters when we are absent, we will be in our actions when we are present" (II Corinthians 10:11). The antithesis of Paul's reasoning applies to Kennard's writing an authentic self in contrast to a tragic persona as constructed by others telling his story. We must therefore consider just how Kennard tells his own story using writing as a form of activism to assert his civil rights, promote social justice, and advocate for racial equity in higher education. And, as I discuss in the chapter's final section, understanding Kennard's education at the University of Chicago explains the decision to look closely at his writing. His experience there serves as a precursor to the tragedy, and it is an important part of the story that is rarely, if ever, told.

THE INTEGRATIONIST CREED

Without even announcing his own case for integrating MSC, Clyde Kennard begins the first letter, aptly entitled "Mixing," to address a complex issue—"race" and school integration—by making it plain and simple, as presented in this chapter's epigraph: "It is interesting to me that subjects which are most widely discussed are those which seem to be least understood by the public whom these discussions are designed to inform." It is a confident gesture of an intellectual pondering the situation at a tense historical moment with racial integration battles waging. Kennard therefore takes a stand and delivers a lecture that could alter public opinion. He appears poised to explain what has not been addressed by others, especially in the pages of a local news weekly. If the public seemed misinformed about the Supreme Court ruling in *Brown v. Board of Education*, or if the white Southern majority refused to acknowledge its legitimacy, Clyde Kennard wants to assure them of the practicality of school integration. "Mixing" was published on the first Friday in December 1958; in a nearly four-column spread, the essay dominates the page framed by advertisements mostly for holiday sales to distract readers.[30] Perhaps this layout design was strategic, but bold labeling of the Letter to the Editor headline seems to direct readers to Kennard on the lectern.

It had been more than three years since his first enrollment attempt, which was blocked when Kennard could not get the endorsement of local white alumni to support his application.[31] Now he could address white readers as equals about the importance of seeking higher education for all. Race relations, he assures them, had been the subject of much debate in the South since the passing of *Brown v. Board*, and thus he enters the public forum as an ordinary citizen with just as much at stake as any of the readers holding the newspaper with rapt attention. Neither bitter nor defeated, Kennard felt instead "a great sympathy for the people who truly believe that the interest of both the White and Negro people would be served best by a system of complete or partial segregation."[32] Signs of change were evident by Kennard even being featured in the white press. David R. Davis explains that "before the Supreme Court transformed desegregation into a national imperative, black Americans had long been virtually invisible in the pages of the nation's daily presses. By and large, blacks did not merit a mention in most white-owned newspapers unless they committed a crime or died a violent death."[33] Kennard's epistles are remarkable, embodied narratives of Blackness; readers must see him / "us" as a person / "people" falsely represented in the press as deviant, disposable, and despised.

Kennard's integrationist creed is a hallmark of African American liberalism as traceable to the nineteenth century. Harold Cruse thought of Frederick Douglass as the prototypical leader, whose Black liberalist approach to solving America's race problem was predicated on securing freedom, equality, and civil rights. And "integration," thus, became the mission of the modern civil rights movement in the twentieth century with the NAACP as the vanguard. Separatists, in Cruse's logic, offered the alternative experience of Blacks' existence as a nation within a nation, functioning within the reality of a racist America not as it is imagined constitutionally. While dismissive of the liberalist and advocating the nationalist, Cruse's critique does not fully consider historical contexts for comparative analysis.[34] Admittedly, I read Kennard's letters through the lens of a post–civil rights movement (a stance Cruse had yet to anticipate) and the effectiveness of a liberal approach marked by the passing of major legislation.[35] Looking at the individualism and group consciousness of Kennard's philosophical reasoning (antithetical to Cruse's estimation of the "crisis" of the Black intellectual), Kennard understands how race functions in a "closed society," acknowledging, "Although I am integrationist by choice, I am a segregationist by nature, and I think most Negroes are. We prefer to be alone, but experience has taught us that if we are ever to attain the goal of first-class citizenship, we must do it through a closer association with the dominant (white) group."[36] To his credit, Kennard anticipates criticism for writing the letter by being honest about race relations as they existed under segregation and how one becomes naturalized by this hostile environment. He continues to explain the race problem and how it affects the state and nation at large.[37]

A system of "separate but equal" seems absurd, Kennard argues, when you examine the real costs of a segregated society. Dual public-school systems, for instance, if funds were distributed equally (which he knows was not generally the case), would bankrupt the state. More importantly, Kennard asks his readers to consider long-term consequences of the race problem. How to sustain a parallel system that will affect every facet of private life and public service for all residents? How to retain the best educated African Americans within the state if they are not allowed access to career opportunities befitting their training? Kennard's appeal for integration exposes the complexities of a segregated society—its distorted educational, political, and economic systems. The letter's tone is relaxed and casual as Kennard cautions readers to consider how easily they could be manipulated by racist propaganda.

Character building is what mostly concerns Kennard: "What we [integrationists] request is only that in all things competitive, merit be used as a measuring stick rather than race. We believe that for men to work together best, they must be trained together in their youth. We believe that there is more to going to school than listening to the teacher and reciting lessons. In school one learns to appreciate and respect the abilities of the other. . . . We believe when merit replaces race as a factor in character evaluation, the most heckling social problem of modern times will have been solved."[38] Such idealistic, integrationist sentiments are most famously echoed later in Dr. Martin Luther King Jr.'s 1963 "I Have a Dream" speech:

> I have a dream that one day even the state of Mississippi, a state sweltering with the heat of injustice, sweltering with the heat of oppression, will be transformed into an oasis of freedom and justice.
>
> I have a dream that my four little children will one day live in a nation where they will not be judged by the color of their skin but by the content of their character.[39]

It is easy to draw comparisons between the two men, though King casts a broad shadow over lesser-known civil rights pioneers such as Clyde Kennard.

Both Kennard and King wrote open letters like those found in the New Testament, epistles written by the apostle Paul for a public audience to fortify its moral conscience.[40] King began using the open-letter format by responding to racial injustice, for instance, while still attending Morehouse College in 1946; he penned a brief letter, "Kick Up Dust," to the editor of the *Atlanta Constitution*, addressing racial violence, miscegenation, and civil rights violations.[41] Being keenly aware of his audience, even a young King understood how to cull Southern white liberals from the lot by disassociation: "I often find when decent treatment for the Negro is urged, a certain class of people hurry to raise the scarecrow of social mingling and intermarriage. These questions have nothing to do with the case. And most people who kick up this kind of dust know that it is simple dust to obscure the real question of rights and opportunities." Appealing to a sense of civility and moral ethics, King brings attention to the absurdity of segregated society and culture—especially as veiled by a thin guise of bigotry—just as Kennard reasons in his letters. King speaks frankly about the generational trauma of Black girls and women being raped by "both white toughs and white aristocrats," which broadens the case for all his readers to consider the creation of a race problem caused not by those advocating racial justice and civil rights for Black Americans. King then issues an integrationist creed calling for equal opportunities in education and public services as well as voting rights protected by laws that would bring about real changes in the nation.

With his pragmatic boldness in the "Kick Up Dust" editorial, we witness the evolution of Dr. King's formulaic writing; the use of the open letter serves to amplify King's voice long before he ever mounts platforms to address throngs of audiences.[42] We see evidence nonetheless of logical reasoning found in the longer expositions about basic civil rights King would most famously deliver later in print and at the podium. By 1956, for example, King had crafted a sermon, "Paul's Letters to American Christians," as he imagined it having been written by the apostle to address the nation as being technologically advanced but spiritually backward.[43] In the double-voiced epistle, King as Paul condemns America's capitalist greed and bankrupt morality, which exacerbate the race problem:

> And so, Americans, I am impelled to urge you to get rid of every aspect of segregation. The broad universalism standing at the center of the gospel makes both the theory and practice of segregation morally unjustifiable. Segregation is a blatant denial of the unity which we all have in Christ. It substitutes an I-It relationship. The segregator relegates the segregated to the status of a thing rather than elevate him to the status of a person. The underlying philosophy of Christianity is diametrically opposed to the underlying philosophy of segregation, and all the dialectics of the logicians cannot make them lie down together.[44]

Kennard may have acted in similar ways writing epistles like King and Paul, but not as a pastor delivering a sermon.[45] Kennard though wanted the same outcome of reaching a complex, hostile audience, including the editor of the *Hattiesburg American* and a broader white public.

To understand and better appreciate Kennard's compositions as civil rights epistles, we might look to a more familiar template as found in King's "Letter from a Birmingham Jail" (1963), illustrating a hybrid of the Pauline tradition and of the Black sermonic tradition.[46] Rich with theological and historical allusions, King wrote to address the criticism of white clergy's opposition to his visit to Birmingham, Alabama, as an "outside agitator." Like the apostle Paul, King felt "compelled to carry the gospel of freedom" anywhere necessary.[47] As an open letter, the document appeals to the masses as it became widely circulated in the press. King explains the stages of his nonviolent campaign and, ultimately, the importance of civil disobedience to achieve justice and racial equality. In response to the clergy's call for negotiation, King counters: "Nonviolent direct action (like boycotts) seeks to create such a crisis and foster such a tension that a community which has constantly refused to negotiate is forced to confront the issue."[48] King's eloquence and philosophical tone allow him to act as a "moral force" in getting America to "embrace its past, to become more inclusive and accepting of humanity."[49] The Baptist preacher appeals to the public as an activist-intellectual with a clear agenda.

So too does Clyde Kennard. "Just as Socrates felt it necessary to create a tension in the mind so that individuals could rise from the bondage of myths and half-truths," as King proclaims, Kennard uses similar rhetorical strategies in his open letters. He makes a public appeal for justice by providing the truth about the race problem and its detrimental effect on all Mississippians and the nation at large. The second letter Kennard penned is entitled "The Race Question," and the *Hattiesburg American* published it on September 25, 1959. He strikes a more philosophical tone in this letter, lecturing on rights and reason. A month prior, Kennard had contacted President McCain to inform him that he intended to reapply for the fall semester at MSC. He had also written a seven-page letter to Admissions Director Aubrey Lucas in which he issued a rebuttal to all the traditional arguments used to defend segregation.[50] Thus, Kennard opens "The Race Question" countering charges against integrationists; he uses logical reasoning and American history to state the case plainly:

> If there is one quality of Americans which would set them apart from almost any other peoples, it is the history of their struggle for liberty and justice under the law. [Abraham] Lincoln has rightly said that this nation was conceived in liberty and dedicated to the proposition that all men are created equal. Truly, the history of America is inseparable from the ideals of John Locke, John Stuart Mill and Jean Rousseau.[51] "We hold these truths to be self-evident, says our Declaration of Independence, that all men are created equal." How different that statement is in spirit from the one which says: Before I see my child go to school with a Negro, I will destroy the whole school system. How different in virtue is the statement of Patrick Henry which says, "I know not what course others may take, but as for me give me liberty or give me death," and the one which says, "before I see a Negro with liberty, I had rather see him dead."[52]

His delivery is punctuated with passion, and Kennard is certain that the truth must be proclaimed. He cites influential Western philosophers and political theorists to ground his own arguments, but he also illustrates their ideas. Rousseau's belief in the corrupting influence of historical circumstance on human beings, Mill's belief in freedom and equality, and Locke's belief in limiting government control over citizens and pragmatism are all brought to bear on the entire segregated South. Kennard interrogates the founding principles of American democracy also in ways like David Walker in his *Appeal* (1829), which cites the Constitution as source of contention to dispute proslavery arguments.[53] Kennard continues his exposition on the modern race problem with a series of questions or by using the Socratic method to engage readers in a critical dialogue about the distinctions between integrationists and segregationists. The repetitious questioning is an effective rhetorical strategy, which leads his readers to ponder the ultimate dilemma: "Can we achieve this togetherness in our time?" he asks.[54]

On January 23, 1960, Clyde Kennard's last letter, entitled "School Mix," was published in the *Hattiesburg American*. It is the only one that explains his attempts to integrate MSC. This letter is more contemplative than the others, more personal, with raw emotions.[55] He admits, "My situation at home makes it very difficult for me to leave home to continue my education." An awkward sense of place and belonging haunts Kennard; he had not been able to attend the school of his choice because Mississippi's discriminatory policies mark him as a native son without a *home* to claim.[56] Kennard's final letter then is not just another plea for justice; it is a love letter to the state of Mississippi: "I know that there are those among us who feel that both races would be best benefited by a policy of private and public separation of the races, and that this segregation should be maintained no matter what the cost to ourselves and to future generations. Unfortunately, perhaps I have not been able to convince myself, nor has anyone else been able to convince me that this is really the wisest course for Mississippi to follow at this critical juncture in our history."[57] Kennard continues reciting the fallacies of maintaining "separate but equal" policies for public education as he does in his earlier letters. He concludes with a resounding truth: "The end product of an education is a greater and more useful participation in the art of living in a civilized society. If an education does not help make out of people more useful citizens to themselves and their community, then it has failed. Conversely, if the community fails to provide those whom it educates an opportunity to serve it to the fullest extent, then the community is guilty of self-impoverishment or self-destruction."[58] The maintenance of white supremacy, Kennard cautions, is burdensome. However, the solution is simple: Educate all individuals to improve all of society. Striking the posture of a public intellectual brings

Kennard into focus not as a passive victim of circumstance, but, especially in his last letter, as a voice of reason as he closes with a daunting dilemma to contest (or *not*) the laws of segregation through the courts. Dr. King, likewise, believed that he had a moral obligation to disobey unjust laws: "All segregation statutes are unjust because segregation distorts the soul and damages the personality. It gives the segregator a false sense of superiority and the segregated a false sense of inferiority. . . . So segregation is not only politically, economically, and sociologically unsound, but it is morally wrong and sinful."[59] This was Dr. King's mandate for civil disobedience. The two men shared philosophical beliefs in nonviolence, and, as Kennard considers pushing his case forward beyond the court of public opinion, he remains adamant: "I have tried to make it clear that my love for the State of Mississippi and my hope for its peaceful prosperity is equal to any man's alive."[60]

"INTEGRATING THE LIFE OF THE MIND": THE CHICAGO EXPERIENCE

While Clyde Kennard did not achieve his goal of completing his education at home in Mississippi, we can trace his intellectualism to experiences at the University of Chicago. His enrollment at this elite institution is often cited to make exceptional Kennard's qualifications to attend MSC. But what if this experience could lead to a greater understanding of the man and his message? If indeed "the end product of an education is a greater and more useful participation in the art of living in a civilized society," as Kennard believed, and "if an education does not help make out of people more useful citizens to themselves and their community, then it has failed," so Kennard's educational quest was not simply diploma driven. As his letters evince, a more thorough investigation of the quality of education Clyde Kennard received at Chicago can satiate curiosity about the extent of his intellectual acumen.

For more than a century, the University of Chicago was at the forefront of integrating higher education in the United States, particularly by providing opportunities to African American students. As early as 1870, the university granted a law degree to Richard A. Dawson, the first African American graduate.[61] After the school was reorganized in the 1890s, a steady trickle of Black undergraduates and professional students completed studies across various disciplines. Among its distinguished alumni, Carter G. Woodson, "the Father of Black History," earned an AB and a master's degree in history by 1908. He later completed his PhD at Harvard in 1912, went on to launch the celebration of Black History Month in 1926 (initially Negro History Week), established two journals (*Journal of Negro History* and *The Negro History Bulletin*), and a research forum (the Association for the Study of Negro Life and History).[62] Sociologist Monroe Nathan Work also trained at the University of Chicago, earning an AB (in 1902) and AM (in 1903), before joining Booker T. Washington at the Tuskegee Institute. A notable scholar, Work debated the merits of a liberal versus vocational education to gain racial equality and continued his research on African American life (especially gathering data on lynching) at Tuskegee Institute from 1908 to 1947. Katherine Dunham, famed dancer of African diasporan techniques, studied at Chicago as an undergraduate in anthropology to earn a PhB in 1936; her studies were foundational for a career that spanned decades as a cultural anthropologist, choreographer, and global activist. In the first half of the twentieth century, Charles H. Turner (zoology), Ernest Everett Just (zoology), Lorenzo Dow Turner (English / linguistics), Georgiana Simpson (German philology), Albert Dunham (philosophy), and Benjamin E. Mays (religious studies) were among at least forty-five African Americans who earned doctoral degrees from the University of Chicago, "more than from any other university in the country."[63]

The University of Chicago cultivated "the life of the mind" ethos with a classical curriculum, leading experts on faculty, and administrators committed to elevating the university's ranking among the Ivy league. Attracting high-performing students for which critical thinking, civic engagement, and humanistic ideology lie at the core of their undergraduate studies defines the Chicago experience for most.[64] This commitment to intellectual and philosophical inquiry is traceable to the "golden ages" of its institutional history, especially during the tenure of Robert Maynard Hutchins, the president who revolutionized the university's curricula in the years leading up to Clyde Kennard's enrollment.[65] Creating "the College" as a core curriculum unit for liberal arts and sciences, Hutchins's plan promoted interdisciplinary studies for the undergraduate and shifted the specialized studies for extended research to be acquired optionally either at the senior level or later in professional schools. This general-education plan replaced the then more conventional model of an integrated learning approach inclusive of specialized studies throughout the undergraduate career at the university.[66] Controversial in its planning and implementation, Hutchins's plan envisioned an academic culture that would generate more liberal debate and autonomous study with students given fully to their intellectual pursuits beyond regimental codes.[67] This "New Plan" required only "an intelligent faculty, a flexible course of study, and a system of general examinations for which the student may present himself when in his opinion he is ready for them," Hutchins believed. Radical evaluation practices—"the abolition of credits, grades and attendance records, and the substitution for them of an intimate knowledge of the individual and an enlightened program of examinations," as Hutchison advocated—allowed even greater academic freedom for students.[68] "Students could attend the lectures and discussion sessions, but they could also study the syllabus and its recommended readings by themselves on their own time and take the six-hour examination whenever they felt sufficiently prepared."[69] Such autonomy allowed students to be "free thinkers" and self-disciplined. Adopted in 1942, Hutchins's plan was standardized by the time Clyde Kennard arrived on campus.

Under the New Plan, students could selectively take courses leading to broader understandings of human relations as influenced by politics, law, philosophy, history, religion, science, and art. Using *The Cap and Gown* yearbooks, we can try to reconstruct the curriculum and campus environment that Clyde Kennard likely experienced.[70] In 1953, students were given an orientation to the College to ensure their successful matriculation by first understanding the university's goals:

> The College of the University of Chicago, particularly since the adoption of the "New Plan" in 1942, has been devoted to teaching the three intellectual virtues: clear thinking, intellectual honesty, and wisdom. It has equally been pledged to acquainting the students with the ideas of the great thinkers of the West, and to developing the qualities which are cardinal in the formation of a thinking individual and a citizen in a free society, and which make of a man a successful human being rather than a technician or specialist, ignorant of the world beyond his specialty and unable to communicate with others than fellow specialists.[71]

The university's goal is stated as Hutchins envisioned, for undergraduates to have a more holistic learning experience with interdisciplinary studies. Moreover, the College had specific objectives to achieve this goal: "the development of the ability to read understandingly," "the ability to make considered judgements of arguments and opinions," and "the ability to communicate one's thoughts to other persons." All such objectives Clyde Kennard achieves with his editorials in *The Hattiesburg American*. The details of Hutchins's New Plan appear illustrated for students with photographs of classroom scenes, for instance, to verify that attendance "has been high, and the scholastic performance of Chicago College students is far in excess of most of their peers elsewhere."[72] "Listen," "Discuss," and "Experiment" are captions labeling images in the yearbook that typically feature white students concentrating on lectures or participating in classroom activities with an occasional Black student in attendance. This sort of social isolation was perhaps expected during segregation, especially as Kennard experienced such growing up in Mississippi, but the images of interracial classes also promote the Chicago way of integrating the life of the mind.

That Clyde Kennard was exposed to enlightened principals of equality and justice at an institution that is central to the history of integration in US higher education is most likely the case when you consider the faculty then at Chicago. Notables such as Frank H. Knight (economics), F. A. Hayek (economics), Richard P. McKeon (history / philosophy), Joseph J. Schwab (natural science), David Reisman (sociology), and Reuel Denney (poet) all received academic acclaim in the 1940s and 1950s, publishing what are now considered classic works in their respective fields.[73] Knight and Schwab, along with then president Hutchins and others, formed the Committee on Social Thought in 1941, to promote the "serious study of any academic topic, or of any philosophical and literary work"—using the Great Books series—that facilitates discussions to address problems in the past and of the modern era.[74] Another collaboration between Denney and Reisman on *The Lonely Crowd* (1950), which concentrates on sociological problems at midcentury, may also help us to understand the atmospheric incubation of Kennard's enrollment at the university. And, considering McKeon's work in the social sciences and the humanities, Chicago's core curriculum bears his imprint as much as that of Hutchins.[75]

Interdisciplinarity research and teaching practiced at Chicago allowed students to gain knowledge from an eclectic roster of professors in an experimental curriculum. Kennard likely would have studied under some of the professors mentioned since they taught general courses in the "Chicago plan for liberal education."[76] The curriculum laid out three sequential, year-long sessions of courses in the humanities, social sciences, natural sciences, English, mathematics, foreign language, and history before students could take final comprehensive exams as required in each area. Students could take the exams after independent study of subjects (without attending classes, with only the syllabi provided) or from enrolling in classes. One unique offering in Chicago's program was the "organizations, methods, and principles of knowledge" course as scheduled for the fourth year of study to integrate the knowledge gained from general courses using theoretical and practical applications to address basic questions.

Curriculum records show that Clyde Kennard enrolled as a typical student in the general education program, though it is often cited that he was a political science major.[77] Under the College's New Plan, undergraduates could not specialize in any subject or declare a major but instead had to complete the degree requirements progressively as outlined in the course catalog. Kennard enrolled at Chicago on February 7, 1953, during the winter quarter, and he began taking the three-part sequences of English and social science courses. Other than covering basic reading and writing skills, the English courses Kennard took over the winter and spring quarters focused on argumentation and persuasive writing. The cycle of social sciences courses introduced students to democratic principles and ideas of citizenship with these purposes in mind: "to give students a scientific understanding of his own and other cultures, and of how the individual comes personally to learn and embody the norms of a given culture. A third purpose is to analyze and clarify the kinds of problems involved when society or the individual tries to apply theoretical knowledge to social action."[78] The application of this knowledge to address the race problem in the South is evident in Kennard's own writing about his attempts to enroll at MSC. Consider, for instance, when Kennard opens his first letter to the editor in 1958, he asks readers to think about the illogical "policy of perpetual segregation" as backed by state officials. He recognizes group affiliations—integrationists versus segregationists—as personal choices to understand differences along racial binaries. Kennard writes his essays about segregated culture as informed apparently by his Chicago studies since the curriculum was designed to specifically examine Black life in the United States as a case study within the broad outline of social science courses: "Primary attention is devoted to an analysis of the effect on the personality of the Negro of his social status, both as a Negro and as a member of one of the classes within the Negro group itself."[79] So, Kennard could confidently identify himself as an "integrationist by choice" and "a segregationist by nature" by theorizing that "most Negroes are. We prefer to be alone, but experience has taught us that if we are ever to attain the goal of first-class citizenship, we must do it through a closer association with the dominant (White) group."[80] Kennard, with his Chicago training, offers pragmatic solutions to the race problem. He considers the "tremendous cost of duplication" as white state officials enforced segregation in a separate-but-(un)equal public school system rather than to integrate. Interestingly, Kennard's letters address the relation between personality and culture, as outlined in his studies.[81] That he would use this framework to analyze the race problem in school integration is significant: "The integrationists offer a program which at first seems if not cruel at least awkward. We admit to bring two groups of people together who have different social and ethnic backgrounds presents certain adjustment problems. We should expect that and any intelligent program must allow for these adjustments."[82] This "mixing" philosophy is central to African American liberalism as it had developed by the twentieth century and as we see evident in Kennard's persuasive arguments for integration appealing to the white readership of the *Hattiesburg American*. It is also this kind of thinking easily dismissed later by Harold Cruse in *The Crisis of the Negro Intellectual* (1967) as betrayal to the race. When reconsidered, however, as Jerry G. Watts proposes, we should contextualize such moderate liberalism among African Americans to understand it better as an effective political strategy given their "quest for functional utility."[83] Such methods, as we see in Kennard's campaign, did not involve using radical means of achieving equality and rather valorized persuasion to advocate for social change while working within systems of white hegemony.[84] Thinking about the processes that shape individuals in a segregated culture and the consequences of that culture having produced individuals with distinct character traits (e.g., flaws of racial biases), Kennard proposes a moderate solution of "getting closer" to erase the color line altogether. Taking social science classes as taught by David Reisman and Reuel Denney would have likely exposed Kennard to the kind of American liberalism that he would use to address the race problem back home in Mississippi.[85]

Also, in considering the Chicago factor, traceable influences of Richard P. McKeon's philosophic approach to understanding freedom, power, and history show up in Kennard's letter-writing campaign. With a "talent for making his philosophic learning accessible to college students," McKeon taught popular courses that challenged students to think critically about ideas and study methods used to address societal problems.[86] The courses McKeon began designing in the early 1950s would "institutionalize his conception of education for philosophic invention, interpretation, investigation, and exploration of values."[87] He organized lectures that proposed varied definitions of key concepts—like freedom, power, and history—and deep analysis of such concepts when studying human behavior and communal relations.[88] Philosophizing about "the race question," as a nod to the syllabi designed by McKeon, Clyde Kennard grounds his argument in American history, pondering the values of freedom and equality as fundamental principles for integration:

> Most basic to our beliefs about the race question in America today is that there can be no racial segregation without some racial discrimination, and that there cannot be a complete racial equalization without some racial integration.... Now this principle is an easy one for us to follow, for it holds as true in human history, especially American History, as it does in logic. Reason tells us that two things, different in location, different in constitution, different in origin, and different in purpose cannot possibly be equal. History has verified this conclusion. For nearly a century now the State of Mississippi has been under a supposedly separate but equal system. Let us ask ourselves, does the history of the system support the theory of the segregationists or the theory of the integrationists? What segregationist in his right mind would honestly claim that the facilities for the two races are equal? Still segregationists say, give us a little more time, we are really making progress. Perhaps they are making progress of some kind, but human life is not long enough to extend their time. They have had nearly a hundred years to prove their theory, and so far they are no closer to proof than when they began.[89]

Kennard knows that the history of segregation is based on illogical reasoning that belies democratic freedom. His perspective is drawn from experience (e.g., perhaps using segregated facilities), and his progressive theories draw from the past to create a better future. McKeon taught students to use knowledge to engage in *debate, dialogue, inquiry*, and *deduction* as four modes of thought for resolving philosophical problems in the social sciences.[90] Kennard used the *Hattiesburg American* as a public forum to debate the principles of integration based on the realities of racial segregation, its prejudicial laws and social customs, in Mississippi. "Reality" thus "conceived of as references, circumstances, or assumptions, or as a combination of these" is the deciding factor to launch the race problem debate, when "the agent or speaker—the knower—is the point of departure."[91] Given his mode of thought (what McKeon classified as *discrimination*, in its typical form of debate and aphorism), Kennard uses the *operational* method to address the problem. It is a "two-voiced" approach where "the assumption is that the orientation of each disputant affects their point-of-view" and how Kennard positions himself against segregationists structures the debate as he presents the oppositional views. McKeon lectured on the function of such debate in philosophic problem solving: "In discrimination, you need to discriminate between the positions taken by means of a debate among the disputants, which involves refutations of opposed positions; and you end the debate by refuting your opponent or by showing it is the better position. Throughout this approach of debate and aphorism, it is important to preserve the matrices of the different perspectives or the frames of reference."[92] Kennard's use of aphorisms is his most effective rhetorical device to counter the beliefs and actions of segregationists. In "Mixing," he requests firmly that "in all things competitive, *merit be used as a measuring stick rather than race*" (emphasis added). He concludes "The Race Question" letter with a famous quote from Mahatma Gandhi: "In the midst of death, life persists; in the midst of untruth, truth persists; in the midst of darkness, light persists."[93] Kennard is inspired to continue his campaign though his final plea for an opportunity to attend MSC is pragmatic. The simple solution is to attend the school closest to his home. The problem of race removed from the equation brings a resolution for Kennard as he regrets not being able to attend school for almost five years since his days at the University of Chicago. His last letter, "School Mix" (January 23, 1960), refutes the segregationist's claims of interracial relations (with implicit sexual taboos), disparity of job opportunities (for Black teachers), morality (citing Black criminality as the charge), and the cost of separate-but-equal facilities, all from the framework of McKeon's philosophic reasoning to solve social problems.

Careful examination of Clyde Kennard's letters reveals how much he wanted to educate the public about systemic racism in higher education and how such problems were endemic to the South and the nation at large. More importantly, his letters also focus on how to create a fair and just society more broadly. This is clearly the sort of practical application that McKeon had in mind with his "structural-relations" philosophical concept. So, what Kennard's letters also reveal is the imprint of the Chicago curriculum that was designed to liberate students from conforming not only to traditional academics but also to social norms, especially in a segregated society.[94] The two years Kennard spent at the school, from February 1953 to May 1955, was a tumultuous era in its history as marked by the transition from Robert Hutchins's administration to Lawrence A. Kimpton's (1951–1960). Kennard transferred to the school during its financial crisis, a period of low enrollment for undergraduates, and the tarnished reputation of "the College" as being too demanding.[95] Realizing how students were affected by the campus climate, it becomes even more apparent how circumstances at Chicago could have also necessitated Kennard's departure for home. With negotiations between undergraduate and graduate divisions in the College at an impasse, "the final outcome of which was that some College students found themselves forced to take almost five years of courses in order to fulfill the demands both of the College and of their respective departments."⁹⁶ Clyde Kennard had taken only general education courses at Chicago under Kimpton's revised plans. Likely, then, he would still need additional course work to complete the requirements of a more conventional BA degree plan. Or, if he'd remained at Chicago, it appears also that he may have only needed to take his final comprehensive exams by the summer of 1955 to complete his studies there.⁹⁷ Unexpectedly, Kennard is featured in the *Cap and Gown* yearbook among the list of undergraduates with an AB degree. This portrait of Kennard, poised and self-assured, brings into focus his tenacity and perseverance. Even with a few failing grades and the need to retake comprehensive exams for some courses (as were common among students), Kennard apparently anticipated graduating from the university that year since he took a class photo before leaving Chicago abruptly.

BOOKS AND BLOOD

Sometime in the summer of 1955, Clyde Kennard returned home to Hattiesburg with plans to run his family farm while suspending his formal studies. He may have left the campus in Chicago but not the life of the mind he had cultivated there. We know of his multiple, unsuccessful attempts to enroll at MSC, but what of other intellectual pursuits that fulfilled his thirst for knowledge and his quest for social change? Kennard's final years were spent not only fighting systemic racism, but he also remained committed to being a "useful citizen" to his community while still acquiring what education he could.

On August 25, 1955, Clyde Kennard was appointed by the Forrest County Board of Education to serve as a trustee for the Bay Springs School, a county school in the Kelly Settlement just a few miles north of Hattiesburg. This is the same rural community in which Kennard had grown up and where he had returned to manage his family farm. The announcement of trustees appeared in the *Hattiesburg American*, listing Clyde Kennard on a committee with several others, including Vernon Dahmer Sr., a local civil rights activist and one of Kennard's close friends and mentors.⁹⁸ The Bay Springs School was one of hundreds funded by philanthropist Julius Rosenwald, who began a partnership with Booker T. Washington in 1912 to build public schools for African Americans throughout the segregated South. Rosenwald officially launched the initiative in 1917 to fund the building of Black schools after the initial trials in rural Alabama, where

Washington had several schools built to demonstrate the need for providing quality education for African Americans.[99] Rosenwald schools became a nucleus for Black achievement within these communities: "By 1928, one of every five rural schools for black students in the region was a Rosenwald School, and they accommodated one-third of the region's rural black schoolchildren and teachers. By the end of the initiative in 1932, Rosenwald had spent $28,408,520 to construct 4,977 schools, 163 shop buildings, and 217 teachers' homes to aid 663,615 students in 883 counties in 15 states. Mississippi's 637 Rosenwald-assisted buildings trailed only North Carolina."[100] The Bay Springs School was built in 1925, and the original campus included a two-story high school building, an auditorium, a cafeteria, a vocational agricultural shop, and the superintendent's house.[101] That Clyde Kennard and Vernon Dahmer served on its board of trustees demonstrates their invested interest in providing young African Americans with at least a primary and secondary education.[102] Too often, when Rosenwald schools would fall under the control of the county superintendent of education, the communities "lost a measure of control over their children's education."[103] The Bay Springs School remained open in the community until 1958, closing in the aftermath of *Brown v. Board of Education*, when most public schools were integrated.[104] A year later, Kennard would lose his own struggle to enroll at MSC, but he continued to seek higher education through less formal means.

Of the various accounts of Clyde Kennard remaining vigilant in his studies—especially about his reading and writing while at Parchman penitentiary (often for illiterate prisoners), it is most unexpected to discover traceable evidence that leads back to the University of Chicago. In the pages of the *Daily Maroon*, the student publication on campus, Kennard's tragic circumstances ironically reveal more his tenacity of seeking an education against all odds.[105] One headline reads, "Kennard needs blood" (February 14, 1963), calling for student contributions following his release from Parchman and during his stay at the Billings Hospital, the medical school at the University, where he was being treated for cancer. The article recounts the experiences of "the former UC student" to make the contributions more urgent: "Any type of blood may be contributed. Males under 21 or females under 18 must have signed notes of permission from their parents in order to make donations." There is no real concern about racially mixing blood contributions apparently.[106] A couple of months later, another desperate plea appears, "Kennard needs books" (April 17, 1963), suggesting his studies continued even though his health was failing.[107] Written as an open letter to the editor, the request comes from Celia Towne, who had followed all the coverage of Kennard in the *Daily Maroon*: "It has come to my attention that Mr. Kennard would welcome the gift of books about the America Negro, in the fields of history, political science and government, natural sciences, philosophy, and sociology since the year 1955, as well as the great classical novels. He has an abundant supply of books but not the sort he wants to read."[108] Most telling of this request is the dated interruption of Kennard's formal education, having left the University of Chicago unexpectedly in 1955, and the stated desire for "the sort [of books] he wants to read," the kind of materials likely introduced to him while a student there. These were subjects familiar to him as such appeared in the College's core curriculum then. After all, he had been trained to be a free thinker, studying independently within the experimental, interdisciplinary program at the University of Chicago in the early 1950s. That the life of the mind remained a constant for Clyde Kennard is thus evident in this simple request to have books forwarded to his home address at "Rural Route One, Box 70, Hattiesburg, Mississippi," hundreds of miles away from his alma mater, while he remained just a few miles away, isolated from the school's campus, which even today has not reckoned fully with his legacy.

CHAPTER 3

THE STUDENT PRINTZ AND ARCHIVAL RECOVERY OF A SEGREGATED PAST

LOREN SAXTON COLEMAN AND CHERYL D. JENKINS

James Meredith's desegregation of the University of Mississippi (Ole Miss) in 1962 was widely covered in the news across the country, but seven years prior, in 1955, Clyde Kennard attempted to integrate Mississippi Southern College (MSC).[1] Even though Kennard's case did not receive similar media attention, the same racist, segregationist structures that conditioned Meredith's experience at Ole Miss in Oxford governed MSC in Hattiesburg. As was historically the case in most university systems, student newspapers were used to chronicle many of these instances of racial injustice. Student newspapers are traditionally recognized as agents of change and can be examined to help understand the formation and constantly evolving university community, particularly during the era of segregation and immediately following the implementation of desegregation at many universities in the South.

Additionally, the student press in this era often served as the channel for information and perspective regarding race, segregation, desegregation, and student activism on college campuses. The distinct narratives found in student papers have historically positioned them to serve as both "university ambassador" and "social crusader," especially when the papers highlight these particularly complex issues during the late 1950s and 1960s. Such was the case for MSC / the University of Southern Mississippi (USM), whose history as it relates to race and race relations provides distinct historical context for coverage in its official on-campus student newspaper, *The Student Printz,* and also for the emergence of *The Unheard Word,* an alternative publication created by the first Black editor of *The Student Printz* during the 1990s.

The 1990s is a significant period in USM's history as the Clyde Kennard story was "reintroduced" in an article in the state's largest mainstream newspaper, *The Clarion-Ledger*.[2] The article piqued the interest of students and others at the university during that era. Although the *Printz* did include stories in the 1990s about the Kennard case, *The Unheard Word* added broader context to not only the Clyde Kennard story, but also to the overall tone on campus in relation to race and racism. The alternative publication played a role in Black student activism on USM's campus during the 1990s, and its content contrasted the often-problematic narratives about race found in the official on-campus newspaper.

Newspapers help make sense of the intricacies of the nexus of social, political, and economic structures necessary to build and sustain community. Student newspapers, in particular, have traditionally been recognized as agents of change and can be examined to help understand the formation and constantly evolving university community. Unfortunately, the often-monolithic racial makeup of a typical college newspaper staff and coverage that tends to mirror their analogous concerns and perspectives can create and perpetuate racial narratives that have historically permeated predominantly white college campuses in this country. In response, many college campuses have provided opportunities for the emergence of alternative newspapers.

These alternative papers typically tell stories of difference and diversity in sometimes perceived homogenized, local, and small communities and often do not need to adhere to the formalities of a traditional student publication that functions not only as a voice for students, but in most cases for the university as well. To examine the role of alternative newspapers on college campuses and their narrative function in that culture, this chapter investigates two distinct texts, USM's alternative newspaper, *The Unheard Word*, published from 1990 to 1993, and the university's official student newspaper, *The Student Printz*, established in 1927. More specifically, this chapter investigates *The Student Printz* and *The Unheard Word* as cultural artifacts, and their coverage of the complex, even controversial issues of Kennard's attempts to desegregate the university. We identify and examine racial narratives perpetuated in the coverage of racial issues in *The Student Printz*, specifically its coverage of his attempts to enroll at MSC. attempts to enroll at MSC. Also, we examine how *The Unheard Word* used racial narratives to challenge dominant coverage on issues of race and race relations on USM's campus.

STUDENT NEWSPAPERS AND ALTERNATIVE VOICES

Alternative papers typically tell stories of difference and diversity in sometimes-perceived homogenized, local, and small communities. Alternative media provide a public space for people to debate politics and celebrate cultural heritage. Chris Atton and James Hamilton state that it's important to understand alternative journalism as a set of activities, rather than a specific kind of news story.[3] This emphasis on activity is paramount to our concept of media, specifically newspapers. Atton and Hamilton's emphasis on alternative journalism's goal to challenge dominant forms of journalism inform this chapter's examination of the role *The Student Printz* played in the construction of racial narratives at USM, and how these narratives helped produce the conditions of emergence for *The Unheard Word*.

Students are more likely to engage with college newspapers when there is some kind of connection to the community. Stevie Collins conducted a study on a college campus to see if the students' connections/involvement would be predictors of student newspaper readership. He found that the more engaged students were on campuses (e.g., involved in student organizations, participating in on-campus activities, and living on campus), the greater the likelihood that students would read the paper. Therefore, his research helped conceptualize college campuses as "community" and student newspapers as "community newspapers."[4]

Student newspapers provide news to both the campus and local communities.[5] While traditional student newspapers have been known to include more editorial coverage on controversial issues, such as antiwar protests, university budgets, and race relations, student newspapers are still largely conditioned by institutional structures and regulations.[6] In her research on the coverage of campus unrest in the 1960s, Kaylene Armstrong explains how traditional student newspapers often function as public relations tools, promoting college campuses instead of criticizing university administration or practices.

Despite the traditional campus newspaper's function to promote the institutional brand, it is common for alternative student-run publications to emerge to provide a more niche perspective about issues on college campuses. Alternative campus newspapers operate outside of institutional norms.[7] These publications are typically not funded or endorsed by the institution.[8] However, they typically emerge to promote a specific political agenda. This chapter is a study of alternative campus media.

Atton and Hamilton state that alternative media have specific goals aligned with democratizing communication or the expansion and inclusion of diverse voices and power among people.⁹ Alternative journalism content should be relevant and of vital interest to its audience.¹⁰ This content often explores the social meaning of community by highlighting the commonalities and communal practices of community and telling stories of difference and diversity in sometimes, perceived homogenized, local and small communities. On the USM campus, *The Unheard Word* was published to engage with a perceived homogenized and local audience on campus, Black students and faculty, and to provide distinct alternative narratives not found in *The Student Printz*.

STORYTELLING, NARRATIVE, AND MYTH IN NEWS

Narratives function to help organize social and cultural life. They help establish and use common knowledge for a particular purpose. Narrative theory proposes that all people are active participants in the creation and evaluation of messages. Therefore, in some sense, they are all storytellers. According to Walter Fisher, narratives help individuals see themselves as part of a larger context and relate to one another through story.¹¹ Daniel Deslauriers explains how narratives help individuals form connections.¹² These connections eventually lead to a quest for meaning.

Narratives must be accurate and credible to establish meaningful connections and commonalities among people. According to Deslauriers, narratives help organize human life into episodes.¹³ Similarly, Fisher argues that life is comprehended through a series of beginnings, middles, and ends. Fisher postulates that there are two basic principles of a good narrative—coherence and fidelity. Coherence is defined as the logical order of the elements within a narrative, and fidelity is the level of truthfulness of the story and its reasoning and values. Therefore, if the elements in a narrative are consistent, presented in a logical order, and credible, then the narrative is more effective in establishing relationships that have contextual and cultural relevance.¹⁴

News reports summarize factual events involving "real" people and thrive on repetition of themes and events.¹⁵ In the news, according to Jack Lule, "real" facts are reported using inherent contextual patterns to help explain origins, promote order, and represent social beliefs and values.¹⁶ Therefore, Lule states that news is reported and understood through universal stories, also known as myths.¹⁷

Lule identifies seven different universal stories, or myths, that permeate news outlets.¹⁸ One of the myths, "the trickster," is typically about Black people in the white, mainstream news. According to Lule, the "trickster" myth is consistent with literature that states that Black people, specifically African American men, are typically portrayed as "stupid" criminals across varying media platforms.[19] This myth is usually perpetuated in two different forms—the savage or animal and the victim. According to Lule, the savage perpetuates the stereotype that African Americans are unfit to function as civil and lawful human beings in society.[20] The victim narrative perpetuates the stereotype that wealthy Black people from lower-class environments cannot escape the social and cultural norms of their class or caste.[21] If a Black person transitions from lower class to middle or upper class, mainstream news overwhelmingly still stereotypes them as poor and unsuccessfully "tricking" society into thinking that they have achieved wealthy status. According to Lule, the use of stereotypes in myth builds a coherent, almost natural narrative that in the case of the trickster is also demeaning and limiting for Black people.[22] To help examine the influence of *The Unheard Word* on Black student activism, we pay specific attention to how *The Student Printz* perpetuated racial narratives at USM, such as the trickster, and how these narratives helped create a climate of Black student activism and the conditions of emergence for the publication and dissemination of *The Unheard Word*.

MYTH IN USM'S STUDENT NEWSPAPERS

Traditional practices that define what constitutes news are embedded in the structures of newspapers.[23] Both Stuart Hall and Lule examine how news is produced and understood through the use of specific patterns. Hall defines newspapers as literary and visual constructs that are shaped by rules, have symbolic meaning, and consist of traditions that are integral to the use of language.[24] Further, Hall conceptualizes newspapers as discursive activity.[25] Newspapers do not just report the news. Instead, newspapers make the news stories meaningful through their conscious and deliberate choice of style, tone, linguistics and rhetoric.

David Paul Nord suggests that newspapers can be examined to help understand the formation and constant evolution of community.[26] Nord discusses how newspapers are cultural artifacts that provide evidence of the complexities of culture.[27] Armstrong states that college newspapers are archival records that detail student perspectives on university or college life.[28]

Hall outlines how to engage in a critical textual analysis. First, immersion is necessary in historical and cultural analyses.[29] He goes on to say that researchers hone in on a specific area by doing a "long preliminary soak," which is helpful in selecting meaningful and significant evidence.[30]

Methodologically, we historicize *The Unheard Word* by identifying and analyzing racial narratives in *The Student Printz* at distinct historical moments that mark Kennard's multiple attempts to enroll at the university (1955, 1958, 1959), the desegregation of USM (1965), and the emergence and publication of *The Unheard Word* (1990–1993). Specifically, we focus on the October 1991 issue of *The Unheard Word*, which featured the first on-record interview about Kennard from university president Aubrey Lucas.[31] *The Unheard Word*, provides a distinct and unique perspective as a "social crusader" rather than as a traditional "university ambassador" *The Student Printz*.

Clyde Kennard Denied

The first historical *moment* is Clyde Kennard's attempts to desegregate Mississippi Southern College (MSC) in the late 1950s. At this historical juncture, the research examines the role of myth in perpetuating racial narratives in *The Student Printz*. Like most Southern cities in the 1950s, Hattiesburg was governed by law and practices of segregation. Public schools were legally segregated until the *Brown v. Board of Education* ruling in 1954. Just two years after this ruling, schools in Hattiesburg remained segregated.[32] Still, Kennard attempted to enroll at MSC in the aftermath of *Brown v Board*, and it is the first on-record attempt by a Black person to desegregate the institution. In the 1950s, *The Student Printz* was printed weekly. Four articles explicitly mention Kennard and his attempts to enroll at the school. The first article mentioning Kennard was printed on the front page on March 2, 1956.[33] The article clearly presents the facts of the story, which primarily include a statement from then university president William McCain on Kennard's attempt to enroll. Dr. McCain detailed that Kennard submitted an incomplete application, and therefore, the administrative offices did not take any action on his enrollment attempt. The end of the article reveals that "despite rumors to the contrary, he (McCain) had no knowledge of any other formal applications by Negroes."[34]

The placement of the article helps convey the prominence of the topic of race but more specifically the first attempt to desegregate the university. Although a short article, its appearance on the front page suggests that it was a matter of importance and urgency to the student body at the time. The clarification on attempts to enroll "despite rumors" also helps validate that there was conversation about Kennard's attempts to enroll at the college, at least among students. Additionally, this first article begins to show consistent, albeit subtle, language with the stereotype of the "trickster." The article's emphasis on the incomplete application is consistent with Lule's emphasis on the trickster's inability to follow established societal norms and rules, such as submitting a complete application for consideration of admission.

The second article appeared in *The Student Printz* on December 7, 1956.[35] The general focus of this article grapples with the idea of college access, almost alluding to the idea that MSC *may have* to be desegregated: "Also, a pertinent consideration for institutions in the South is whether a flood of Negro students would impair the standards which have existed. This consideration, although not pressing at the time, must be kept in mind."[36] Unlike the first article, the second article details how desegregation may be more of a reality for MSC and should be "kept in mind." Both articles are brief and do not seem to convey that desegregation was a material reality. *The Student Printz*'s seemingly disconnected tone in the first two articles is consistent with literature that suggests that college campuses generally functioned in silos separate from what was happening off campus.[37] While student activism in response to larger societal issues was much more prevalent in the 1930s as a result of the Great Depression, that momentum dissipated and would not broadly reemerge until the Vietnam War era.[38] Although *Brown vs. Board* legally mandated the desegregation of all public schools, including those in higher education, MSC, like other Southern public universities, continued to function as a segregated institution. Therefore, Kennard's story was not given much attention in the *Printz* until December 1958, when his admission to MSC seemed more plausible to the administration and students alike.

The third article about Clyde Kennard's attempt to enroll appeared on the front page on December 12, 1958. The headline read, "Negro Warns He Will Seek Admission to MSC."[39] The secondary headline reads, "Wants to Transfer from Chicago U, NAACP May Help." Unlike the first two articles, this *Printz* article provides a much longer story about Kennard. It details that Kennard had a good record at the University of Chicago, and it was speculated that he was taking instructions from the NAACP as it related to his second attempt to enroll at MSC.[40] The article plainly states that the Mississippi Sovereignty Commission was investigating Kennard, and "the issue" should be handled quickly without too much trouble. Maurice Malone, director of the Mississippi Sovereignty Commission, is quoted in the article stating, "We will do anything legal to prevent his entering."[41]

Unlike the first two articles, this third article includes details about what MSC was doing to prevent Kennard from being admitted to the college, such as the Mississippi Sovereignty Commission's involvement. The paper's inclusion of this racist undertone is consistent with the racial narrative about Black people in mainstream media during this period. Catherine Squires explains how mainstream news coverage about civil rights (from 1950 through 1980) typically reinforces negative stereotypes of Black Americans, uses conflict frames to report stories, and deemphasizes Black concerns, ultimately perpetuating a very biased perspective of civil rights cases and protest.[42] In this third article, it was made clear to the student body that the administration did not want Kennard to desegregate the institution, therefore, conveying the institution's complacency and even support of racist, segregationist laws.

The last article that detailed Kennard's attempts to enroll in MSC was printed on September 25, 1959. In "Negro Is Again Refused Entry," *Printz* provides specific details on Kennard's failed attempts.[43] According to *Printz*, Kennard was denied because of incomplete records and failure to meet admission requirements. Additionally, the article provides details on Kennard's arrest on campus for illegal possession of liquor and reckless driving. The language of this article is consistent with the stereotypes aligned with the trickster myth, as Kennard is described as a criminal. Kennard was arrested, sentenced, and eventually sent to the state penitentiary for these charges.[44]

In specific relation to the role of student-run newspapers in the creation and sustainment of universal stories and the promotion of the institution, our research shows how the trickster myth helped create a racial narrative that deprioritized the institution's overt racist strategy to keep Kennard from entering MSC. Moreover, it used the trickster myth to emphasize Kennard's perceived lack of compliance with rules of admission and laws within the city of Hattiesburg. This trickster myth helps legitimize MSC's refusal to admit Kennard based on lack of compliance, not the color of his skin.

Desegregation

The second historical moment of USM's racialized past used to historicize *The Unheard Word* is the desegregation of the university in the mid-1960s. In the fall of 1965, USM was integrated by Raylawni Branch and Gwendolyn Chambers Armstrong. Their admittance was fairly quiet, in regard to media attention. There was no formal story published indicating any "concern" about their enrollment on campus. There were no protests or outward expressions of distress indicated in the student newspaper. There was only one letter from President McCain to the students, faculty, and staff regarding the desegregation of the university. The letter appeared in *The Student Printz* on September 6, 1965, on page 1: "Ladies and Gentlemen: Two negro students have been admitted to this institution. These students will be participating in various orientation activities on campus beginning Monday, Sept. 6, 1965. It is expected that all personnel connected with the university will go about their affairs in a 'business as usual' manner. We are certain that fine conduct and spirit of our people will manifest itself during these times of change and that the university community will continue to show that we are 'the biggest and the best.'"[45]

The brief announcement mirrors most of the publication's coverage centering on race during this time. Even with all that was happening in the South with the civil rights movement during the 1960s, the *Printz* seemed to adhere to a "business as usual" tone in most of its coverage about the atmosphere on campus. In fact, the examination of articles published during the 1960s about race or racism was quite limited as there were very few stories that delved into the issue at all. With the increase in college student protests around the country and universities being integrated in the South, the *Printz* seemed to focus mainly on what was going on inside the campus community with little regard to what was going on outside of it. One exception was the *Printz*'s coverage of the integration of Ole Miss by James Meredith in September 1962.

In "Dean Grantham Lauds Southern Miss Students for Sound Judgment in Ole Miss Crisis," Grantham, the dean of men, praised students for their "sound judgment" and "lack of violence" during the week of racial clashes in the state and praised students for their lack of demonstrations.[46] The story was in reference to the rioting and demonstrations that were taking place in Oxford, Mississippi, after Meredith was admitted to Ole Miss. Grantham was quoted in the story as saying, "We hope and feel assured our students will continue to be a credit to this institution."[47] The quote speaks to a general tone that permeates *The Student Printz*'s coverage of racial issues during this period, particularly as it relates to integration efforts that were happening across the South. McCain, still the university's president at that time, was admittedly a segregationist but often asked for student cooperation in matters of race and expressed his desire to follow the rules of that day. In one university address that was featured in a 1963 issue of *Printz*, McCain stated that if a racial matter happened on campus, he would "call the students together and keep them informed" and discouraged any "outside disturbance or disorder."[48] The theme of following the laws or rules of the day was rarely challenged as indicated by editorials from

Printz and letters to the editor. It was apparent that McCain set the tone for the university, and the student newspaper reflected that. This follows the vein of the "ambassador" or role traditionally taken on by student-run college newspapers.[49]

Another example of how the paper may have perpetuated the "status-quo" ideology of the university happened in 1964. The March 20, 1964, edition of *The Student Printz* originally contained an article titled "Frazier's Attempt to Matriculate Is Unsuccessful." The article was about the enrollment attempt by John Frazier, a Black student who was also denied admittance almost a decade after Clyde Kennard's attempt. According to the notation beneath the article that is only accessible through the university archives (McCain Library), copies of the issue were confiscated, and a replacement issue was printed that did not contain the Frazier story. In 2007, a surviving issue of *Printz* with the Frazier story in it surfaced and was added to the USM archives.[50]

The Student Printz was consistent in sustaining the narrative that USM was neutral in regards to race relations during the period of desegregation on campus. Any issues related to race were published in the form of either an official letter from an administrator or in the form of a standard news story with little to no context about the unrest that was happening around the country, particularly in the Deep South. This journalistic omission was critical in continuing the myth that noncompliance with rules or laws subvert the status quo. The school's integration proceeded with little fanfare and university officials praised the actions of students who did not behave "unlawfully" in comparison to students in Oxford following the integration of Ole Miss. This "lawlessness" in the face of racial unrest was counter to the university's seemingly dispassionate stance on the issue.

The 1990s

The next historical moment this chapter examines is between 1990 and 1993, which also includes the period when the *Printz* hired its first Black student editor, Riva Brown. Unlike the first two moments we examine, this third moment yields several more articles that explicitly discuss race. Articles in *The Student Printz* during this period covered issues in Black popular culture, such as the premiere of the critically acclaimed film *Boyz N' the Hood*; national and international culture, such as the Ayers case in Mississippi that brought attention to systematic discrimination against historically Black colleges and universities (HBCUs) in the state; and President

Bush's foreign policy on Somalia. It seemed that with the first Black editor, *The Student Printz* devoted more news coverage to help raise awareness about issues on and off campus, specifically as it relates to race and culture. In "Discussion Brings Out USM Racial Problems," writer Daniel Mungai describes a tense discussion about racism in academia during a panel held on Clyde Kennard Day, which had been instituted by the university in October 1991.[51] The editorial juxtaposed another that seemed to offer an "alternative" perspective—"Black Conservative Stresses Diversity," by guest columnist David Bernstein—which railed against the "race monitors" on campus and their demand of "diversity of every kind" except diversity of thought. Bernstein writes, "As a black conservative, I was ostracized by the very people who claim to value difference because I was, well, different."[52] In addition to *Printz* coverage on political and popular culture between 1990 and 1993, there were some articles printed about Clyde Kennard relating to the university's administration and students' responsibility to honor Kennard's legacy. The article titled "Lucas Appoints Committee for Memorial Proposals" reported on efforts by the university to recognize the legacy of Kennard in some tangible way.[53]

Statistical data from USM's Office of Planning, Evaluation and Institutional Effectiveness' *Fact Book* reveal a surge in enrollment of Black students at USM in the early 1990s, signaling a recognizable change in student demographics on campus.[54] Following the publication of a story about Clyde Kennard in *The Clarion-Ledger*, the state's largest newspaper, many Black students became increasingly outspoken about racial issues on campus. With Brown as its head, the student newspaper began to reflect these concerns but continued to adhere to traditional journalistic practices and norms that often hindered the nuance necessary to address critical issues of race. The student newspaper, which had historically avoided any real coverage of racial stories, could not be the "voice" in these matters. As a result, Black students turned to a small alternative publication created by Brown in the fall of 1990 aptly named *The Unheard Word*.

The Unheard Word

The Unheard Word was distributed from October 1990 to March 1993 and included articles such as "The Black Student Agenda for the 21st Century," "The Five-Year Plan for Black Greek Eradication," "The African Concept of Personhood," and other Afrocentric commentary. The publication included a list of Black faculty members on campus, which at the time, was very small, and advertisements from local Black churches and the Black newspapers in the state. It was justly an alternative to what students would find in *The Student Printz* up to that point.

Brown's most noteworthy accomplishment with this publication was the inclusion of an interview with then university president Dr. Aubrey K. Lucas.[55] In the Q&A-style article, Lucas, who was director of admissions at Mississippi Southern College in the 1950s, described incidents surrounding Clyde Kennard's attempts to enroll at the school.[56] Although *The Student Printz* did document the enrollment attempts by Kennard when they occurred, there was never an explanation (at least in print) given by the main players at the university who denied Kennard's admittance. It is also significant that the editor of *The Unheard Word* was able to get this interview with Lucas while he was the sitting president since he was director of admissions when Kennard's application was denied.[57] Another key witness to the case still at the university in the 1990s was William McCain. Though McCain was president emeritus at the time of the interview, he did not speak openly about the case.

When asked how Kennard's case affected him, Lucas replied, "It's difficult for me to remember my reactions at the time. It appears to me that Clyde Kennard was framed, and I think it's horrible. I think it's terrible that Clyde Kennard could not come to the University of Southern Mississippi."[58] Though Lucas expressed slight contrition about Kennard's death, he was emphatic in this interview that the university would not name a building or erect a monument on campus in his honor. Lucas acquiesced: "I don't think Clyde Kennard would want that. Clyde Kennard would rather we take that money and put it in a fund that would do something good ... Clyde Kennard would want whatever monies we raised used to benefit people to help them do what he didn't get to do."[59] This sentiment was not shared by many of the Black students and student leaders on campus. In fact, what happened following that interview was a renewed vigor by students and members of the community not only to fight for Kennard's exoneration and have his memory recognized on campus in some tangible way, but to also address the cloud of white supremacy under which the university had functioned for so many years.[60] *The Student Printz* in 1991 called for the creation of an African American Studies Department and an endowed chairmanship in Kennard's name.[61] The student interviewed in that article suggested that the endowment should take the place of one of the endowed professorships named for officials whose history at the university was marked with racial intolerance or complete silence when those issues arose in the community. *The Unheard Word* followed the Lucas interview with additional stories and commentary about Kennard and suggestions about how the university should position itself in the matter. The publication provided a space for students to finally voice opinions about racial issues and did not limit that space to just Black students.

In "White Students Should Be Outraged at Kennard's Death Too," published in *The Unheard Word* in October 1991, the contributing writer considers how much has changed (or not) with race relations at USM decades after segregation:

> As a young, white student at the University of Southern Mississippi, I am ashamed at what my race did no more than 30 years ago. I am more ashamed that the people who surround me are not ashamed. I see the very people who were responsible and complicit in the killing of Clyde Kennard in high and respected positions at USM. Just as bad, I see many of my peers who, as white students at USM, cannot understand how this aspect of our history concerns them. Their souls are in danger.[62]

The Unheard Word was able to counter the racial narratives that had been perpetuated for many years on the USM campus. As the trickster myth was laid out in early published stories about Kennard in the student newspaper, the creator of *The Unheard Word* utilized the influence of an alternative voice to respond to that narrative. Through the use of positive language and imagery describing Black people and blackness, *The Unheard Word*'s editor, contributing writers, and followers pushed forward the aspect of "human action" within "social struggle." There was engagement because students connected to and identified with the stories that were published in *The Unheard Word*. This platform provided an avenue for diverse perspectives that were not limited by the ideals of the institution in which it was created.

Further, alternative newspapers tell the stories of difference and connect individuals who share specific political agendas. Although connected by race and ideology, many Black students on the USM campus also rallied around efforts to honor Clyde Kennard and to finally bring justice in the form of full exoneration. Stories and commentary published in *The Unheard Word* about Kennard were passionate, nuanced, and served as a democratizing agent for change. With the creation of this publication, the "Black agenda" finally had a visible and viable "voice" leading the way.

As stated earlier, Fisher explains that narratives must possess two main characteristics—coherence and fidelity.[63] This chapter showed that *The Student Printz*'s coverage of the first attempt to desegregate the institution was consistent with the universal story of the trickster, with the student newspaper's portrayal of Kennard as a criminal, unable to follow the rules or obey the law. The four stories about Kennard's attempts to enroll conveyed a coherent and accurate trickster narrative. The beginning of Kennard's trickster narrative detail his failure to submit complete applications to the institution. The second and third articles represent the middle of the narrative. In *Printz*'s coverage about his second attempt, although inclusive of more favorable details of his character, like his good standing at the University of Chicago, the story emphasizes that the situation was being handled legally. The end of the narrative was the *Printz* coverage on Kennard's final failed attempt to enroll.

The distinct beginning, middle, and end told a story about Kennard that ultimately perpetuated the status quo of the trickster myth. If someone does not follow the rules or breaks the law, there must be negative consequences, such as in Kennard's case: the denial of admission and later, arrest and time in prison. The accuracy of the story was conveyed using official sources in the news articles, such as the inclusion of quotes from the university president at the time, Dr. William McCain, and the Mississippi Sovereignty Commission. The racial narrative created and perpetuated via *The Student Printz* was one that deemed Kennard unworthy of admission to the institution, not solely because of his race, but because of his alleged incompetence. Kennard, who was "caught" with illegal liquor while driving recklessly, was portrayed as a trickster—the "stupid" thief, who got caught by authorities. Kennard's coverage in *Printz* as the trickster justified a separatist, segregationist, and white supremacist structure at the university.

Although there was limited coverage on the desegregation of the university in 1965, it still told a specific narrative about race and race relations on campus. The narrative of neutrality regarding race relations during the period of desegregation perpetuated the idea that the university was only following the rules or laws of the day and that the more overt effects of white supremacy were not at play at USM during the heightened period of racial unrest on college campuses across the country. Students at USM were even praised for their lack of involvement with the growing social movements across the country attached to racial equality. It's in this historical moment that the analysis provides evidence of the "hero" myth, which Lule explains reminds news audiences that they have "potential for greatness." While this greatness can be conceptualized as the university's desegregation and "forward" progress in race relations on campus, it also perpetuates a narrative on how white college campuses in the South should proceed in desegregation efforts. *The Student Printz*'s praise for students' lack of involvement in larger social movements and civil unrest across the Southeast worked to decontextualize USM's desegregation from nationwide efforts for racial equality and civil rights. It labeled the university as a "hero" because of its seemingly apolitical participation in the school's desegregation.

The emergence of *The Unheard Word* and concomitant coverage in *The Student Printz* in the 1990s challenges the trickster myth of Kennard and the hero myth conveyed in the coverage of the school's desegregation efforts. Brown, publisher of *The Unheard Word* and editor of *The Student Printz*, calls into question the coherence and fidelity of Kennard as the trickster. She challenges the distinct beginning, middle, and end of the story conveyed in the 1950s *Printz* coverage She includes the official source, the president of the university and admissions officer at the time of Kennard's attempts to enroll, Dr. Aubrey Lucas, in her interview that was published in *The Unheard Word*.

The Unheard Word as an alternative voice provides a different narrative to the homogenized stereotype that was constructed in the 1950s. The content was indeed political, thus challenging the "hero" myth perpetuated in the 1960s that praised the university's tamed involvement in the fight for civil rights and racial equality. *The Unheard Word* engaged Black communities, on and off campus, with relevant content and ultimately spurred people to explicit action in the continued fight for racial justice, reconciliation, and equality.

What *The Unheard Word* adds to the inquiry about student voice, specifically in relation to sensitive or controversial issues that affect campuses and society at large, is that outside of the parameters of institutional boundaries (be they bureaucratic or systemic, racialized ones) the coverage in alternative publications tends to be in broader strokes when articulating the concerns of students. *The Unheard Word*, in particular, actually broached many aspects of the student voice that are traditionally found on college campuses. For one, Riva Brown was also the first African American editor of the school's official student newspaper. Newspapers at predominately white institutions traditionally have poor records of racial diversity on their editorial staffs.[64] As a result, she was in a unique, visible position when she began reporting on the Clyde Kennard story. That position coupled with her own unique perspective as an African American student garnered a more personal investment in the outcome of her coverage. Second, the publication was created during a climate or period of increased student activism and discontent on college campuses. With popular films such as *Higher Learning*, Spike Lee's *School Daze*, and television shows such as *A Different World* illustrating the frustrations of the post–civil rights generation coming to a head, students at USM in the 1990s were speaking out about issues that had permeated the campus culture and attitudes for decades leading up to that point.

This is also reflective of actions we see today by students who feel they must look outside of their official or traditional means of expression to have their voices heard. Katherine Knott writes in *The Chronicle of Higher Education* about how the current political climate has brought a surge of publications run by Black students as they seek to cultivate a distinct voice on their campuses.[65] Knott's article cited *DOWN Magazine* at Yale University and *Black Hurricane* at Purdue University as examples of alternative publications with strong oppositional voices on predominantly white campuses. Those publications build community and give marginalized groups a platform to talk about issues important to them. *The Unheard Word* was a tool used in that same vein. *The Student Printz* and *The Unheard Word* at USM each played an important and distinct role in student life. In addition to existing research that calls for more diverse newsroom staffs at predominantly white institutions, this work offers a different perspective on the importance of on-campus student newspapers.

First, *The Unheard Word* helped fill a void for the USM's Black community. It challenged the universal stories that oversimplified and glossed over the lived experiences of Clyde Kennard, Raylawni Branch, and Gwendolyn Armstrong-Chambers, who each played a critical role in the desegregation of the institution. *The Unheard Word* called attention to the university's active role in the erasure of Kennard's legacy, prompting Black students to demand institutional change on issues of race and diversity. In the 1990s, there was a renewed urgency for students and Hattiesburg residents and city officials to tell Kennard's story. There was an influx in media coverage across the state about Kennard's story in both on-campus and off-campus newspapers.[66] As more people learned about Kennard's story, a collaborative effort was organized to exonerate Kennard for what people learned were false charges that led to his incarceration and ultimately his untimely death.[67] Although we cannot draw a causal relationship between *The Unheard Word* and Kennard's exoneration in 2006, it does show the significant role the alternative newspaper played in helping to ignite renewed interest in the Kennard case and his important role in USM, the city of Hattiesburg, and the state of Mississippi's history.

As college campuses are grappling with how to serve student populations that are wrestling with current political, economic, cultural, and racial crises, this chapter suggests that universities should reinvest and encourage the production of alternative student newspapers. Both forms of newspapers, traditional and alternative alike, can help prepare future journalists, and alternative student newspapers specifically, help build communities of action and activism among marginalized groups.

CHAPTER 4

"MAKING SURE HIS LEGACY DID NOT DIE WITH HIM"

Black Student Activism and the Memory of Clyde Kennard

REBECCA A. TUURI

On a Saturday evening in April 1972, John Ellis Price (BBA 1973, MS 1976), a junior accounting major from Vicksburg and the former president of the Afro-American Cultural Society (AACS) at the University of Southern Mississippi (USM), was honored for his work within the AACS. The society was less than four years old as an organization, yet it was a lifeline for Black students on campus. Black students had only been able to attend USM since fall 1965, when Gwendolyn Elaine Armstrong and Raylawni Branch became the first two students to enroll. It was not until fall 1968, though, that Black students created their own organization in the AACS. By the time that Price won his award, the organization had begun to call for significant changes at USM, including teaching Black history and literature classes, having Black sororities and fraternities on campus, and removing racist symbols on campus. As AACS president in spring and fall 1971, Price himself was a part of this work, and he was honored with a new award from the organization. The award was presented to a member of the AACS who had "given outstanding service" and who was the epitome of a community servant. Notably, the award was named for Clyde Kennard.[1]

Kennard, with his remarkable intelligence, character, courage, and determination to attend the predominately white institution was someone whom USM's Black students revered. As alumnus Anthony Harris (BA 1974; MA 1976) recalls, "it was a no brainer to call it the Clyde Kennard . . .

award.... We considered it an honor to be part of the tradition ... of making sure his legacy did not die with him." Harris won this award in 1974.[2] As he wrote in his 2013 memoir, *Ain't Gonna Let Nobody Turn Me 'Round*, he considers the Kennard award "the most meaningful award I have ever received or ever will receive," and it is so important that it continues to hang in his office at Prairie View A & M University today.[3]

Like Harris, many of the first Black students to attend USM hailed from Hattiesburg, where they either knew Kennard or learned about his story. Once on campus, they shared their knowledge of Kennard's courageous efforts, unjust imprisonment, and tragic death. Still, Kennard's case was not well known nationally and was overshadowed by James Meredith's higher-education-integration case.[4] USM former professor Monte Piliawsky asserted in his 1982 expose of USM, *Exit 13*, that Clyde Kennard's case had been forgotten.[5] Historians have echoed this claim and only recently included his story in examinations of the civil rights movement.[6] However, this claim ignores the memory keeping of those in the local Black community and on campus. Even students who were not openly involved in activist work viewed Kennard as a role model and pushed fellow students to know his story. Black Students at USM drew a direct ideological line between Kennard's attempt to integrate and their continuation of his efforts on the campus. Later students also used his bold insistence on racial equality as a model for Black pride.

Building on the work of recent scholars of the Black campus movement, this chapter will highlight the experiences and activism of Black students at a predominantly white state university or college (PWI) in the Deep South.[7] Unlike students in the Black campus movement in hotbed areas in the North, West, and Midwest, students at USM from 1965 through 1975 rarely protested and never engaged in any actions that resulted in a militarized response.[8] Like students at many PWIs around the country, USM's integration story is a slower, quieter, and more cautious one.[9] Still, they did push an agenda that mirrored those at more radical campuses, such as insisting on the creation of an Afro-American Cultural Society to preserve and celebrate Black culture, demanding the removal of racist symbols on campus, and promoting self-determination through the hiring of Black faculty and staff. Though their activism was limited, Black students at USM did engage in Black Power, and this chapter offers a nuanced concept of its meaning at a predominantly white state university in the Deep South.

This chapter also builds upon memory studies to highlight the importance of local Black freedom fighters, including Kennard, as counters to university-sanctioned white supremacist heroes, including Nathan

Bedford Forrest at USM, that continued to be revered on PWI campuses between 1965 and 1975.[10] While many white students facing integration at USM still upheld Lost Cause symbols such as the General Nat mascot and the anthem "Dixie," Black students carved out their own cultural spaces and upheld not only high-profile national Black Power leaders such as Malcom X and Dick Gregory but also Kennard. In this way, they were similar to Black students in the Memphis student movement who upheld Ida B. Wells as their own local militant hero.[11] Through its examination of Kennard's influence on USM's students, this chapter emphasizes the power of local civil rights heroes to inspire Black students for decades after the civil rights movement.

Finally, this chapter breaks new ground by highlighting the intergenerational evolution of both activism and memory keeping on campus. Students' relationship to Kennard changed as the racial environment shifted both on and off campus. Students from 1965 through 1968 mainly sought to take classes and integrate quietly into preexisting groups on campus.[12] As white resistance to Black students on campus softened, and Black students became a critical mass on campus, they took bolder actions to memorialize Kennard. Starting with the establishment of the AACS in 1968 through the late-1970s, a second generation kept Kennard's memory alive by carving out a space for themselves and creating their own organizations; a third generation of students, roughly from the mid-1980s through the mid-1990s, broke open the story of Kennard campus-wide; and a fourth generation in the mid-2000s prodded the State of Mississippi to eliminate the white-sanctioned narrative about Kennard's criminality, have him exonerated, and lay the groundwork for him to be publicly recognized as a hero. Far from being forgotten, Kennard was remembered and cherished by USM's Black students.

THE FIRST GENERATION: QUIETLY INTEGRATING

The earliest generation of Black students at USM strove to quietly take classes but did not have the critical mass necessary to create separate organizations for students of African descent. This first generation of Black students came from Hattiesburg and the surrounding areas and continued to live at home. The first two African American students to attend USM, Elaine Armstrong and Raylawni Branch, were both from Hattiesburg and had family demands. Armstrong's mother was disabled, and Branch had to care for her family.[13] Central to both the local preservation of Kennard's memory and the integration of USM in 1965 was the local NAACP, which aided both Gwendolyn Elaine Armstrong and Raylawni Branch in their integration efforts. Gwendolyn Elaine Armstrong had just graduated from Rowan High School, one of two all Black high schools in the area, in May 1965, and the local NAACP supported her bid to enter Southern Miss.[14] Raylawni Branch was the secretary of the local NAACP and was recruited to help Armstrong with the integration attempt. Branch had graduated six years before Armstrong and already was married with three children, but she agreed to attend Southern to support Armstrong. Branch knew Kennard well, as he would bring eggs to the café where she worked. In fact, she recalls seeing Kennard on the morning of his integration attempt at Mississippi Southern College in September 1959.[15]

Black students in this earliest cohort at USM had to steel themselves for the isolation and discrimination that they faced on campus. Much like other first-generation Black students at white institutions in the South, Black students at USM were still seemingly few and far between and were largely excluded from campus life.[16] The USM yearbook, *The Southerner*, from 1965 through 1966, when Armstrong and Branch were the first students, showed no Black students in any campus organizations. Meanwhile, the yearbook highlighted a "maid of cotton" and Confederate battle flags in many pictures. In the next year's *Southerner*, there were a few more Black students. Armstrong served as an editorial assistant for the yearbook and was visible in one awkward and uncaptioned photo on a page in which all other photographs include staff names.[17] The only Black students to have features written about them in the student newspaper, *The Student Printz*, in the late 1960s were Elaine Armstrong and Gwendolyn Jordan, the two winners of the Panhellenic talent shows in 1968 and 1969.[18] This mirrors the experiences of other "student heroes" of the first generations at predominantly white colleges around the South, where Black students were only reluctantly let into the university and were still blocked from campus culture, either informally or sometimes still formally.[19] Students at other Mississippi PWIs, Ole Miss and Delta State, also recall being taunted, called derogatory names, and isolated both within their classrooms and on their broader campuses.[20] However, this earliest cohort also trusted in their aptitude, emotional resilience, and faith to tolerate the experience.[21]

White student and faculty reactions on campus ranged from hostile to supportive. When Armstrong attended class, students would not sit close to her. They would make sure to sit in the front of the room if she sat in the back or in the back if she was in the front. She was called names, and her family received threatening calls at home. Her one white friend was nearly run over by a car. Armstrong mentioned that some faculty would never call on her but also that the majority of faculty were supportive and some even extremely supportive.[22] Branch has echoed the idea that most of the faculty were supportive, including Dr. Geoffrey Fish, an oceanography professor who volunteered to be the faculty advisor to both Armstrong and her. In addition, Branch has said that students would sit alphabetically in the classroom, and because her last name began with *Y* (her surname was then Young), she sat in the back and was not harassed in class like Armstrong. Branch did recall that she was once asked by girls in the locker room if she had a tail and that she was called the "n" word once in P.E., but she has also stated that she did not face a significant amount of racism on campus.[23] Jacqueline Hayes (BS 1969, MS 1972) has said that when she attended as an undergraduate between 1967 and 1969, students were mostly ambivalent toward her on campus and that faculty were supportive.[24]

THE SECOND GENERATION: CREATING BLACK CULTURAL SPACES

Following this earliest generation was a second cohort that began to advocate for Black cultural spaces on campus. This cohort began with the establishment of the AACS and continued through the 1970s with the swift growth of the Black student population and campus organizations. Black leadership and participation within mainstream organizations also occurred in the 1970s. Like the earliest group of African American students, this second generation was keenly aware of Kennard's ultimate sacrifice which made their enrollment possible. They honored his legacy in two main ways. First, they kept the story of his enrollment attempt alive through conversations with one another. Melvin Miller (BS 1972), who also was from Hattiesburg, did not recall really understanding Kennard's story until he came to USM, where he was encouraged to read stories about and discuss the case of Kennard.[25] Deborah Gambrell (BS 1972), then Deborah Jones, lived in Wiggins and was forced by her parents to attend USM because it was the closest college to home. Jones learned about Kennard from Elaine Armstrong during the summer before Jones started at USM.[26] Second, the members of this generation sought to continue the work that Kennard had started by completing their education and creating new physical, social, and intellectual spaces through which Black students would feel welcome on campus. As Miller recalled, "The hero is Clyde Kennard because we all stand on his shoulders. You know, he never got to graduate, but we graduated for him, that's how we feel about Clyde Kennard." Miller went on to say that although there was never any push from this cohort of students for a large-scale commemoration of Kennard, they believed that they should continue his work by "making sure that we get Black fraternities and sororities; making sure that the culture is present there so that we have something to relate to; making sure that we have Black faculty members, administrators, and staff; and . . . [that] Black . . . students [are] involved in the perks" such as getting the best on-campus jobs.[27]

Some members of this generation also knew about Kennard through their connection to the Hattiesburg community. As Eddie Holloway (BS 1974, MS 1975, MS 1984, PhD 1997), who enrolled in 1970, earned undergraduate and graduate degrees from USM, and later became an administrator at the school, recalls, "Since I was a little boy growing up in Hattiesburg's Mobile-Bouie neighborhood—going in and out of my mother's beautician shop, attending club meetings, watching the women quilt in the living room of my house, and listening to their conversations while they fished—I have always remembered the stories about Clyde Kennard. Kennard and his attempts to integrate Mississippi Southern College were the topics of conversations in many African American households."[28] Anthony Harris had an even more direct connection to Kennard. He first learned about Kennard from his mother, Daisy Harris Wade, who had been an ardent supporter of the civil rights movement in the mid-1960s. Harris's father, James Harris Sr., and Rev. John Cameron had brought Kennard back from the hospital in Jackson to Hattiesburg after he was released by Governor Barnett in late January 1963. Anthony Harris himself attended a freedom school in 1964, worked with voter registration, led civil rights meetings in song, and helped to integrate Thames Middle School in 1966. He was arrested for picketing, and his family also risked their safety by housing civil rights workers in the mid-1960s.[29]

Like other Black students who were among the first to integrate PWIs, these students in the first and second generations were very focused and academically gifted.[30] Many of them were valedictorians, salutatorians, and other high-achieving students at their high schools. Since graduation, the members of this cohort have gone on to work as professors and administrators in higher education; lawyers and judges; medical doctors, nurses, and veterinarians; and teachers and principals in secondary education. Jones became a judge; Miller became the director of development at Jackson State and director of public relations at the Piney Woods School; and Harris became an Educational Leadership and Counseling professor and administrator at Prairie View A & M University.

This second cohort, much like Kennard, and later Branch and Armstrong, decided to attend USM because it was the only four-year college close to home. While most had contemplated going to the closest HBCUs (Jackson State College, Alcorn Agricultural and Mechanical College, and Tougaloo College), which their parents and siblings had attended or were attending, many could not leave behind their loved ones while they pursued their education.[31] Melvin Miller decided to attend USM after his mother had a stroke and remained very ill. His twin sister went to Jackson State, and his older sister transferred from USM to Tougaloo College. He had also considered attending Jackson State or Alcorn but instead decided to go to USM because it was close to home. Melvin knew that it would be difficult at USM because he saw the difficulties that his older sister faced while on campus: "We [Lorma and Melvin] never talked about the racism or anything like that, I just knew that she was having a tough time, and so, when she went to Tougaloo, she just blossomed. But at USM, it was just the opposite, so I knew then that it was not going to be just a stroll in the park for me."[32] Anthony Harris lived at home and then took the bus to campus for a dime.[33] Others, such as Deborah (Jones) Gambrell, lived on campus but went home on the weekends.

White students on campus continued to harass Black students. When Deborah Gambrell first arrived on campus, she had asked to be housed with another Black student, but the dorm matron insisted that she room with a white student. When the white student saw Gambrell, she threw a fit, and Gambrell's parents had not gotten more than thirty miles down the road when the university called her parents to let them know that she would be moving to a new room.[34] Melvin Miller recalls that his classroom experience was awkward, as he often was the only Black student in classes, but he did not face overt racism in his classes. However, in the public social spaces such as the Hub, bookstore, and mailroom, white students would call him the "n-word."[35] Anthony Harris's brother James, who began at USM in 1969, received hate mail every week and had racist notes tacked to his door.[36]

There was no character more offensive to this second cohort than the Southern Miss mascot of General Nat, short for General Nathan Bedford Forrest, the Confederate general who led the Ft. Pillow Massacre that slaughtered scores of surrendering Black Union soldiers. Forrest is the namesake of Hattiesburg's county (founded in 1908), and he made his wealth as an antebellum slave dealer in Memphis, was an early leader of the Ku Klux Klan, and ran a convict leasing farm late in his life.[37] General Nat was still the mascot in 1971, when Anthony Harris arrived. Harris recalls that at every USM touchdown at the football games, General Nat would race up and down the sideline on horseback letting out a shrieking rebel yell and striking the air with his saber. As Harris recalls with a chuckle, "Thankfully we weren't very good." The band also played "Dixie" at every game. While the white students would cheer for the song, Black band members refused to play.[38] Harris's experience was echoed at other universities across the South. Markers of white supremacy were embraced by those clinging to massive resistance, including at the University of Mississippi (Ole Miss), with its own Colonel Reb mascot (another Confederate icon), which officially survived as the university's mascot until 2003, though an effort to keep him as an unofficial mascot remains two decades later.[39]

Some faculty also were unsupportive or even openly racist, well into the 1970s, but others continued to be supportive. When Anthony Harris informed his academic advisor that he wanted to change his major from political science to Spanish, his advisor tried to dissuade him by telling him that Black people had something wrong with their tongues that prohibited them from making the proper sounds in Spanish. Harris changed his major immediately to foreign languages (including Spanish) and completed his degree in 1974.[40] But other accounts were positive. Melvin Miller recalls that white students and faculty attended his wedding in 1972.[41] Alvin Williams (BS 1974) says that he felt welcomed by white professors. In fact, his professors were so impressed with him as an undergraduate that they later funded his PhD in marketing at the University of Arkansas if he agreed to come back to teach at USM, which he did for nearly thirty years.[42]

Much like with the first generation, family and community ties helped this second group navigate the challenges of being at a PWI. Miller grew up surrounded by the supportive environment of the Mobile-Bouie neighborhood. His church was within a few blocks of his home. His mother worked at the local elementary school, also a few blocks from his home. Holloway also was a child of the community. When he was only eleven years old, Holloway's mother died, and the Mobile-Bouie neighborhood looked after him. He was strengthened by teachers who lived in his neighborhood and by his participation in Mt. Carmel Missionary Baptist Church. The people in his community gave students like him school supplies or extra toothbrushes, combs, or clothing. Holloway decided to attend USM in order to live locally to care for his father.[43] Like Holloway, Anthony Harris also wanted to be close to his family members and community, including the fellow parishioners at Starlight Missionary Baptist Church, who had supported him since his youth.[44] These strong local ties provided an important support network for those like Holloway and Harris who could return home in the evenings and weekends and be rejuvenated. The community also served Black students who were new to the area. Representatives from community churches would pick up students on Sunday, take them to the service, and feed them before taking them back to campus.[45]

A crucial step for nurturing Black students on campus was the creation of the Afro-American Cultural Society (AACS).[46] In fall 1968, students Charles McArthur (BS 1969) and Charlie Jones (BS 1970) founded the group as a safe haven for the Black students at the time to offer friendship, social activities, and cultural events, especially when Black students were not welcomed, either officially or informally, in the other organizations.[47] This mirrored what other Black students were creating at other PWIs around the South around the same time. While some other Black student groups used some variant of the name *Black Student Union* or *Afro-American Association*, students at USM chose to highlight cultural aspects of the Black Power movement with their group's name.[48] By the time of Anthony Harris's arrival in 1971, the organization had grown to more than two hundred students, with most of the Black students on campus joining. The AACS brought Black students together to socialize, especially because the student activities council on campus created programming geared to white students, and Black students felt that "we had to find our own outlets," Harris recalled.[49]

AACS hosted pageants, talent shows, and "record hops," which were dances held in the student union, and students, including Harris, served as DJs. Harris's mother, civil rights activist Daisy Harris Wade, worked for the first Black radio station in the region and had access to a portable stereo system and records.[50] Harris also recalls playing the speeches of Malcolm X or Dick Gregory publicly on the lawn. The social events were "an important part of maintaining sanity and maintaining networks and just having a sense of belonging," according to Harris.[51] Though the club did not have a picture in *The Southerner*, at least four seniors proudly listed their participation in the Afro-American Cultural Society in their biographies in the yearbook.[52]

The late 1960s was a time of great creativity and action on university campuses around the country as northern and western universities—in response to the demands from Black students on their campuses—hired Black faculty, admitted Black students, and created Black studies departments.[53] In contrast, USM was slow to make changes to embrace Black culture and intellectual contributions. Much like at other PWIs around the country, Black students were the ones driving change on campus.⁵⁴ In fact, the AACS was the group that pushed the History Department to offer a new class on Black history. In October 1969, the Academic Council, the faculty body that approved new courses, overwhelmingly approved the new history course as well as a Black literature course for the winter 1970 quarter. USM had to hire part-time faculty members from Jackson State to teach these courses. However, by May 1970, USM still had no permanent Black faculty members.⁵⁵

Although the AACS had not envisioned itself as an activist organization initially, that changed in 1970 in the aftermath of the Jackson State murders, according to Miller, who had been elected president of the AACS only a short while before the murders.⁵⁶ In the evening of May 14, 1970, Jackson police and highway patrol came to Jackson State's campus after a dump truck was burned and a crowd of students gathered at the men's dormitory. The authorities then marched up to Alexander Hall, the women's dorm. When a bottle crashed on the sidewalk shortly after midnight, the police and highway patrol fired 150 rounds into the dorm. The police and highway patrol claimed that they thought there was a sniper. Two young people—high school student James Earl Green, seventeen, and JSU student Phillip Lafayette Gibbs, twenty-one—were killed, and twelve other JSU students and other young people were injured by the police and highway patrol's bullets.⁵⁷

The horrifying violence against young people at JSU caused Black students at USM to demand change. Many had personal ties to the JSU campus. Miller's twin sister lived in the women's dorm that the police shot into. In addition, Black Hattiesburgers had significant ties to JSU. Many of the teachers in Hattiesburg's schools had gone to JSU. In addition, any time there was a band or other type of competition in the state, Black students from Hattiesburg and south Mississippi would travel to JSU to participate. Such an attack hit very close to home for students at USM, and the tensions that had been building for more than four years "bubbled up to the top."⁵⁸

Students demanded that USM have some response to the tragedy and were prodded to action after Julian Bond, Student Nonviolent Coordinating Committee leader and representative of the Georgia House of Representatives, cancelled a talk that was scheduled for the evening of Sunday, May 18. Bond said that he could not speak when two students had been murdered at Jackson State and six Black people had been murdered in Augusta, Georgia, after an uprising in response to the killing of a teenager in a local jail. He also said that he assumed USM would close in honor of the JSU victims. Black students then took this as an opportunity to bring their larger grievances to President William McCain at his on-campus home that same evening. When he did not show up, students decided to come back the following morning to meet with him.[59]

In that subsequent meeting, sixty students shared their frustrations and demands. They insisted that no disciplinary action should be taken against those protesting, the school should close for a day in honor of the JSU students, and the flag should be lowered to half mast. Students also wanted to implement changes to make them feel more welcome on campus. They wanted the hiring of Black faculty, staff, administrators, and student workers as dorm matrons and proctors, campus security, and workers at the on-campus café and bookstore. They also wanted Black fraternities and sororities on campus, the removal of General Nat as the mascot, and cessation of "Dixie" at athletic and university events.[60]

The students were met with platitudes. President McCain did not cancel classes or fly the flag at half mast, but university official Forrest Tucker announced, over the university's loudspeaker system, "Dr. McCain respects your feelings and is sympathetic with your problems. They are problems of the entire university and the nation." McCain offered to speak with protest representatives in his office. Miller and other Black students were not satisfied with McCain's watered-down response. They wanted to be recognized for the pain that they were feeling and the injustice of what had happened but felt that their pain was met with nothing. As Miller said, it was hard to focus on his final exams in the aftermath of this shocking event, in which students just like him were killed.[61]

Despite their efforts to ensure their right to protest, Black students, and their white allies, were not protected. Deborah Gambrell recalls that campus officials took note of the protestors, and advisors tried to sway students away from protesting.[62] Students such as Melvin Miller were also tracked by agents of the Sovereignty Commission, who interviewed Willie V. Oubre, the director of campus security at USM. Oubre claimed that Miller was a troublemaker and may have been trying to purchase explosives. Oubre also reported falsehoods about other Black students who were a part of the Afro-American Cultural Society and other white students who had been involved in campus protests.[63] While thankfully no students were imprisoned for their protesting, one Black student, Milton W. Forte, and three white students, Ernest E. Gregory, Phillip R. Speake, and Richard A. Peters, were permanently suspended for supposedly handing out pamphlets that called for cancelling classes on Monday, the 18th, and Tuesday, the 19th.[64] The students took their case before the Board of Trustees of the Institutions of Higher Learning and before Judge Walter Nixon Jr. in the

US District Court, Southern District of Mississippi, but ultimately Judge Nixon confirmed USM's decision.⁶⁵

USM students' protest echoed that of other protests at PWIs in Mississippi in the late 1960s and 1970s, though USM's students escaped imprisonment for their activism. In 1969, Black students at Delta State University, in the heart of the Mississippi Delta, had protested the poor treatment that they received from both fellow students and faculty members and were jailed at Parchman penitentiary in response. Although Black students had been frustrated by racism on campus since they first attended Delta State in 1966, they finally decided to protest after Black student James Kennedy was struck on the head by a white student during a fight in the cafeteria. Kennedy subsequently had a seizure and died a few days later. In response to this tragedy, students in the Black Student Organization (BSO), which was founded in early 1969, crafted a list of ten demands for administrators to address on March 6, 1969. Much like what students around the country, and later those at USM, demanded, Delta State's students wanted more Black faculty, a Black counselor, more Black history resources, and an end to racial discrimination in classes and campus culture, among other changes. When Delta State's president, James Ewing, refused to meet with the students, they sat outside his office, but he never met with them. A few days later, fifty-two students, led by the BSO, went to sit on the lawn of Ewing's home and later went to his office, where they refused to leave. Ewing eventually called the police, and the students were arrested and sent to Parchman penitentiary, where they spent a night in jail. Much like how Black students at USM were supported by Black Hattiesburgers, Black locals supported Delta State's protesting students by raising money for their bail.⁶⁶

About a year later, protesting students at Ole Miss were also sent to Parchman prison when they protested discriminatory treatment on campus. On February 24, 1970, students in Ole Miss's Black Student Union, also founded in early 1969, crafted a list of twenty-seven demands that included more Black faculty and better treatment for Black students on campus, and they delivered the demands to university chancellor Porter Fortune. Some students danced on tables in the cafeteria while others burned a Confederate flag on campus. The next day, a group of eighty-nine students were arrested when they disrupted a concert by Up with People, an interracial group. These students were arrested and sent to Parchman, where they also stayed overnight. Ultimately, eight students were suspended from the university.⁶⁷

Still, Black students at USM saw in their own protest a historic parallel that those at Delta State and Ole Miss did not have. As Melvin Miller recalls, the students felt helpless to push back against the unjust treatment of these students, including Forte, who had been a model student and was set to graduate that May. Though only Forte was Black, the suspended students' treatment seemed to mirror Kennard's treatment eleven years prior. Miller recalled, "All of us [Black students at USM] were still in a state of shock—this [arrest and suspension of the four students] was like two or three days after the killings, and after the request to assist us and acknowledge this, [nothing] was done, and the response for us was ok, we're gonna kick these kids out for some trumped up [charges], you know, the Clyde Kennard syndrome, if you will." However, unlike after Kennard's arrests, significant changes began on campus after this protest. In the aftermath of the protest march, the AACS took McCain up on his call to meet with representatives. Black students pushed hard to open opportunities that had not existed for the earlier students.[68]

BLACK STUDENTS ENTER THE MAINSTREAM

While this second generation of students used the Afro-American Cultural Society to build support among themselves, by the mid-1970s, Black students found community in other settings as their numbers drastically increased. According to USM institutional research data, there were 1,027 Black students out of 11,081 total, or 9.27 percent of students enrolled in fall 1974.[69] This was a tremendous increase from the handful of students in the first generation. In the late 1960s, Black students from around the state began to consider USM as an option after their siblings, neighbors, and classmates attended.[70] In addition, with these larger numbers, Black students began to found other organizations on campus to support themselves. By fall 1970, USM's Panhellenic Council voted unanimously to invite the Black sorority Delta Sigma Theta to campus. By this time, eight young women had already formed a chapter, but it had not yet been formally incorporated.[71] Although it was invited on campus in 1970, it was not until spring 1975 that Black fraternities and sororities officially appeared on campus, when twelve women pledged Alpha Kappa Alpha and twenty-one men pledged Omega Psi Phi.[72]

Black students also were elected to mainstream offices and honors. In the 1972–1973 year, Juanita Sims became the first Black senior homecoming maid through the AACS's block voting.[73] Both Juanita Sims and John Ellis Price became students honored by Who's Who in 1973.[74] In the 1973 through 1974 academic year, football star Fred Cook was captain of the 1973 team, selected to USM's Hall of Fame and as Mr. USM, and was recruited by the Baltimore Colts. In that same academic year, Roderick Posey was inducted into USM's Hall of Fame, while Alvin J. Williams and Melvin Hawkins were inducted into Who's Who. Roderick Posey was the treasurer of the Student Government Association, Betty Dahmer and Ron Jordan were representatives on the Student Senate, and Melvin Hawkins was the chief justice of the Student Supreme Court. Posey and Hawkins were also on President William McCain's advisory board.[75] Black students were both creating additional Black organizations and becoming more involved in the mainstream organizations on campus.

Students also continued to push against the most egregious public racism and won gains in the early 1970s. According to Anthony Harris, after foot dragging from the administration about changing the campus culture, the local Forrest County NAACP brought US Justice Department officials down to USM to speak with the Black students about their grievances, especially about the playing of "Dixie" at football games and the lack of Black faculty and staff on campus. Unfortunately, the Black investigators admonished the students, arguing that they should not be so concerned with the playing of "Dixie," and nothing changed immediately. Harris was disappointed that Black officials seemed to make light of the students' grievances, but in recalling the situation, he pointed out that these officials worked for Republican president Richard Nixon.[76] As a strategy, Black students on campus did allow white allies, like the three white students who were suspended after the 1970 protest, to join in their causes. When the Black students complained about discrimination, administrators had ignored them, but when more white students started issuing those concerns, the university began to listen. Eventually the AACS's concerns about General Nat were heard. The mascot was removed in November 1972 and replaced with the Golden Eagle.[77] However, General Nat remained an unofficial presence for all of Harris's time as an undergraduate student at USM (through 1974).[78]

As more Black students began to attend USM in the 1970s and create new organizations, they also continued to uphold Kennard's memory. Black Greek organizations were formed in the 1970s and 1980s. Delta Sigma Theta was officially established on campus by fall 1975, and Kappa Alpha Psi, by fall 1976.[79] Alpha Phi Alpha, Zeta Phi Beta, Phi Beta Sigma, and Sigma Gamma Rho were all established by the early 1980s.[80] These groups became powerful on campus. They partnered with the AACS to sponsor programming for Black History Week and later Month (starting in the late 1970s).[81] This growing group of students and alumni continued to honor Kennard. The AACS and Phi Beta Sigma held a commemoration program for

Kennard on campus in February 1981. In the late 1970s or 1980s, a group of Black alumni gathered and raised $3,500 in one evening to start a Clyde Kennard scholarship. Although the group was unable to distribute scholarship funds immediately because of university regulations, the Kennard scholarship fund was revitalized decades later.[82] In addition, several Black alumni stayed at USM to pursue graduate degrees and even to work in administration. Alumnus and dean of students Eddie Holloway was pivotal to ensuring that the Kennard scholarship was nurtured. Today the Kennard scholarship endowment has $170,000, which is enough to pay for tuition and some expenses for four students every year. As both an alumnus and longtime administrator, Holloway always tried to keep Kennard's story alive on campus.[83]

GAINS WON AND STILL TO BE WON BY THE THIRD GENERATION

By the late 1970s, Black students, mainly through the AACS and the Black Greek organizations, were able to offer cultural programming that was much more radical and Afrocentric. The AACS helped bring Nikki Giovanni to campus in 1979 for Black History Month, and in 1980, Stokely Carmichael.[84] Black students continued to support one another's bids for elected offices. In 1980, Jacqueline Kay Redd was elected the first Black homecoming queen at USM. By the 1980s, a third generation of students who had attended integrated schools for most of their secondary school careers decided to attend USM. These students did not have the benefit of all-Black community schools with Black teachers and principals who nurtured them. Instead, at elementary and high schools in the 1970s, Black teachers and principals often were fired, reassigned, or demoted as schools integrated. Many of this third generation of Black students at USM had been singled out for their academic talent years earlier and had been placed in advanced classes with white students. This was still uncommon for Black students in white-dominated school systems even into the 1980s, as many other Black students in the era of early integration were placed in remedial classes.[85] By the late 1980s, many more African American students attended USM, and there were a handful of Black faculty and administrative staff on campus, but much remained to be done to address racism on campus and uphold Kennard's memory.[86]

While Black Greek life and other Black organizations such as the Minority Engineering and Technology Club thrived in the 1980s, the

Afro-American Cultural Society's power lessened.[87] Between 1984 and 1987, the AACS had become seemingly defunct, but by fall 1988, a new generation of students wanted to reconstitute the organization. This time, the group was known as the Afro-American Student Organization (AASO).[88] And they chose as their future leader Isaac Bishop (BS 1990), an engineering student who had recently been elected to the Associated Student Body (ASB), USM's student government association. As a newly reconstituted organization, the AASO wanted to help elect a Black homecoming queen. The AASO decided upon the young woman to support, Angela Odom, who ultimately won the crown in 1988. Like its predecessors, the AASO held cultural events and parties and found other ways to relax and find community.[89] While the group mainly focused on social events, the goal of such programming was to "bring about a greater awareness and understanding of multicultural issues and concerns, as they relate to the University and other areas of concern."[90]

In addition, students also worked outside of USM-sponsored organizations. As discussed in the previous chapter, Riva Brown (BA 1993, MS 1998, PhD 2013), the first Black editor of USM's newspaper, *The Student Printz*, began an independent newspaper, *The Unheard Word*, in the fall of 1990 to draw widespread attention to Black voices and the concerns of the Black community locally and nationally. It was through *The Unheard Word* that Kennard's story was first shared widely across campus. Without Brown's honest and influential writing, it is doubtful that the university would have truly acknowledged its role in Kennard's death. As Robert Taylor (BS 1990) has reflected, while he and others helped Riva Brown by writing stories, distributing newspapers, or helping to fund her newspaper, *The Unheard Word* was really a singular effort by a remarkable student.[91]

Sometimes activism was more spontaneous. Issac Bishop (BS 1990), the young man chosen as the new president of AASO, was a natural leader. While he was a part of both the AASO and Kappa Alpha Psi fraternity, he also took up an activist cause even if it was outside of the planned events for these organizations. In the late 1980s, Fred Horne, a longtime USM student, brought racist signs on campus and caused a nuisance for the university. Bishop saw his signs and, deeply offended, asked him to take the sign away. Horne refused, stating that he had the right to free speech. Bishop responded, "Just like you have the right to free speech, I've got the right to freedom of assembly, and I'm going to assemble right in front of your sign." Within an hour, between one hundred and two hundred people gathered. After a while, university police handed Bishop the phone. Aubrey Lucas, the president of the university was on the line. He had called to ask what the problem was. After speaking with Bishop, Lucas agreed to have the police remove Horne from campus.[92] Taylor was also involved in protesting in front of Horne.[93] These spontaneous acts of courage by students reclaimed the space from a white supremacist on campus.

THE THIRD GENERATION: PUSHING FOR RECOGNITION FOR KENNARD

It was also this third generation of students who pushed the university to finally recognize the history of Clyde Kennard in a significant and sustained way on campus. The timing was ripe for students to push the university to face its own racist legacy, as Mississippi publicly grappled with its racist past. Since 1975, Black plaintiffs, led by Jake Ayers Sr., the father of a student at Jackson State University, had sued the state and predominantly white institutions, including the USM, arguing that Black students, former students, parents, and employees of Historically Black Colleges and Universities (HBCUs) in the state had received unequal treatment and were owed compensation. The lawsuit was heard in federal district court in 1987 and at the Fifth Circuit Court of Appeals in 1990. After years of losing their case, the plaintiffs scored a win when in 1992 the Supreme Court sided with them that Mississippi HBCUs deserved compensation for the unequal conditions their institutions and Black students in the state had faced under segregation. It would take another ten years before the three HBCUs in the state would receive $503 million to be paid over seventeen years.[94]

Another important topic in the early 1990s was the legacy surrounding the Mississippi Sovereignty Commission, which officially ended in 1977 but retained its files that same year after Mississippi Department of Archives and History director Elbert R. Hilliard, former lieutenant governor William Winter, and state secretary Heber Ladner helped convince the legislature not to destroy these records. Although the files were originally ordered to remain closed until 2027, Ed King, John Salter, and the American Civil Liberties Union (ACLU) filed a lawsuit almost immediately to open access to the files. The suit went through several twists and turns, mainly to open access in a way that respected the privacy of those victimized by the Sovereignty Commission, and made headlines from 1989 through 1998, when the files were officially opened to the public.[95]

Seven years before the Sovereignty Commission records were opened, Jerry Mitchell, investigative reporter of *The Clarion-Ledger*, leaked some

Mississippi State Sovereignty Commission papers that highlighted that in September 1959 after being rejected admission to USM, Kennard had been framed by two Forrest County constables for driving too fast and having illegal liquor in his car. The Hattiesburg Black community had always maintained that Kennard was framed since he did not drink alcohol, but now they had confirmation. Though the Sovereignty Commission knew about the framing, they did nothing to counteract it. In addition, Mitchell highlighted how "state officials," according to former president McCain, secretly had altered Kennard's medical certificate on his application. McCain then used the "fraudulent" medical certificate as justification for rejecting Kennard in 1959. In addition, Mitchell highlighted that Constable Lee Daniels Sr. not only had arrested Kennard in 1959, but he arrested him again for stealing chicken feed in 1960. These were the first of many revelations to come to light on the role of state, local, and university officials not only in blocking Kennard's integration attempts but also in falsely arresting him. In addition, Aubrey Lucas, the USM president in the 1990s, was named in the files as having been the admissions officer who delivered Kennard's rejection letter in 1959.[96] As discussed in the previous chapter, *Student Printz* and *Unheard Word* editor Riva Brown then interviewed Aubrey K. Lucas for *The Unheard Word* in his first published interview about his role in denying Clyde Kennard entry.[97]

After Mitchell's story and Brown's interview with Lucas, university leadership began to heed the call of Reverend John Webb, the widower of Kennard's sister Sara, and began to consider commemorating Kennard on campus. Former president William McCain pushed back on this idea, arguing that Kennard was never a student, so there should be no memorial for him. However, President Aubrey Lucas began to entertain the possibility of something widespread on campus.[98] The AASO became a significant part of this effort to commemorate Kennard. As AASO president and vice president of the Associated Student Body, Marcus Cathey, stated at the time, "We need to acknowledge who [Kennard] is and what he did because for so long it's been denied and swept under the rug, and that makes the situation worse."[99] Under Cathey's leadership, the AASO pushed for the creation of the first Clyde Kennard Day in October 1991. The first Clyde Kennard day brought Webb, James Meredith (who had integrated the University of Mississippi), and Charles Tisdale (the editor and owner of *The Jackson Advocate*) to campus. The program also included a panel entitled "The Legacy of Racism in Academia," featuring Forrest County Justice Court Judge Deborah Gambrell, attorney Alvin Chamblis, and the AASO election commissioner. A candlelight vigil held for Kennard was a symbolic gesture of yet another generation of USM students being torchbearers for his legacy.[100]

With all the attention and pressure provided by the AASO and Riva Brown's *Unheard Word*, the university created a committee, chaired by Black alumnus Alvin Williams, who was also then the chair of USM's marketing department, to oversee the university's response to the commemoration of Kennard. Although there had been many reconciliation ideas, including creating a marker and/or an endowed Black history chair named for Kennard, the committee settled on four recommendations: a yearly lecture series, which became the Armstrong-Branch Lecture Series; a Clyde Kennard scholarship; renaming the Student Services Building Kennard-Washington Hall, honoring both Kennard and Walter Washington, the first Black PhD graduate of USM (in 1969) and later longtime president of Alcorn; and integrating the story of Kennard into the curricula of the university in a significant way.[101]

The first three recommendations were embraced, including the renaming of the Student Services Building during a "Celebration of Diversity" in February 1993. Although some students felt that it was wrong that Kennard had to share the building name with Washington when there were no other buildings named for Black students, others thought it was still a worthwhile gain. At the Celebration of Diversity, Aubrey Lucas publicly apologized for the treatment of Kennard on campus. Honored guests at the event included Rev. John Webb, Kennard's brother-in-law; Walter Washington; and Alvin Williams. The AASO student choir sang at the event, led by alumna and then assistant professor of music Kimberly Davis. In addition, the university recognized twenty-two alumni who were the first African Americans in significant categories at the university: Armstrong and Branch; Charles McArthur, founder of the AACS in 1968; Wilbert Jordan, the first Black athlete when he joined the basketball team in 1968; John Berry, the first Black faculty member in 1970; and many others. The inaugural Armstrong-Branch lecture was held with 1989 Pulitzer Prize–winning columnist Clarence Page speaking about the need for unity at USM, while respecting everyone's differences. Black students and alumni saw these steps as progressive but not the end to their work to memorialize Kennard.[102] Riva Brown continued to push everyone on campus to remember Kennard through funding the Kennard scholars' program and pushing to ensure that all students at USM learn about him, especially at orientation.[103]

THE FOURTH GENERATION: EXONERATING KENNARD

While the university had made some tangible steps to memorialize Kennard on campus in the 1990s, a fourth generation of Black students worked to clear Kennard of his criminal record. This time, students were influenced by the recent successful efforts to reopen the cases of Medgar Evers and Vernon Dahmer's murderers in 1994 and 1998, respectively. Mississippians, including Ellie Dahmer herself, and their nationwide supporters believed that perhaps Kennard could be exonerated.

In 2006, students of the AASO once again mobilized to push for Kennard's exoneration. In the previous fall, *The Clarion-Ledger* investigative reporter Jerry Mitchell was back to work on the Kennard case, this time with the aid of Raylawni Branch, who helped to pressure Johnny Lee Roberts, the young employee of the Forrest County Co-op who claimed that Kennard had directed him to steal chicken feed in 1960, to publicly tell the truth. As an employee, Roberts had been allowed to take damaged feed for a reduced price or even for free from the co-op and then sell it to farmers at a discounted price. After Kennard had tried to integrate MSC, the co-op would no longer sell him feed. The co-op also directed Roberts not to sell even damaged feed to Kennard, but Roberts had wanted to help Kennard by stealing the feed and taking it to him. Though Kennard knew nothing of Roberts's plans to steal the feed, after Roberts was arrested, he claimed that Kennard had masterminded the theft. This was the evidence that helped an all-white grand jury convict Kennard—in only ten minutes—of a felony. Judge Stanton Hall then sentenced Kennard to seven years in prison, while Roberts only received probation.[104]

After Mitchell's news article revealed the truth about Roberts's testimony, Roberts filed an affidavit in January 2006 in which he admitted, "Kennard did not ask me to get him feed 'on the side.' Kennard did not ask me to steal. Kennard did not ask me to break into the co-op. Kennard did not ask me to do anything illegal. Kennard is not guilty of burglary or any other crime."[105] Roberts had told Raylawni Branch and other members of the NAACP as early as in 1962 that he had lied but was worried that someone would hurt him or his family if he told the truth.[106] The Mississippi State Sovereignty Commission ceased to exist in 1977, and its papers were released in 1998 (with leaks to Mitchell years earlier), but it took Roberts more than forty years to reveal the truth publicly.

In response to Roberts's public declarations of Kennard's innocence, students of the AASO began to mobilize. First, LaKeisha Bryant (BS 2006), president of the group, supported an effort in early January by Senator John

Horhn of Jackson to sponsor a resolution that Haley Barbour or Attorney General Jim Hood exonerate Kennard.[107] Center for Human Rights student coordinator Tangee Carter (BA 2008, MS 2010) then spearheaded a petition effort on campus and ultimately gathered fifteen hundred signatures of faculty, staff, and students around Mississippi to exonerate Kennard. Student leaders organized many opportunities for students and faculty to sign the petition.[108] Governor Haley Barbour had expressed his belief that Kennard was innocent, but he said that he could not be pardoned posthumously according to Mississippi state law. Bryant then led a delegation of thirty-six USM students to Jackson to attend a March 30 celebration in honor of Kennard and deliver the petition to the governor. According to *The Hattiesburg American*, Bryant emphasized, "We want his spirit to be free." In addition, she highlighted the importance of remembering Kennard. "We want to show we haven't forgotten about (Kennard's) sacrifices."[109] Meanwhile the AASO sponsored a Kennard prayer breakfast on April 22 that kept Kennard's story front and center both on campus and in the state at large.[110] Still, Kennard's name had yet to be cleared. Although many leaders in Mississippi supported exonerating Kennard, there were roadblocks at every turn. The Mississippi State Supreme Court, Governor Haley Barbour, and the Mississippi Parole Board all repeatedly rejected requests to clear Kennard's name, saying that they were procedurally unable to do so because Kennard was deceased and no longer a prisoner.[111] For more than a year, Barry Bradford, a teacher at Adlai E. Stevenson High School in Illinois, had encouraged his students to look into the case of Kennard. He then sought the help of Professor Steve Drizin of Northwestern University Law School's Center on Wrongful Convictions to collect data about the case to find avenues to exonerate Kennard.[112] Bradford and Drizin worked with retired judge Charles Pickering, with the blessing of local district attorney Jon Mark Weathers, to create a petition with support from high-profile Mississippians, including the governor, Aubrey Lucas, Shelby Thames (then the president of USM), former governor William Winter, Reuben Anderson, and Ellie Dahmer (Vernon Dahmer's widow), among others, to clear Kennard's record.[113] On May 17, 2006, Forrest County circuit judge Robert Helfrich listened to a twenty-minute hearing and then declared Kennard innocent of the fabricated charges of stealing chicken feed. Helfrich said that the story of Kennard was "not a black/white issue. It's a right/wrong issue. And to correct that wrong, I am compelled to do the right thing, and that is to declare Mr. Kennard innocent, and to declare that the conviction of Mr. Kennard is hereby null and void."[114]

CONCLUSION

Without the courageous efforts of students in the AACS, the AASO, and students who worked independently like Riva Brown, the university likely would have never acknowledged its violent history in denying admission to Kennard. His story would not have received the same local and statewide pressure that it did and possibly would never have resulted in his exoneration. The first and second generations of Black students courageously entered the campus and drew strength from and shared Kennard's story. The third generation of activist students pushed the university to acknowledge Kennard's path-breaking attempts in a sustained way on campus, and the fourth generation helped him become exonerated.

Kennard provided an inspirational model for later student activists, but spotlighting his unjust treatment and publicly memorializing him as a hero became causes for the third and fourth generations of students at USM. Contrary to popular belief outside of the local Black community, Kennard's memory did not die but lived on in the work of USM students. The story of students' work to honor Clyde Kennard's legacy broadens our understanding of integration, student protest, and activism, as it illuminates the importance of taking a local approach when studying Black power on campus. While many Black students in the late 1960s in the North and West turned to international pan-Africanist ideas to shape their activism, Black students at USM also found strength in their own local integrationist hero. This story also highlights the importance of considering the historical framing of Kennard's story. Students and local community members recognize his victimization but also celebrate his bravery and intelligence. Later students took courage from Kennard's character and actions and viewed their attendance at USM as the fulfillment of his efforts.

This story also illuminates the evolution of demands of Black students at Southern PWIs in the first decades after integration. While the earliest students at USM fought for survival at the institution in the mid-1960s, a second generation in the late 1960s and 1970s pushed not only to be welcomed into white-dominated spaces but also to bring in Black organizations, such as the AACS, fraternities, and sororities. As the state reckoned with its racist legacy in the late 1980s and early 1990s, especially in public discussions about the Ayers case and the Sovereignty Commission, another generation of students pushed for the university to reckon with its own racist past. Finally, Black students in the 2000s, buoyed by the larger push to reexamine Kennard's case, helped join the effort to exonerate him. The memory of the hero Kennard was ever present for Black students on campus, pushing them to first complete their degrees, then to improve the conditions on campus for their peers, and later memorialize and clear the name of the man who had been their torchbearer.

EPILOGUE

HONORING CLYDE KENNARD

A building, a historic marker, and, finally, an honorary degree represent efforts the University of Southern Mississippi (USM) has taken to atone for its role in the injustice that Clyde Kennard experienced while trying to receive an education. Generations of students, however, deserve much of the credit in commemorating Kennard as he remains an inspiration to succeed against all odds. It is fitting then that we conclude our collection by reflecting on our role as educators having had the privilege to work at the same university that once denied Kennard the opportunity to study here.

The Freedom50 Research Group conducted archival investigations to document Clyde Kennard's story for current and future generations of students at institutes of higher learning and to promote public dialogues about race. Starting in 2015, our research led to the production of a short documentary film, *Measure of Progress: The Clyde Kennard Story*, in partnership with Alysia Burton Steel and Bobby D. Steele Jr., faculty members at the University of Mississippi. The documentary was funded by the Mississippi Humanities Council with a Racial Equity Grant.[1] Our work is a continuation of prior efforts to bring attention to the case of Clyde Kennard. We follow in the path of Dr. Eddie A. Holloway, who established the Kennard Scholars Program at USM in 2014 to provide eligible students with scholarships that help pay for tuition/fees, provide mentors, and make available other resources for the duration of their enrollment at USM. We recognize protests and a diversity campaign initiated by USM students that led to the dedication of the student services building on campus to honor Kennard in 1993. While this is not the same building where Kennard made his attempts to enroll in the 1950s, this is the building that houses the university's admission services.² A historic marker was unveiled on February 2, 2018, in front of the Kennard-Washington building recognizing Kennard's contribution to the greater public as an "unsung hero" of the civil rights movement. Chairman of the Mississippi Freedom Trail Task Force, civil rights scholar, and guest speaker for the unveiling ceremony, Dr. Leslie McLemore challenged the university to consider Clyde Kennard as essential to "the DNA of the university."³

Indeed, the legacy of Clyde Kennard is evident in the diversity of the student body, faculty, and staff at USM. The generations of African Americans who have studied and worked at the university are certainly a testament to Kennard's sacrifice. Perhaps a building and a historical marker acknowledging his ubiquitous presence on campus are measurable milestones of progress. However, many supporters of the movement that began with Kennard's initial enrollment attempt believed that the ultimate tribute had yet to be given. We believed that not granting Clyde Kennard a degree was both ironic and tragic. Petitions to grant him an honorary degree began circulating around the planning for the historic marker. Some people were inspired to write letters to state and local officials, administrators at USM, and the Board of Trustees of the Mississippi Institutions of Higher Learning. More than eighty USM faculty and staff signed a petition asking that we honor Kennard by posthumously bestowing upon him a doctorate of humane letters. Politicians, businessmen/women, artists, and prominent activists are most often granted honorary degrees by institutions of higher education to which they may have little or no connections, though their contributions may have impacted society at large. Clyde Kennard is worthy of such recognition, however, because his sacrifice and contributions to USM are immeasurable. It had been almost fifty-five years since Clyde Kennard died and almost sixty-three years since he made his initial enrollment attempt when he was finally awarded an honorary degree during USM's Spring Commencement on May 11, 2018.

Continually inspired by Kennard's voice, so well-preserved in his writings in the *Hattiesburg American*, USM's Center for Black Studies created The Clyde Kennard Lecture Series in 2023. Key goals for the public lecture were defined by an interdisciplinary committee of faculty and staff: examine educational equity for underrepresented minorities in higher education and in K–12 schools; present interdisciplinary studies about the experiences of Black people; and promote campus and community partnerships to create sustainable and equitable relations. On October 17, 2023, Harvard professor Jarvis R. Givens was the inaugural speaker, paying a fitting tribute to Kennard by acknowledging the role of Black teachers as unsung foot soldiers in the civil rights movement and by preserving generations of students' collective memories as "witnesses" to such struggles. Kennard having served as a trustee for the Bay Springs School is a testament to his commitment to providing an education to Black youths even as his own journey was thwarted by others. As the namesake of the lecture series, we are hopeful that USM continues to honor Kennard for years to come.[4]

None of these efforts, however, would have been possible if not for the continued support of the community, which kept Clyde Kennard's memory ever present. Throughout this project, we have tried to preserve the oral histories shared with us by the people who knew Kennard as a childhood friend or as a neighbor, as a church member or as an activist. It is impossible to live in Hattiesburg and not ever hear mention of Clyde Kennard, especially now that there's a memorial highway named in his honor.[5] Even the curious tourist can now be guided to campus to understand better how "a little man ... has done a lot of big things." To experience more of Clyde Kennard's legacy, we direct attention to the historic Mobile-Bouie neighborhood near downtown Hattiesburg where he is featured on the Generations Strong Commemorative Wall.[6] Clyde Kennard is best remembered as one of the many African Americans who lived with dignity in the era of segregation. We honor him for his persistence and determination, and we believe in his foresight to inspire future generations.

The Colored American Magazine, appearing around the turn of the twentieth century was the most immediate predecessor to *Jet*. *The Colored American Magazine*, June 1900, vol.1, no.2. The Digital Colored American Magazine, project directors Eurie Dahn and Brian Sweeney, https://coloredamerican.org/.

Cover of the very first issue of *Jet* magazine, November 1, 1951.

Clyde Kennard in his military uniform around the time of his enlistment in the army on March 28, 1946. This picture was used in the October 1959 *Jet* issue that depicted Kennard as a dignified soldier after his first false arrest. Permission granted by the Kennard family.

Clyde Kennard's sister Sarah Tarpley and her husband Jesse Tarpley. Also, Kennard is pictured with Sarah. *Jet* included these pictures of his family members in an article by Larry Still in a January 1963 issue. Permission granted by the Kennard family.

Clyde Kennard's brothers Melvin Kennard and Albert Kennard along with his stepfather Silas Smith with his mother Leona Smith. *Jet* included these pictures of his family members in an article by Larry Still in a January 1963 issue. Permission granted by the Kennard family.

On February 2, 1963, just days after his release from the Mississippi State Penitentiary in Parchman and a brief visit home, Clyde Kennard arrived at the O'Hare Airport in Chicago and was escorted by his sister Sarah Tarpley. Kennard was admitted to Billings Hospital on the campus of the University of Chicago, where he would undergo more extensive medical treatments for intestinal cancer that had developed while imprisoned. His condition worsened despite the medical care he received for months in Chicago. Clyde Kennard died there on July 4, 1963. Bettmann via Getty Images. Printed by permission.

Headline about Clyde Kennard's imprisonment and illness on cover of *Jet* magazine, February 7, 1963.

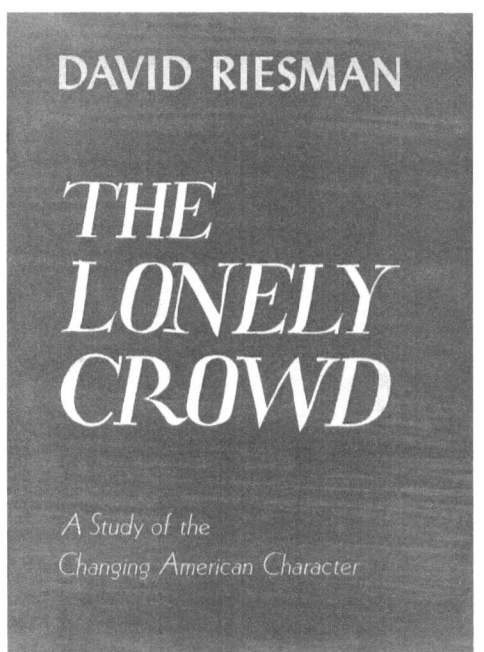

David Reisman (sociologist) and Reuel Denney (poet) were faculty members at the University of Chicago when Clyde Kennard attended. Reisman (in collaboration with Denney and Nathan Glazer) wrote *The Lonely Crowd: A Study of the Changing American Character* (1950), which examines conformity and individualism in society at midcentury. Reisman and Denney, like their peers, introduced their ideas in classes likely attended by Kennard.

Clyde Kennard's class photo as published in the yearbook just before his return home to Mississippi. Clyde Kennard, *Cap and Gown*, 1955. Hanna Holborn Gray Special Collections Research Center, University of Chicago Library.

David Reisman (right) in his office with Reuel Denney (left) at the University of Chicago in 1950. Both were faculty members when Clyde Kennard attended the university. Hanna Holborn Gray Special Collections Research Center, University of Chicago Library.

At the University of Chicago, philosophy professor Richard McKeon taught popular courses that challenged students to think critically about ideas and study methods used to address societal problems. Traceable influences of McKeon's philosophic approach to understanding freedom, power, and history show up in Clyde Kennard's letter-writing campaign about Mississippi's race problem. Richard P. McKeon, *Cap and Gown*, 1954. Hanna Holborn Gray Special Collections Research Center, University of Chicago Library.

Robert Maynard Hutchins, University of Chicago president (1929–1945) and chancellor (1945–1951). Under his administration, Hutchins instituted the radical "New Plan" for the curriculum with general education courses (no grades nor course requirements) and comprehensive exams, which allowed students more flexibility for intellectual development. Clyde Kennard experienced such freedom during his studies at Chicago. Hanna Holborn Gray Special Collections Research Center, University of Chicago Library.

Joseph J. Schwab (pictured here in 1952), a professor of Natural Science, along with President Robert M. Hutchins and others formed the Committee on Social Thought in 1941 to promote interdisciplinary studies at the University of Chicago. This curriculum was standardized by the time Clyde Kennard enrolled on February 7, 1953; he began taking general courses in the "Chicago plan for liberal education" as taught by Schwab. Joseph J. Schwab, *Cap and Gown*, 1954. Hanna Holborn Gray Special Collections Research Center, University of Chicago Library.

1st Negro Attempts To Enter School

President W. D. McCain issued a statement Wednesday concerning an application for admission to Southern, by a Negro. The statement follows:

"Last November, Clyde Kinard (or Kinnard) of Hattiesburg, a Negro, requested information concerning admission to Southern. He then submitted a partial application for admission. Since his application was not complete, the administrative officers of the college did not feel it necessary to take any action."

Dr. McCain added that, despite rumors to the contrary, he had no knowledge of any other formal applications by Negroes.

Student Printz reports on Kennard's first attempt to enroll at Mississippi Southern College in 1956. *Student Printz*; 1956 mus_032_0001, University Archives, The University of Southern Mississippi.

Negro Is Again Refused Entry

Clyde Kennard, a Negro farmer from the Eatonville community near Hattiesburg, was for the second time refused admission to Mississippi Southern College when he applied registration day to Aubrey K. Lucas, director of admissions.

Dr. John Allen, dean of the school of arts and sciences said Kennard's Sept. 15 application was refused for incomplete records and failure to meet admission requirements.

Unknown to campus officials, Kennard was arrested on the campus by two Eatonville constables and charged with illegal possession of liquor and reckless driving.

Kennard's lawyer from Jackson, who has at one time represented the National Association for the Advancement of Colored People, said he is not representing Kennard in a case against MSC but in the defense case on illegal possession and reckless driving.

Allen emphasized that Kennard did not create any trouble and left the school quietlyy.

Student Printz reports on Kennard's attempts to enroll at Mississippi Southern College in 1958 and 1959. *Student Printz*; 1958 mus_rg032_0002 and 1959 mus_rg032_0003, University Archives, The University of Southern Mississippi.

OCTOBER, 1991

LUCAS TALKS ON BLACK ISSUES

Front page of *The Unheard Word*, the alternative student publication created by Riva Brown in the early 1990s. This October 1991 edition features an interview with University of Southern Mississippi president Dr. Aubrey K. Lucas, describing incidents surrounding Kennard's attempts to enroll at the university. *The Unheard Word*, October 1991; mus_rg006_0001, University Archives, The University of Southern Mississippi.

Gwendolyn Elaine Armstrong was one of the first two African American students to enter the University of Southern Mississippi in Fall 1965. 1966 *Southerner*; mus_YB1966_001p, University Archives, The University of Southern Mississippi.

Raylawni Young, later Branch, was one of the first two African American students to enter the University of Southern Mississippi in Fall 1965. 1965 mus_m335_001p, University Archives, The University of Southern Mississippi.

Gwendolyn Elaine Armstrong was one of a handful of Black students in the 1966–1967 academic year. Here, she is depicted in the 1967 *Southerner* yearbook, but there is no caption accompanying her picture at the bottom of the page spread. 1967 *Southerner*, spread pgs. 96 and 97, mus_yb 1967, RG 032, University Archives, The University of Southern Mississippi.

General Nat, the mascot of the University of Southern Mississippi until the early 1970s, stood for Nathan Bedford Forrest, the Confederate general and early leader of the Ku Klux Klan for whom Hattiesburg's Forrest County was named. White students at USM clung to General Nat as a cultural icon after integration. This cover of the 1968 *Southerner* yearbook depicts a silhouette of General Nat. 1968 *Southerner* cover, mus_yb 1968, RG 032, University Archives, The University of Southern Mississippi.

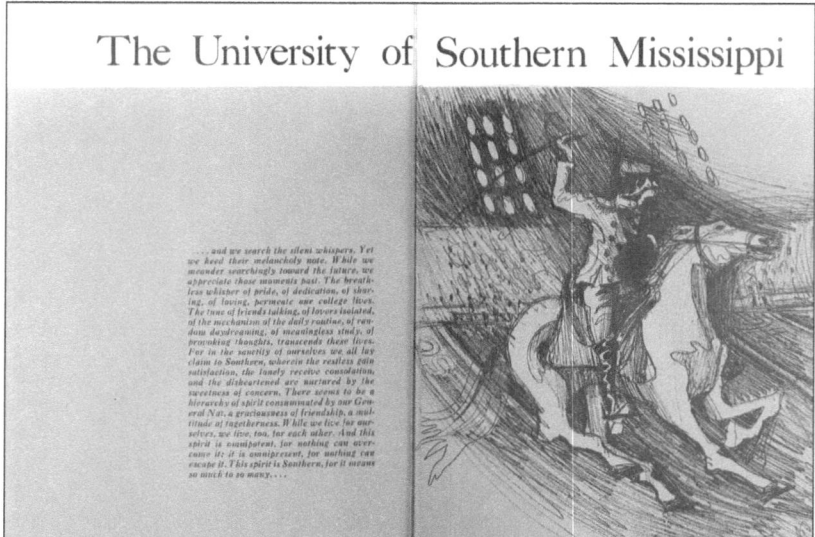

The first few pages of the 1968 *Southerner* yearbook highlight the reverence that white students at USM continued to hold towards General Nat after integration. 1968 *Southerner*, pgs. 4 and 5, mus_yb 1968, RG 032, University Archives, The University of Southern Mississippi.

TOP: Joyce Ann Street, Deborah L. Jones, Chris Angela Pack, Elbert Soloman, Samson Byrd, Alfred Herron, Lillie Walker—Parliamentarian; Rhonnie Gilmore. BOTTOM: Verna Alford—Secretary; Milton Forte, Melvin Miller—President; Alfredia Dampier, Jean Dillon, Frankie Benton, Jr., Sidney McArthur—Vice-President.

Afro-American Cultural Society

By 1970, the Afro-American Cultural Society, which was founded in 1968 as the first organization for Black students, was thriving. 1970 *Southerner*, page 259 (all), mus_yb 1970, RG 032, University Archives, The University of Southern Mississippi.

The Afro-American Cultural Society

"More Power to The People"

From left, first row: Alice Whitehead, Doris Thomas, James Cooley, Belinda Shaw, Linda Baker. Second row: Casey Price, James Simmons, Jimmie L. Hooker, Kelly Cooper, Melvin Hawkins, Linda Ross, Roderick B. Posey, Richard L. Lockett, Gary Donaldson. Third row: Watson Street, Lee Vaughn Martin, Phyllis Qualls, Doris Jones, Mona Taylor, Demetria Davis, Gayle Hall, Rhonda Hearn, Oscar Young, Bettye Ferguson, Margie Gaddy, Norweda L. Moore, Alvin R. Cooley, Eugene Henderson, Mary Ann Adams, Cecile A. Gaines, Peggy Ray, Elvie A. Willis, Linda Jordon, Sheila Johnson, Vivian Gore, Frankie Benton. Fourth row: Lonnie Johnson, Mattie Watson, Glenn Hearn, Nita Thomas, Lettie Evans, Samson Byrd, Charles Collins, Abram Howle, Carol E. Brooks, Larry Ike Spinks, Jr., Catherine Nelson, Katie Nave, Raymos McMillon, Juanita Sims, Sherron Jackson, Alvin Williams, Cornelius Flowers, Earl E. Nix.

Officers. From left: Sherron Jackson, treasurer; Raymos McMillon, parliamentarian; Linda Ross, secretary; Melvin Hawkins, vice-president; James Cooley, president.

Miss Afro Court. Front: Demetria Davis, Miss Afro. Back: Linda Ross, Fifth Alternate; Elvie Willis, Fourth Alternate, Freddie Singleton, Third Alternate; Betty Price, Second Alternate; Bettye Ferguson.

By 1972 Afro-American Cultural Society was a strong and vibrant organization that drew together many Black students on campus. It hosted a Black beauty pageant, in addition to other cultural events. 1972 *Southerner*, page 282 (all), mus_yb 1972, RG 032, University Archives, The University of Southern Mississippi.

In 2023, the Clyde Kennard Lecture series was organized by the Center for Black Studies at the University of Southern Mississippi. Dr. Jarvis R. Givens, Professor of Education and African American Studies at Harvard University, was the inaugural speaker. Permissions granted by the Center for Black Studies.

Clyde Kennard's gravesite at the Mary Magdalene Baptist Church cemetery in Hattiesburg, Mississippi (Forrest County). Kennard is buried in the Eatonville community where he grew up. Photo taken by Sherita L. Johnson.

The Mississippi Freedom Trail Marker to honor Clyde Kennard was unveiled on February 13, 2018, at the University of Southern Mississippi. The marker is located near the Kennard-Washington Hall, the student services building named after Kennard and Walter Washington, the first black student to receive a doctoral degree from Southern Miss. Photo taken by Sherita L. Johnson.

Members of the Freedom50 Research Group standing with Clyde Kennard's Mississippi Freedom Trail Marker on February 13, 2018. Members of the Freedom50 (left to right) includes Dr. Cheryl Jenkins, Dr. Loren Saxton Coleman, Dr. Sherita L. Johnson, and Dr. Rebecca Tuuri. Photo taken by Sherita L. Johnson.

APPENDIX A

Clyde Kennard's Letter to the Editor series: We provide copies of Kennard's letters as published by the local newspaper, the *Hattiesburg American* (Hattiesburg, Mississippi). Kennard informs the public about his attempts to attend Mississippi Southern College not to launch an integration campaign (as organized by civil rights organizations) but more to plead his case for trying to complete his education. In doing so, Kennard brings attention to the school's unfair enrollment policies.

"MIXING," *HATTIESBURG AMERICAN*, DECEMBER 6, 1958

LETTER TO EDITOR

MIXING

Editor, *The American*,

It is interesting to me that subjects which are most widely discussed are those which seem to be least understood by the public whom these discussions are designed to inform.

It would not surprise me if more words had not been spoken and written on integration and segregation in the last four years than on any other subject, especially in the South.

In our state the officials spend much of their time and perhaps much of our money trying to convince the integrationist, and reassure the segregationists, that the policy of perpetual segregation is the wisest course for us to pursue, in spite of the tremendous cost of duplication.

Somehow I feel a great sympathy for the people who truly believe that the interest of both the White and Negro people would be served best by a system of complete or partial segregation. Although I am integrationist

by choice, I am a segregationist by nature, and I think most Negroes are. We prefer to be alone, but experience has taught us that if we are ever to attain the goal of first class citizenship, we must do it through a closer association with the dominant (White) group.

Now it is this "getting closer" attempt by the Negro group that has aroused too much attention throughout the world, and no doubt a temporary animosity between the two groups.

There are two schemes for the solution of the present race problem. The first, spearheaded by the National Association for the Advancement of the Colored People, and given authoritative backing by the Constitution of the United States as interpreted by the Supreme Court in its 1964 decision says that Negroes are American citizens and are entitled to the same rights and privileges, the same opportunities and duties as other citizens, and that the best way to secure these rights and duties on a fair and equal basis would be to (in all things public) subject both races to identical conditions of life.

The second scheme championed primarily by the Southern States, says that Negroes are American citizens and are entitled to the same rights and privileges, the same opportunities and duties as any other citizen, and that the best way to secure these rights and duties on a fair and equal basis would be (in all things public and private) to subject both races to different conditions of life.

As the public schools are the essential organs for general intellectual discipline, and the preparation for private life and public service, let us superimpose the plan of separate but equal on the public school system.

It is my understanding that separate but equal means that in matters where public funds are involved every time a dollar is spent for the development of Negro students, a dollar will be spent for the development of White students, and vice versa.

This plan is to be followed through Junior college, Senior college, medical schools, law schools, divinity schools, graduate schools and all supported by public funds.

After our paralleled graduate schools, where do our parallels of separate but equal go? Are we to assume that paralleled hospitals are to be built for the two groups of doctors? Are we to build two bridges across the same stream in order to give equal opportunities to both groups of engineers? Are we to have two courts of law so as to give both groups of lawyers the same chance to demonstrate their skills, two legislatures for our politically inclined, and of course two governors?

The folly of such a conclusion is perfectly obvious. Yet the question remains, what is to become of the doctors who are not allowed to treat their patients in public hospitals? What will the engineers do when there are no roads or bridges for them to build? How must the lawyers occupy their time when the state courts restrict their opportunities to practice? How shall young statesmen, who can't even get their names on the ballot, ever hope to be elected to the legislature?

Segregationists whose convictions are based on reason rather than passion might agree that the most honorable and actually the only path to our goal would be to allow integration at some level, if not on the school level, then surely on the "job" level.

In utter desperation, I can see one other possible solution to which segregationist might resort, short of integration. They could do in theory what our state now does in fact, namely, raise and educate young people for the benefit of other states. While they get richer, we get poorer.

The integrationists offer a program which at first seems if not cruel at least awkward. We admit to bring two groups of people together who have different social and ethnic backgrounds presents certain adjustment problems. We should expect that and any intelligent program must allow for those adjustments.

What we request is only that in all things competitive, merit be used as a measuring stick rather than race.

We believe that for men to work together best, they must be trained together in their youth. We believe that there is more to going to school than listening to the teacher and reciting lessons. In school one learns to appreciate and respect the abilities of the other.

We say that if a man is a good doctor though his face be white as light or black as darkness let him practice his art. We believe that the best engineer should build the bridge or run the train. We believe that the most efficient secretary should get the best paying job and the greatest scholar the professorship. We believe in the dignity and brotherhood of man and the divinity and fatherhood of God, and as such, men should work for the upbuilding of each other, in mutual love and respect. We believe when merit replaces race as a factor in character evaluation, the most heckling social problem of modern times will have been solved.

Thus, we believe in integration on all levels from kindergarten to graduate schools; in every area of education: in government, federal, state, local; in industry from the floor sweeper to the superintendent's office; in science from the laboratory to the testing ground.

This, I believe, is our creed. And though it is not perfect, still I had rather meet my God with this creed than with any other yet devised by human society.

Respectfully submitted,
Clyde Kennard
RFD 1, City

"THE RACE QUESTION," *HATTIESBURG AMERICAN*,
SEPTEMBER 25, 1959

LETTER TO EDITOR

Route 1, Box 70
Hattiesburg, Mississippi
September 25, 1959

THE RACE QUESTION

Editor, *The American*:

The charge that any person who believes in any form of integration of the races is a Communist or an outside agitator has been made so constantly and with such force that it would not surprise me if there are some people who are innocent enough to believe, if not all, at least some portion of that charge. It is for the benefit of these unfortunate people that I review, briefly, the fundamental principle upon which the conviction of the integrationists is based.

Most basic to our beliefs about the race question in America today is that there can be no racial segregation without some racial discrimination, and that there cannot be a complete racial equalization without some racial integration.

Now this principle is an easy one for us to follow, for it holds as true in human history, especially American History, as it does in logic. Reason tells us that two things, different in location, different in constitution, different in origin, and different in purpose cannot possibly be equal. History has verified this conclusion. For nearly a century now the State of Mississippi has been under a supposedly separate but equal system. Let us ask ourselves, does the history of the system support the theory of the segregationists or the theory of the integrationists? What segregationist in his right mind would honestly claim that the facilities for the two races are equal? Still segregationists say, give us a little more time, we are really making progress. Perhaps they are making progress of some kind, but human life is not long enough to extend their time. They have had nearly a hundred years to prove their theory, and so far they are no closer to proof than when they began.

The differences which we now have over this matter of segregation versus integration have, unfortunately, been characterized by some as a

APPENDIX A

mortal contest between outside agitators and-or Communists, and peaceful law-abiding citizens. This is furthest from the truth. The question is whether or not citizens of the same country, the same state, the same city, shall have equal opportunities to earn their living, to select the people who shall govern them, and raise and educate their children in a free democratic manner: or whether or not because of the accident of color, one half of the citizens shall be excluded from society as though they had leprosy?

If there is one quality of Americans which would set them apart from almost any other peoples, it is the history of their struggle for liberty and justice under the law. Lincoln has rightly said that this nation was conceived in liberty and dedicated to the proposition that all men are created equal. Truly, the history of America is inseparable from the ideals of John Locke, John Stuart Mill and Jean Rousseau. "We hold these truths to be self evident," says our Declaration of Independence, "that all men are created equal." How different that statement is in spirit from the one which says: Before I see my child go to school with a Negro, I will destroy the whole school system. How different in virtue is the statement of Patrick Henry which says, "I know not what course others may take, but as for me give me liberty or give me death," and the one which says, before I see a Negro with liberty I had rather see him dead.

I find it indeed interesting that the people who come closest to the thinking of Fascists and Communists in their activities should accuse the integrationists of that very thing. Is it the segregationists or the integrationists who are employing secret investigators to search the records and to apply pressure on any one suspected of opposing the present dictatorship of the minority by the majority? Is it the segregationists or integrationists who are preaching the doctrine of the superiority of one race over another? Is it the segregationists or integrationists who are dogmatically suppressing the aspirations of nearly half the people of this great state for their inalienable right to participate in their government?

The segregationists give as their reason for not allowing Negroes to participate more fully in the general community activities that ninety-five percent of the Negroes are not interested, which would leave only five percent of the Negroes in the state who are interested. Now, assuming that their statement is correct, and knowing that no person nor group of people in the United States has the right to forbid even one single person his constitutional rights, what accounts for their actions? Some declare that the northern states can permit integration because they have only a few Negroes, but the South can't do that because the South has so many Negroes. Well, according to their own estimates, only five percent of the Negroes in the South are interested in participating in the gernal [sic] community activities, and five percent of the Negroes in any community would certainly not weigh very heavily in any critical issue, even if we were to assume that they would all vote the same way. On the other hand, if a majority of the Negro people in this State desires to participate to the fullest extent in the general community activities and are being forbidden to do so either through fear or ignorance, then the segregationists of this State are guilty of one of the strangest and probably the most tragic dictatorships yet recorded by history.

It is an easy matter, I suppose, for White people to misunderstand the aspirations of Negroes; this is understandable. But we have no desire for revenge in our hearts. What we want is to be respected as men and women, given an opportunity to compete with you in the great and interesting race of life. We want your friends to be our friends; we want your enemies to be our enemies; we want your hopes and ambitions to be our hopes and ambitions, and your joys and sorrows to be our joys and sorrows.

The big question seems to be, can we achieve this togetherness in our time? If the segregationists have their way we shall not. For instead of preaching brotherly love and cooperation they are declaring the superiority of one race and the inferiority of the other. Instead of trying to show people how much they are alike, they are busy showing them how much they differ. Instead of appointing a commission to study the problem to determine whether integration or segregation is the best policy for Mississippi at this time, they appointed a commission to try to maintain segregation at all cost whether it is the best policy or not the best policy.

In this matter I like to quote from the great Indian leader, Mahatma Gandhi, in his discourse on the existence of God. He says: "In the midst of death, life persists; in the midst of untruth, truth persists; in the midst of darkness light persists."

So, let it be, in our case.

Respectfully submitted,
Clyde Kennard

"SCHOOL MIX," *HATTIESBURG AMERICAN*, JANUARY 26, 1960

LETTER TO EDITOR

Route 1 Box 70
Hattiesburg, Mississippi
January 23, 1960

SCHOOL MIX

Editor, *The American*:

The discussion of the problem of integration which faces our state at this time prompts me to offer a statement, not in defense of my efforts to enroll at Mississippi Southern College, but as an explanation of our position on public school integration.

Mississippi Southern College is the only State supported four year college in this area and my situation at home makes it very difficult for me to leave home to continue my education. On this account I have been unable to attend school for nearly five years. By attending Mississippi Southern College my problem would be solved, as I could live at home and attend school.

From a general point-of-view I am keenly aware of the race problem entailed, as nothing has so constantly occupied my thoughts during the past three years. I know that there are those among us who feel that both races would be best benefited by a policy of private and public separation of the races, and that this segregation should be maintained no matter what the cost to ourselves and to future generations.

Unfortunately, perhaps, I have not been able to convince myself, nor has anyone else been able to convince me that this is really the wisest course for Mississippi to follow at this critical juncture in our history.

Those who advocate the separation of the races theory generally say: To teach Negro and White students in the same schools would mean, in part, mixing of White and Negro blood to the extent of destroying both races; Negroes as a result of their economic and social history, have developed such low moral habits until it would be tragically degrading to White youngsters for them to associate with Negro youngsters; since White students are so much more advanced scholastically than Negro students it would be a grave injustice to Negro students to have them compete in the same classroom, for since Negroes are so inferior in development to

White students this would end even the little development which they are capable of making when left to themselves; if schools are racially integrated, Negro teachers would have to turn to some other income source here in Mississippi or leave the State completely for employment; and if schools maintained for Negro people are equal in facilities and teachers to those maintained for White people, then the schools are equal in total essence.

Although I have tried never to underestimate the importance that many people attach to being of a certain racial group, I have not been able to discern a noticeable difference, other than color, between a good White man and a good Black or Yellow man.

I would be in favor of a commission of eminent social scientists to make a careful study of colleges and universities which have practiced total integration over a long period of time to determine whether or not the purity of any races involved has been greatly diluted, and if so, to what extent this dilution has actually impaired the effectiveness of those involved.

The study of such a commission would show, I believe, that the percentage of interracial courtships which led to anything as serious as marriage or reproduction would be so small as to be completely negligible. Should such a commission report a contrary result, however, then I would be among the first to about-face and join, actively, the segregationists among us.

The second major objection which segregationists advance against racial integration is the question of morality. No thinking person would pass lightly over this problem; for it is no secret that the percentage of Negroes who are accused of crime is higher than the Whites. I admit that we have had and still have, to a large extent, lower economic and moral standards than many of our White neighbors. However, we must realize that this condition is not a cause for segregation, but the effect of segregation and discrimination. The more segregation and discrimination we have in our community the more we shall continue to have ignorance and immorality and poverty.

To those who think that it would be an injustice to Negroes to have them compete with White students: the answer is found in the fact that our plan is to establish a system of education and not a temporary scheme to relieve ourselves of a problem which we are not willing to face. Certainly, there will be injustices at first where Negro students are behind White students in development; though not because of any natural inferiority, but because the society in which we live has long failed to abide by its own contract to provide equal educational facilities for all of its children. There will be scattered instances where Negroes might fall behind White students, but shortly this problem would be, for the most part, eliminated.

Others maintain that integration is all right, but it would put an end to the employment of Negro teachers. Those who feel this way seem not to correctly appraise the transition. In the first place, it will take many years to drastically change the present patterns of our community; for years we shall continue to have areas predominantly White, and areas primarily Negro. The law will not have to require this arrangement; the pride which people have in their homes, churches, and schools will motivate this stability.

What seems to be the second major defect in their argument is the idea that the same prejudices which are leveled against Negroes before integration will remain after integration. This will not be the case. We are entering a period in which merit must rule the selection of teachers. There was a time when a person could get through college by hook or crook, and if he could do nothing else he would reach. This practice is rapidly becoming a thing of the past; in tomorrow's world it will be unheard of. Thus, if a teacher has mastered his profession, and has made the proper adjustments, and is willing to dedicate himself to man's biggest calling, though he is yellow, black or white, there will be a place for him.

Finally, let me mention the argument for separate but equal facilities in public education as being superior to a non-restricted system. This argument may seem more plausible if getting an education were an end in itself, and not a means to an end. The end product of an education is a greater and more useful participation in the art of living in a civilized society. If an education does not help make out of people more useful citizens to themselves and their community, then it has failed. Conversely, if the community fails to provide those whom it educates an opportunity to serve it to the fullest extent, then the community is guilty of self-impoverishment or self-destruction.

This is why I have not been able to understand what good an equalization program would serve, if no sincere plans are being made to equalize employment opportunities. If there are to be no jobs in government, science, or industry, the time and money spent in educating the child are in vain. The question seems to be what part will the educated Negro play in our society in future years? If we plan to continue our policy of employing all White on our hospital staffs, all White in government service, all White on engineering staffs, all White in anything which requires the least amount of brain-power, what will the thousands of Negroes do who will be graduating each year? On the other hand, if we decide to be realistic and fair about the whole thing, and employ people according to merit, would it not be much more sensible and certainly more economical to permit the lawyers, doctors and engineers who are to be working on the same staffs just after graduation, to go to the same schools where they could learn to respect and appreciate each other?

Questions of this kind have led me to request that I be permitted to enroll at Mississippi Southern College, without a court order to do so. I, too, am a solid believer in the ability of the individual States to control their own affairs. I believe that if this State should lead out with only the smallest amount of integration, it would never have to worry about Federal intervention.

I have done all that is within my power to follow a reasonable course in this matter. I have wanted the State to see that our position has at least some validity. I have tried to make it clear that my love for the State of Mississippi and my hope for its peaceful prosperity is equal to any man's alive. The thought of presenting this request before a Federal Court for consideration, with all the publicity and misrepresentation which that would bring about, makes my heart heavy. Yet, what other course can I take?

Respectfully submitted,
Clyde Kennard

APPENDIX B

Hattiesburg American published an official response by President William D. McCain to Clyde Kennard's enrollment attempts. Kennard uses the newspaper as a platform later for his open letters to the public.

"NEGRO ENTRY INQUIRY ANSWERED,"
HATTIESBURG AMERICAN, FEBRUARY 29, 1956, 1

Negro Entry Inquiry Answered

In response to a number of inquiries, President William D. McCain of Mississippi Southern College today issued the following statement concerning application of Negroes for admission to the college:

"Last November Clyde Kennard (or Kinnard) of Hattiesburg, a Negro, requested information concerning admission to Mississippi Southern. He then submitted a partial application for admission. Since his application was not completed, the administrative officers of the college did not think it necessary to take any action on it."

Dr. McCain said that to his knowledge there has been no other formal request for admission to Southern by a Negro.

Negro Entry Inquiry Answered

In response to a number of inquiries, President William D. McCain of Mississippi Southern College today issued the following statement concerning application of Negroes for admission to the college:

"Last November Clyde Kennard (or Kinnard) of Hattiesburg, a Negro, requested information concerning admission to Mississippi Southern. He then submitted a partial application for admission. Since his application was not completed, the administrative officers of the college did not think it necessary to take any action on it."

Dr. McCain said that to his knowledge there has been no other formal request for admission to Southern by a Negro.

APPENDIX C

After his return home to Mississippi, Clyde Kennard's experiences were covered by the *Chicago Maroon*, a student publication at the University of Chicago considering his prior enrollment at the institution. One letter was written and submitted to the editor by Celia Towne, whom we have not been able to identify or explain her relations to Kennard. He is credited for writing (or perhaps having dictated) the final notice about blood donations thanking both students and the staff at Billings Hospital (located on the university's campus) where Kennard received cancer treatment following his release from prison.

CHICAGO MAROON, APRIL 17, 1963: CELIA TOWNE,
"KENNARD NEEDS BOOKS," LETTERS TO THE EDITOR, 2

Kennard Needs Books

TO THE EDITOR:

I write to you in reference to Clyde Kennard, the Negro about whom you have carried stories, who was formerly a U. of C. student and was later imprisoned in Mississippi following his attempt to enter an all-white segregated university in Mississippi and who is now dying of cancer of the liver.

It has come to my attention that Mr. Kennard would welcome the gift of books about the American Negro, in the fields of history, political science and government, natural sciences, philosophy, and sociology since the year 1955, as well as the great classical novels. He has an abundant supply of books but not the sort he wants to read.

Mr. Clyde Kennard's address from now on will be Rural Route One, Box 70, Hattiesburg, Mississippi.

CELIA TOWNE

APPENDIX C

EDITORIAL

Hits apathy on college aid

Among the many reasons behind the lack of Congressional action on aid to higher education is one directly attributable to the students of the University of Chicago as well as to their counterparts across the country. Since very few letters from those who stand to benefit most directly from education legislation have been received in Washington, a general impression prevails there that such legislation is neither very pressing nor very important.

In light of the general agreement of educators that the challenges facing our nation's schools are too immense to be successfully met without large scale and immediate federal assistance, and in light of the increasing financial burdens being placed on students who wish to pursue their education through college, we cannot understand this deplorable lack of concern. After all, federal aid legislation means more and better fellowships, scholarships, loan funds, libraries, research facilities, classrooms, and teachers.

An education bill will get through Congress only if there is enough sentiment for it among the students and teachers of the country, according to Phillip DesMarais, who is on the staff of Secretary of Health, Education, and Welfare Celebrezze. Nonetheless, he said, and Dr. Deborah P. Wolfe, education staff chief for the House Committee on Education and Labor, confirmed, almost no letters from college and university students have been received.

Illinois Senator and former UC Professor Paul Douglas agrees that letters from the student community would have a favorable effect on legislation, but noted that he, too, has not seen much interest in pending education bills.

Adam Clayton Powell, chairman of the House Committee on Education and Labor, said he has received "very little mail on education bills."

And even Representative Edith Green, sponsor of the only general college aid bill that is acknowledged to have any chance of passing this session, said she has not received much mail from students. Mrs. Green suggested that letters of support from students who find it financially difficult to get through college would serve as a valuable impetus to legislators.

What sadly remains, then, is for students of this university to do something to make a point of finding a few moments to write to their Congressmen and other key legislators and to stand up for education. We are confident that their demonstrated interest will have a very great effect. And, while it would be disgraceful if this country were to go one more year without tangibly facing up to its responsibilities in the field of education, it would be even more so if the students of the nation allowed this to happen by their lack of concern for their own education.

Letters to the editor

Kennard needs books
TO THE EDITOR:

I write you in reference to Clyde Kennard, the Negro about whom you have carried stories, who was formerly a U. of C. student and was later imprisoned in Mississippi following his attempt to enter an all-white segregated university in Mississippi and who is now dying of cancer of the liver.

It has come to my attention that Mr. Kennard would welcome the gift of books about the American Negro, in the fields of history, political science and government, natural sciences, philosophy, and sociology since the year 1955, as well as the great classical novels. He has an abundant supply of books but not the sort he wants to read.

Mr. Clyde Kennard's address from now on will be Rural Route One, Box 70, Hattiesburg, Mississippi.

CELIA TOWNE

Welfare key to election
TO THE EDITOR:

I read with interest Mr. Herman Finer's analysis of the Daley victory in the mayoral election. (Maroon April 5). While his statement listing the immediate causes for the decreased Daley plurality seems correct, the analysis of the basic causes leading to the decline is questionable. Mr. Finer is certainly, as a private citizen, able to revere Mr. Daley and the Democrats and to despise Mr. Adamowski and the Republicans, indeed this thought is the desirable verdicate of the moral. However, this emotionalism obscures the basic problem which Mr. Finer, as a political scientist, is trying to answer; why people voted as they did.

The problem is, as Mr. Finer saw it, the increase in government expenditures. The city today is obliged to build more schools and roads. In addition the city must provide for the traditional services; police and fire protection, sewage disposal, water purification, etc.; these costs increase each year.

There is also the problem of the great pariah class, the unemployed and the underemployed; the class a comprised chiefly of Negroes. This group creates a great economic problem since, although it has smaller than average tax bills, it requires far more than the house city services. To support this class the city must put the payroll, allocate a personnel funds to control the increased fire and crime rates, build many new schools to educate the large numbers of youngsters, and spend far more than normal for an employment compensation and aid for dependent children. This staggering cost is compounded since the city now feels obliged to provide new housing for the pariah class. Mr. Finer considered only this one segment of the total welfare bill and here his analysis becomes emotional.

The cost of Chicago's huge expenditures for relief are partially borne by the local taxpayers and they do not like it. The Chicago property tax rate is over $5.50 per $100 of assessed valuation and in addition the city directly receives 1/7 of the state sales tax. It is little wonder the local taxpayers oppose the bond issue and urban renewal programs which take from the property owners and give to the low-income pariah class. A vote for Adamowski might well be considered as a simple, unqualified prejudice" against the high cost of urban renewal and the whole set of services the city performs for the low income class. Such a vote may represent an unqualified prejudice" but it is not irrational.

Mr. Finer believes there is an approaching national conflict in urban affairs; we would do well to study Chicago and Illinois as a costly example. The federal government provides many millions annually for the support of the welfare programs, the unemployment compensation program and the urban renewal program. The state of Illinois is nearly bankrupt and yet it must increase its welfare budget, most of which goes to Chicago, to nearly one billion dollars for the next biennium. Employers must pay part of the cost of the unemployment compensation program. Finally the local citizens must pay their property taxes. For a city and a state who are both economically sick. The cool air staggering; voters revolt.

Here we are at the heart of the problem. Why are we providing these services for the low-income class? How do these services aid the class? Are the members of the class better able to rise economically and socially? Do welfare funds help life people over temporary crises or does the welfare check become a permanent alternative to gainful employment? There is also the related question of taxes; given the presumably unlimited present need for welfare funds, how much more financial support can and should be expected from each employer and property owner? And finally, will there ever be an end to the welfare programs or are they an ever growing economic cancer as is the defense program.

In light of the voter revolt in Chicago and the one Mr. Finer sees approaching throughout America, I would suggest the whole set of welfare programs needs a complete reappraisal. The programs must be continued but we must reappraise them in light of growing tax payer opposition. Only through calm study can we formulate the best possible welfare programs. We must not engage in useless name calling.

CHARLES R. KEEN

Hits dogmatic liberalism
TO THE EDITOR:

It seems that both dogmatic liberalism and dogmatic conservatism may make reference to the same source, J. S. Mill, for support. Liberalism may make such reference in order to support either the free exchange of ideas to the end of progress and need welfare or social irresponsibility in the name of freedom. Conservatism may make such reference in order to support either individual freedom or, by analogy, state as opposed to federal authority to the end of limiting individual freedom as guaranteed by federal law. Neither dogmatism, in either social or political expression, can meet all the needs of a society yet allow for the responsible operation of a newspaper. More often than not, the Maroon represents dogmatic liberalism.

Your "Statement of Policy" regarding advertising in the 29 March edition of the Maroon seems to have been made from the perspective of the dogmatic liberalism to which I refer. You "carefully considered positions" valued both for its enlightenment and its pragmatism" cannot be valued for its responsibility. You neglected to mention fraud as a reason for rejecting advertising. And is there not implicit fraud in the advertising of a poison as a candy even though the poison may taste sweet? If cigarettes are to be advertised with reference to their short range pleasure able effects, should not the reader be given the benefit of reading in the same advertisement reference to their disease-producing potential? Of course, it seems likely that the cigarette industry would consider such a negative reference bad advertising policy. As you refuse to take some kind of action against irresponsible advertising, you are being irresponsible.

If one must graduate directly from thumb-sucking to cigarette sucking, let us at least have the safe filter which Mr. Meehan Mode has mentioned. The Maroon's rejection of implicity fraudulent advertising might help to publicize the need for a harmless thumb surrogate. (Other students of taxes and economics find in newspapers have survived financially without cigarette advertising.)

It seems that Mr. Klein, your advertising manager, will not take a position which someone might call moral because of his fear of seeming unenlightened. Mr. Meehan Mode does not seem to be asking that you help to being back "Old Man Prohibition" in new garb but that you contribute to an activity equivalent to taking the wood alcohol out of the booze.

W. BROWN

The one lotion that's cool, exciting — brisk as an ocean breeze!

Old Spice — the shave lotion men recommend to other men!

BLACK FRIARS
"Aside From All That"

APRIL 26, 27, 28   TICKETS $2.00, $1.50

MANDEL BOX OFFICE

CHICAGO MAROON, APRIL 11, 1963:
"KENNARD RETURNS TO MISS," 3

Kennard Returns to Miss

Clyde Kennard, the Negro former UC student who was jailed for two years after trying to enroll at the University of Southern Mississippi (USM), has announced that he plans to return to his home town of Hattiesburg, Miss. Friends of Kennard also announced the start of a fund to help pay off his debts, which total over $10,000.

Kennard was sentenced to seven years in jail on charges of stealing $25 worth of chicken feed in 1961, after attempting three times to enroll at USM, but was released last January after it was revealed he had cancer.

He was given a suspended sentence and flown to Chicago to be treated at Billings Hospital.

Now living in Chicago with his sister, Mrs. Sarah Tarpley, Kennard will return to Mississippi this month.

After paying his debts, he would like eventually to attend law school, either at UC or at Howard University, if he doesn't decide to try to go to school in Mississippi again.

Dr. Andrew L. Thomas, M.D., a college classmate of Kennard, announced that with the founding of the Clyde Kennard Fund of Chicago, all other funds for Mr. Kennard have been dissolved, including one in Jackson, Miss. Kennard's sister and contributors have already paid off $900 which was owed on a mortgage note on the Kennard farm.

Money raised by the new fund will pay existing debts and prevent foreclosure on the farm's mortgage, help finance any educational expenses if Kennard returns to school, aid any legal procedures needed to clear Kennard of the theft charge, and establish a scholarship fund in Kennard's honor if he cannot resume his studies.

Thomas said the Kennards owe $8,000 to the Farmer's Home Administration on their farm's mortgage, $2,000 to the NAACP state branches on a loan for equipment, and $900 to local businessmen.

Address of the fund is Clyde Kennard Fund of Chicago, Box 4820, Chicago 80, Ill.

APPENDIX C

Russian choir presents concert

The Russian Choir will present a Lenten concert of church music tomorrow at Bond Chapel. Stejan V. Lazarevic, a specialist in Slavonic music, will conduct.

The Choir has been rehearsing since January for the concert, which will begin at 8:15 pm and is free.

Church music from the 18th, 19th, and 20th centuries, including a Byzantine chant, will comprise the program. In addition, Lazarevic will give a short explanatory talk about Russian music, and

UCers get chem awards

The American Chemical Society honored two UC faculty scientists and an alumnus at its recent national meeting in Los Angeles.

Robert S. Mulliken, Ernest DeWitt Burton Distinguished Service Professor Emeritus of Physics and Chemistry, and Director of the Laboratory of Molecular structure and Spectre, received the Peter Debye Award in Physical chemistry.

Stuart A. Rice, Professor of Chemistry, and Professor in and Director of the Institute for the Study of Metals, was presented the American Chemical Society Award in Pure Chemistry.

Martin D. Kamen, a UC graduate, now at the University of California, San Diego, received the Society's award for nuclear applications in chemistry.

songs in the program will be explained.

Russian music is very western in style. The sacred music, which includes many chants, is much like that heard in modern churches on Sundays. Russian church music remains traditional and has stayed away from the changes which affected Russian music as a whole. In the 19th century, there was no native school of Russian music. Then, slavic music resembled Italian music or whatever western European style happened to be modish at the time. In the 19th century, Moussourgsky and Borodin created a new Russian style with an imitation of folk music. Stravinsky and other experimenters are noted in the 20th century. Thomas Riha, assistant professor of history and chairman of the

Midway studio drive begins

The Women's Board of the University has launched a drive to improve the Midway Studios at 6016 Ingleside. The studio, which has been the place of work for sculptor Lorado Taft and many other artists, is now used by the Department of Art of the University.

At a tea yesterday, plans for the drive to renovate the 56 year old studio were announced. The board hopes to be able to raise funds to construct a special exhibit gallery, a new painting studio, and conduct

Russian Civilization course, organized the choir three years ago. Since that time, the choir has boasted 35 regular members who meet each Tuesday night at 7:30 in Ida Noyes.

The members of the choir are people interested in singing. Very few of them speak Russian; the lyrics are transliterated for them. As well as singing Russian music in the original, the choir also attempts Ukrainian and Serbian songs. Their repertoire includes folk and secular music aside from the church music which will be presented at the concert.

The choir's most recent concert was given in January before the students in the Russian Civilization course as an example of Russian art.

a general renewal program in the remainder of the studio, according to Mrs. Harris Ward, Chairman of the Women's Board.

Expansion of the University's art program is also planned, said Mrs. Ward.

At the tea yesterday, Mrs. Paul Douglas, daughter of sculptor Taft, will discuss the history of the building. Mrs. Margaret French Cresson, daughter of American sculptor Daniel Chester French, was also a guest of honor at the tea.

The Women's Board was formed two years ago to acquaint women with the educational and research activities of the University and to provide a channel for them to utilize their skills and energy in University projects.

Kennard returns to Miss

Clyde Kennard, the Negro former UC student who was jailed for two years after trying to enroll at the University of Southern Mississippi (USM), has announced that he plans to return to his home town of Hattiesburg, Miss. Friends of Kennard also announced the start of a fund to help pay off his debts, which total over $10,000.

Kennard was sentenced to seven years in jail on charges of stealing $25 worth of chicken feed in 1961, after attempting three times to enroll at USM, but was released last January after it was revealed that he had cancer.

He was given a suspended sentence and flown to Chicago to be treated at Billings Hospital.

Now living in Chicago with his sister, Mrs. Sarah Tarpley, Kennard will return to Mississippi this month.

After paying his debts, he would like eventually to attend law school, either at UC or at Howard University, if he doesn't decide to

Austrian poems read

Austrian Actress Susi Nicoletti will present readings from a wide range of modern Austrian authors this evening.

Miss Nicoletti, a regular performer at Vienna's famed Burgtheater, will read selections from such authors as Arthur Schnitzler, Ilse Aichinger, Hugo von Hofmannsthal, Franz Werfel, and Anta Wildgans.

The program, sponsored by the Graduate Germanics club, will be at 8 pm in the Law School auditorium.

try to go to school in Mississippi again.

Dr. Andrew L. Thomas, M.D., a college classmate of Kennard, announced that with the founding of the Clyde Kennard Fund of Chicago, all other funds for Mr. Kennard have been dissolved, including one in Jackson, Miss. Kennard's sister and contributors have already paid off $900 which was owed on a mortgage note on the Kennard farm.

Money raised by the new fund will pay existing debts and prevent foreclosure on the farm's mortgage, help finance any educational expenses if Kennard returns to school, aid any legal procedures needed to clear Kennard of the theft charge, and establish a scholarship fund in Kennard's honor if he cannot resume his studies.

Thomas said the Kennards owe $8,000 to the Farmer's Home Administration on their farm's mortgage, $2,000 to the NAACP state branches on a loan for equipment, and $900 to local businessmen. Address of the fund is Clyde Kennard Fund of Chicago, Box 1820, Chicago 90, Ill.

Struve, Fyvie die

Otto Struve, a former head of the University's department of Astronomy, died Saturday in Berkeley, California. Struve had been head of the department of Astronomy from 1932 to 1950, was director of the University's Yerkes Observatory at Lake Geneva.

Struve had been awarded the gold medal of the royal Astronomical Society of London, the highest award in astronomy.

William Fyvie, a laboratory technician at the University for 30 years, also died this week in Billings hospital. Fyvie, 52, had retired in 1961.

Fyvie's funeral will be held Saturday at 3 pm from the Cocoran Funeral home, 1420 East 87th st.

HOBBY HOUSE RESTAURANT

Open Dawn to Dawn

BREAKFAST   DINNER
LUNCH   SNACKS

1342 E. 53rd St.

Bova Florist

5239 Harper Avenue

Happy Easter

20% Discount To University Students and Faculty upon presentation of I.D.

"Where Your Dollar Has Blooming Sense Off the Corner but on the Square"

Classifieds

APTS., ROOMS, ETC

WANTED

PERSONALS

FOR SALE

KELLY! KELLY! KELLY!

Today's Wise Buy

Real Cool Special
'59 LARK WAGON
Fully Factory Equipped

$395.00 FULL PRICE

With This Ad

SOUTH SIDE STUDEBAKER, Inc.
46th & Cottage Grove
BO 8-1111

April 11, 1963 • CHICAGO MAROON • 3

CHICAGO MAROON, FEBRUARY 14, 1963:
"KENNARD NEEDS BLOOD," 1

Kennard Needs Blood

Blood contributions are needed for Clyde Kennard, first Negro to attempt enrollment in a Mississippi University, who is currently in Billings Hospital for cancer treatment.

Kennard, who is scheduled to undergo surgery tomorrow, was released from a Mississippi prison earlier this month in order to get needed medical treatment. Last year, doctors removed a malignant growth from Kennard's intestine and gave him a 20% chance to live five years.

The former UC student was sentenced to seven years in prison for an alleged theft of $25 worth of chicken feed. His conviction was reportedly to prevent him from making further attempts to enter the University of Southern Mississippi near his home. Persons with criminal records are not allowed to attend state universities in Mississippi.

Any type of blood may be contributed. Males under 21 or females under 18 must have signed notes of permission from their parents in order to make donations.

Appointments for giving blood may be made by calling extension 5579.

UC among schools to benefit from aid bill

by Laura Godofsky

There is a "good chance" that at least some parts of President Kennedy's education bill will be passed this year according to UC President George Beadle.

Many people believe that Kennedy's omnibus bill will be broken down and considered in parts, he said. In fact, several bills have already been prepared which would consider various proposals individually.

If the bill is passed, it would affect the University of Chicago in many ways, said Beadle.

The higher education proposals in the bill include one billion dollars in federal funds to be loaned during the next three years to public and private universities and colleges to cover up to 75% of the cost of construction of classrooms and other academic facilities.

It also provides a three-year, $300 million program for buildings, books and equipment in public and private college libraries, technical schools, science facilities, and graduate programs; and expanded grants for teaching and research in science.

In addition, the bill asks for a 50% increase in funds from $90 to 135 million for the National Defense Education Act (NDEA) student loan program; an increase in NDEA graduate fellowships from 1500 to 10,000 a year; a three year $67 million grant program to subsidize part time jobs for students; a program for insuring commercial loans of up to $10,000 for students; and an increase in the number of National Science Foundation awards from 2800 to 8700 a year.

Kennedy's bill would go a long way toward enabling the University to build its planned new library, and hoped for chemistry building, said Beadle.

In addition, the University needs expanded facilities for its physicists (particularly the higher energy physics groups), geophysicists, and psychologists.

Increased stipends and numbers of fellowships would aid the University, said Beadle.

The University would gain from changes in the NDEA too, assuming it would still qualify for the maximum amount, which would be increased under the provisions of the new bill.

Beadle praised the contemplated extension of the forgiveness principle in the bill from students who are planning to go into teaching at the elementary and secondary levels to include those who plan to teach in colleges and universities.

The American Council on Education (ACE) which is comprised of colleges, universities, foundations, and educational organizations, of which Beadle is a director has, in a recent statement, urged a "broad program of federal action to help expand and improve both public and private institutions of higher education." The statement supports many of the proposals in Kennedy's bill and urges still more government aid to education.

Although he did not aid in the drafting of the ACE statement, Beadle attended sessions at which it was discussed and modified.

Logan Wilson, President of the ACE wrote President Kennedy in December of the urgent need for federal action on educational proposals.

Because of the time needed to enact new federal legislation, to get it into effective operation, to plan and then build new facilities, and to complete the graduate education of a college teacher, ACE estimated that the full effect of federal legislation passed this year would not be felt until at least 1965-66, he said.

"The focus of federal action to sustain and develop American higher education as a national resource must be on programs to assist institutions to meet the demand for better higher education for an increasing number of students," said ACE.

"Thus the construction of academic facilities and the recruitment and preparation of qualified college teachers must have first priority for the academic community and should have first priority in the thinking of Congress and the Executive. The need for more student financial assistance holds a second priority."

ACE said "the need justifies a commitment by the federal government averaging $1 billion annually for a program of matching grants and low-interest loans for construction of academic facilities in both public and private institutions."

It urged "federal agencies which support research in colleges and universities" to be "authorized and encouraged to provide appropriate support for the construction of the physical facilities and for acquisition of the equipment for such research."

It urged the government to "make full use" of its authority to make college housing loans, and, if the demand for loans should exceed available funds, to seek additional lending authority." Currently, the College Housing Loan Program is authorized to dis-

(Continued on page 4)

chicago Maroon

Vol. 71 — No. 68 University of Chicago, Thursday, February 14, 1963 31

New nations tied to small firms

by Deidre Holloway

In a paper given before a United Nations Conference being held this month in Geneva, Switzerland, Professor Bert F. Hoselitz of the Division of Social Sciences stated that the successful and rapid growth of private business communities in the new nations of Asia and Africa is dependent upon the small and medium sized firms which they established.

This formula was presented to the UN Conference on the Application of Science and Technology for the Benefit of Less Developed Areas in Hoselitz's paper entitled "The Entrepreneurial Element in Economic Development." Hoselitz was not present at the conference to present the paper in person.

Hoselitz reasons that the very different relative supply of labor and capital in emerging nations necessitates a reliance on small business. He presumed that it was visionary for such nations to hope for immediate Pittsburgs or Burminghams and said they should rather be concerned with the allocation of small capital in various industrial and commercial fields.

His paper also held that private businessmen in the new nations should not be afraid of public aid in the form of a planned economy. "It is quite conceivable," Hoselitz stated, "that the mixed economy (the mixture of public and private planning) as it takes shape in many developing countries, may grow into a new form of economic system with its own distinctive characteristics, one of which would be collaboration between public officials and private entrepreneurs in the development of the economy."

With the growth of the small business through reinvestment of profits, entrepreneurs might exert pressure on the actions of the state, especially the legislature, through their social status and political influence, he said.

This influence, he thinks, is necessary because government assistance is essential to successful business and industry. Hoselitz termed the agencies through which governments would provide aid as "development banks." In addition to monetary subsidies, such banks would also provide information on topics of vital interest to entrepreneurs.

Hoselitz intimated that the success of entrepreneurial performance would yield to the increasing prosperity of the less developed nations because "the interests of government, of the newly emerging entrepreneurial class, and of the mass of the population in a developing nation are closely parallel. The main problem," he said, "is to find a formula by means of which this parallelisms of interests can be put into effect with least friction and greatest likelihood of success."

Hoselitz, who has been on the University faculty since 1945, has been described as one of the world's few "universal social scientists."

UI ends discriminatory list

by Andrew Stein

In an unexpected move Tuesday, University of Illinois (Champaign) officials reversed their policy on the listing of unapproved housing accommodations.

The decision came in a letter from university provost Lyle H. Lanier to housing director Paul J. Doebel, directing him to remove from housing division listings the names of all landlords who will not sign a pledge of non-discrimination by March 15.

The university housing division maintains a central listing of about 1200 landlords who have housing avilable. Undergraduates are required to live in approved housing, such as dormitories, fraternities and cooperative living groups, which are under the jurisdiction of the university. Graduate students, married students and other non - undergraduates may live in unapproved housing.

There are no discriminatory clauses in any approved housing except in fraternities and they have been ordered by the University to remove any so called "white clauses" by 1965.

The official decision came on the eve of a meeting planned Wednesday between a representative of the provost office and an ad hoc student committee. The ad hoc committee, Student Action for Non - Discrimination, was formed to protest what it considered discriminatory practices of the housing division.

The group said that incidents reported to the NAACP and the Association of International Students indicate that wide discrimination continues in unapproved housing. They charged the university was tacitly accepting this situation by listing the housing without requiring a pledge of non discrimination.

The committee had started action Tuesday to circulate petitions calling for the action that was taken by the administration later that day.

The UC student government passed a resolution in last week's assembly calling for the University to exclude discriminatory housing from its housing list.

The bill stated that the University "has neither taken action nor made public announcement of a policy excluding discriminatory housing from its housing list." They claimed that "a discriminatory housing list is detrimental to the University . . .'

Kennard needs blood

Blood contributions are needed for Clyde Kennard, first Negro to attempt enrollment in a Mississippi University, who is currently in Billings Hospital for cancer treatment.

Kennard, who is scheduled to undergo surgery tomorrow, was released from a Mississippi prison earlier this month in order to get needed medical treatment. Last year, doctors removed a malignant growth from Kennard's intestine and gave him a 20% chance to live five years.

The former UC student was sentenced to seven years in prison for an alleged theft of $25 worth of chicken feed. His conviction was reportedly to prevent him from making further attempts to enter the University of Southern Mississippi near his home. Persons with criminal records are not allowed to attend state universities in Mississippi.

Any type of blood may be contributed. Males under 21 or females under 18 must have signed notes of permission from their parents in order to make donations.

Appointments for giving blood may be made by calling extension 5579.

SG will sponsor Spring NY flights

Student Government will sponsor a charter flight to and from New York for Spring Interim.

The flight will leave Friday evening, March 15, from O'Hare and will return Sunday, March 24, from Idlewild. The cost of the flight is $60 including bus transportation to and from O'Hare.

Reservations can be made at the SG office, Ida Noyes Hall, on Monday, Tuesday, Wednesday, and Friday from 3 to 5 p.m. and Monday, Wednesday, and Friday from 10 to 11 a.m. One way flights can be arranged through the flight leaders.

A deposit of $30 is necessary for a reservation and should be made as soon as possible. The deadline for full payment is March 5.

Despres backing gains strength

by John T. Williams

The fifth ward aldermanic campaign enters its final two weeks with incumbent Leon M. Despres showing increasing strength. His opponent is Hyde Park attorney, Chauncey Eskridge.

The Greater Woodlawn Pastors Alliance unanimously endorsed Despres recently; the group's statement said "we cannot stand by quietly when it is so obvious that our community is being used as a battleground by outside forces which are not interested in the needs of our people or the real problems of our community."

Last Sunday, United States Senator Paul Douglas strongly urged Despres' reelection at a cocktail party sponsored by Despres' backers.

Despres is also backed by the Fifth Ward Regular Democratic Organization; the Independent Voters of Illinois; the Fifth Ward Regular Republican Organization, and the Republican Mayoral candidate, Benjamin Adamowski. Despres has also enjoyed generous support from the press. One of the major metropolitan papers singled him out two weeks ago as one of the six or seven aldermen most worthy of reelection. Another newspaper supported him editorially yesterday. The paper hailed him for his independence and his interests in economical city government.

Two weeks ago, the two community newspapers in the fifth ward, the Hyde Park Herald and the Woodlawn Booster published editorials vehemently advocating Despres' reelection.

The **Herald** editorial, which was probably more anti-Eskridge than pro-Despres, charged that the candidates are no longer the chief issue in this campaign. They are overshadowed by that aspect of the political life of the city which they represent."

The **Booster** dismissed Eskridge as "comparatively conservative and uninformed" and endorsed "democracy's greatest local defender"—Despres.

This week, the **Herald** charged that Eskridge did not even know that the Hyde Park-Kenwood Urban Renewal plan existed. This plan, which was initiated several years ago, involved expenditures of nearly forty million dollars. Although it is not yet completed, it has already involved much demolition and rebuilding in the community.

Eskridge was also unaware that the University had presented a specific South Campus plan to the city. The Herald editorial said that the community was bitter because Eskridge presents himself as a candidate for public office "without giving us (the community) the courtesy of finding out what we have been doing. You do not even know enough to say we have been right or wrong, no less to make a judgment about future plans," the editorial continued.

Eskridge's most significant supporters are from outside the ward. Alderman Kenneth Campbell of the 20th ward, has assumed command of the Eskridge campaign. Campbell is not being opposed in the forthcoming election. He is using many of the members of his own ward Democratic Organization in the Eskridge campaign.

James Quisenberry, president of the Democratic Organization in Campbell's ward and administrative assistant to Eskridge during the campaign, appeals for Eskridge on the ground that "no white can know how a Negro feels because no white has ever been jim crowed, suffered the things I've suffered."

Several pro-Eskridge groups have been formed in the past few weeks. Among them are: Labor's Committee for the Election of Chauncey Eskridge for Alderman of the Fifth Ward and the Veterans Committee for Chauncey Eskridge for Alderman.

Eskridge has been endorsed by Andrew J. Hatcher, a press aide to President Kennedy. Hatcher's letter of endorsement said that he had been "the beneficiary of Eskridge's hard thinking on matters affecting the national community and now . . . you should be able to effect many of your ideas for the benefit of Chicago. You have my good wishes for a constructive and victorious campaign."

CHICAGO MAROON, FEBRUARY 22, 1963:
"KENNARD THANKS DONORS," 2

Kennard Thanks Donors

TO THE STUDENTS OF THE UNIVERSITY OF CHICAGO AND THE EMPLOYEES OF BILLINGS HOSPITAL:
I wish to express my sincere gratitude to those persons who donated blood in my behalf at Billings Hospital.

CLYDE KENNARD

(Twenty-five people contributed blood for Kennard as a result of an appeal in last week's *Maroon*. —Editor)

Letters to the editor

Kennard Thanks Donors

TO THE STUDENTS OF THE UNIVERSITY OF CHICAGO AND THE EMPLOYEES OF BILLINGS HOSPITAL:

I wish to express my sincere gratitude to those persons who donated blood in my behalf at Billings Hospital.

CLYDE KENNARD

(Twenty-five people contributed blood for Kennard as a result of an appeal in last week's Maroon.—Editor)

Int Players' director defends Horning's review

TO THE EDITOR:

I am writing this letter to defend Carol Horning, not personally, but as a reviewer. Of the letters appearing in the MAROON of Thursday, Feb. 20th, those of Jerry Mast and Robert Strang, both members, I believe, of UT, attacked Miss Horning's personal relationship with that organization. Beside the fact that they were slightly upset by her unfavorable review of GOOD NEWS, they dwelt with considerable vituperation upon Miss Horning's expressing her personal opinion and her right to do so. In both letters, so it seemed to me, there was the implication that a bad review would destroy the show. Further was the suggestion that Miss Horning's dislike of GOOD NEWS was a result of her alienation from UT and that otherwise she would have been favorably disposed to the production. I do not see that it follows.

Undoubtedly Miss Horning has her biases, both as a knowledgeable person in the theatre and as a newspaper critic; and undoubtedly she expressed these biases in her review. Good. For what else indeed, is the function of the critic, either on a campus or in the city, or anywhere else? I see it as three-fold: to inform and instruct the production, and to stimulate newspaper readership. In a word, the reviewer must be critical, critical according to his or her own subjectivity (I'm not sure that I understand what objective reviewing is) and critical in the most entertaining fashion that he or she can muster.

Certainly I can sympathize with Jerry Mast's feelings over the review, since it was only recently that a somewhat unfavorable review appeared concerning my own production. But I cannot understand why he considers six weeks of work wasted. Miss Horning did state, if I understand her correctly, that she found the show enjoyable. She criticized it upon both artistic and theatrical grounds, decrying the latter and admitting certain praise to the former. Her comments concerning UT seem to me more one of a desire to rectify and build rather than disparage and destroy. I cannot believe that Miss Horning, being as devoted as she is to theatre, would wish either the failure or demise of UT. What she expresses is the wish that it were better. Curiously enough, the very review Mr. Mast found so derogatory has, so I found in conversation with readers, had an opposite effect on many: they are going to see GOOD NEWS as a result of reading Carol Horning's review.

As to Mr. Strang's letter, he is guilty of the fault of which he accused Carol Horning. He states that the reader can rest assured that GOOD NEWS is a show which will evoke laughter, but fails to state anything which supports this appraisal. It seems to me that the attack on Miss Horning is far more personal and subjective in its origin than any part of Miss Horning's review.

In a certain sense I am in competition with UT, and yet I will fervently support all their productions and encourage as many as I can to attend them. But that does not mean that I must find every one of their productions worthwhile and good. That does not mean I will not criticize unfavorably a production which leaves me unfavorably impressed. It will be most unfortunate if the only way Carol Horning can be assured of support is if she gives a good review of UT productions. It will be unfortunate if Carol Horning is personally attacked as disenchanted UT-er simply because she had fault to find with a UT production.

And what is wrong with a relatively well documented unfavorable review? It is my conviction that bad reviews can spur good theatre as well as good ones. The object of UT or any campus theatre is, or should be, to produce good theatre and fill the house. Some intelligent, well-written, wittily biased criticism can help both these aims. I would ask Jerry Mast, for whom I have the highest regard as a director, to reread Miss Horning's review in three weeks and in quiet subjectivity ask himself how far her criticisms are accurate. He might be surprised.

JOE EHRENBERG, DIRECTOR
INTERNATIONAL PLAYERS

We think one fact has been ignored in the recent controversy about Miss Horning's review: she did not pan the play; she merely criticized certain aspects of it. The general tone and content of her review made Good News sound like an evening of fun. We really wonder at all the uproar—Editor

Ex IRP chairman bemoans loss of a 'fun' party

TO THE EDITOR:

My name is Dick Jacobsen. Until last Sunday night I was the last duly elected Chairman of the Independent Reform Party. Now I am no longer Chairman, and the party is no longer independent. A long time ago, Eliot Lilien, founder of IRP, told me, "Show Them that SG can be fun. If it ever stops being fun, quit."

The IRP that I used to know was fun. For the benefit of first year students, I'll quote from the IRP Future History of the University, 1961-1967: "1962 (written a full year before): Tuition raised to $1420 over the summer . . . 1963: Student suspended for missing three days of class while waiting for treatment in Billings Emergency Room . . . 1964: RH&C eliminates food complaints by serving pablum at all meals in six delicious flavors . . . 1965: Twelve students suspended for missing 12 o'clock bed check . . . 1967: The Bookstore buys the University." The campus thought that this was fun too. In 1961 Eliot Lilien was swept into office, outpolling everyone in the college, and becoming the only candidate in recent history to receive more than 500 votes — even more than Axelrod got.

Well, IRP stopped being fun and I got out. But a couple of diehards stuck it out. This shows guts, but no brains. The result of this perversion of the party's principles was the merger with funless UP.

For these exIRPers to whom SG has lost all prospect of being fun, the only gratification of participation is winning elections. Maybe winning is great stuff for power-hungry opportunists, but for the IRP of Eliot Lilien, and even my IRP, winning is small consolation for a merger which sacrifices all the principles for which the Imperial Revolutionary Party (IRP means SEX in Russian), the Imperial Reform Party (IRP won a seat in SG), and the Independent Reform Party (IRP won three seats in SG) stood, in turn for four years.

All that remains now of an intelligent, happy-go-lucky but dedicated group is a few small people who have sold their humorless souls for the promise of power and who betray themselves with every 'lovable' word they utter.

IRP mortuus est, and a eulogy is in order. The most fitting tribute that I can pay to the Grand Old Party is simply: "IRP, R.I.P."

DICK JACOBSON

Hits The Liberal Newsletter

TO THE EDITOR:

In these days of proliferating student political publications, the appearance of yet another such organ prompts the question, "Why?"

In the case of The Liberal Newsletter, the answer is simple: "Because."

Ostensibly issued to "demonstrate (the Liberal Party's) ability to publish an SG newsletter," LN describes the activities and plans of its publishers and attempts to clarify their differences with POLIT; viz: "POLIT's conception of 'fighting for civil rights and liberties' is fighting HUAC, while neglecting other civil liberties issues (see article on the Attorney General's list, p.2)."

So we turn to page 2, expecting to find an article on the Attorney General's list, and behold: an article on the "Guide to Subversive Organizations and Publications," which the liberal Party has mistaken for the Attorney General's list. Tsk, tsk. Surprisingly enough, the "Guide" is published by the House Committee on Un-American Activities.

"Surprisingly enough," says LN, "civil liberties groups seldom mention the List." If the writer of this statement will call on this writer, I shall be happy to furnish him with a rather extensive bibliography dealing in whole or in part with this and other lists.

The writer may also be interested to know that he may get in touch by phone with an outfit located in he Loop which specializes in abstracting and cross filing from this and other lists and from the files of governmental and private organizations. For a price, the American Security Council will furnish a client with a complete dossier on any individual or organization desired.

What I intend by this example is merely to point out to the Liberal Party that, no matter how good their intentions, the incantation of liberal dogma is no substitute for knowledge. If they wish to attack POLIT for its failures, they should do so in areas where POLIT has in fact failed, and not attempt to do what POLIT is more competent to do.

RON DORFMAN

Rockwell extermination policy a new approach

TO THE EDITOR:

As a liberal and open minded student of the University of Chicago, I begin to realize that Rockwell's idea of exterminating certain people is not such a bad solution after all. Please forward to me one ticket of admission to his performance. I'd prefer a balcony seat with a clear vision range of the platform.

EX-INMATE OF KL AUSCHWITZ
KL MAUTHAUSEN, Etc.
TATTOO No. 10001

Past too soon forgotten

TO THE EDITOR:

Swept under humanity's carpeting of indifference is the oh so dim memory of a long war and its many dead. To be a liberal that is the noble virtue. Hate, destruction, power and fear are the proper food for analysis, thought and discussion in our University Community. Forbidden is the duty of rememberance of compassion and love for our dead families, comrades and friends. And those who love, like the pagan Christians are victims of the Roman multitude's pleasure, because one might care to hear Mr. Rockwell and democracy is ruled by the sacrosanct whims of the individual. But I do not like maggots, for I am a tidy housekeeper and I shall sweep away the dirt of Mr. Rockwell's ideology and plant flowers upon the forgotten graves—those monuments of man's inhumanity to man—indifference.

LUBOV BABENO

University should adopt rational hours policy

TO THE EDITOR:

The time has come for an attempt at rationality in the whole emotional realm of women's hours.

We attend a university which we would like to be able to call—without a trace of equivocation—one of the great universities of the world. Yet how can we do this other than with tongue in cheek when the administration of this would-be great university refuses to take a staunch, logical, understanding position on any one of a dozen issues? Must we impute to the administration an inability to come to such a position, a fear of having to defend a position, or an ignorance of the need for clarification in any area?

The question of women's hours is one such area which can now be pressed to the fore because some have begun to talk seriously of them and the administration has shown the beginnings of interest in the problem. It cannot be allowed to die as always from lack of constant, continued, vehement-but-rational, organized, and individual student pressure.

The present situation—the tacit but obvious attempt to cloister all women between 12 pm and 7 am, frantic racing to the time clock, feverish punching of weekly "goody-girl cards," hectic mental tabulation of punches down and punches to go—is slightly worse than childish and slightly less than rational.

It is easy to ridicule an active interest by the men of the university in the extension or, better, elimination of women's hours. Victorian prudery runs rampant in the too-frequently-granted understanding "that we must, of course, keep the little ladies from those breathless beasts who riot continually beyond the walls."

We are men; we are women; we are students at a university we would call great. We will be free! Let those whose contrary sensibilities are offended control their lives as they wish. But don't, DON'T, tell us that our freedom must yield to greater security for them in their ways.

And besides, in all seriousness, the concept that the principles of morality will be violated in direct mathematical proportion to the relaxation of those housing regulations which keep the women away from the men is really rather nonsensical.

When a guy can't see his girl and both are living independently, when a woman can't leave her hall, when contact between men and women is arbitrarily made difficult at arbitrary hours, the freedom of both men and women is being infringed upon.

Let this be discussed: the only position befitting an intelligent university community is one which is rational, and the small scope of rational positions which are solutions to the problem of women's hours makes discussion of the problem on any level, with anyone, unusually clear.

All that is required is pressure. When has the University of Chicago lacked contributors and contributions to well-directed pressure?

MIKHAIL

GANT

COPPER-MAIZE

Copper-Maize—a spirited cotton oxford shirt that lends "color" to dark-tone suits. Versatile—it wears handsomely with blues, greys, olives or browns. Like all Gant shirts, it has elan in a gentlemanly manner.

©1963 Gant Shirtmakers

THE STORE FOR MEN

Cohn & Stern, Inc

Town and Campus Shop

In the New Hyde Park Shopping Center

1502-06 E. 55th St.

Phone 752-8100

"WHEN the White House Press Secretary gets news-managed into a promise to hike fifty miles, that's news. But when he manages to unmanage the news by retracting his pledge, no doubt in return for onsite inspection of his unguided muscles, that's not news, managed or otherwise. It's just a broken pledge. That's not news, any more."

For the current issue of NATIONAL REVIEW write for free copy, 150 E. 35 St., New York 16, N.Y.

Joseph H. Aaron

Connecticut Mutual Life Insurance Protection

135 S. LaSalle St.

MI 3-5986 RA 6-1060

NO LLOOOONNNNNGGGG

food lines at the Wash Prom this year Delicious Buffet expertly catered by Annette's

SAT. NITE—FEB. 23

SECOND CITY STARTS AT 7:30

2 • CHICAGO MAROON • Feb. 22, 1963

APPENDIX D

Black student enrollment at Southern Miss, 1974 through 2023. Source: Southern Miss Institutional Research. Data on the race of students enrolled at the university is not available before 1974.

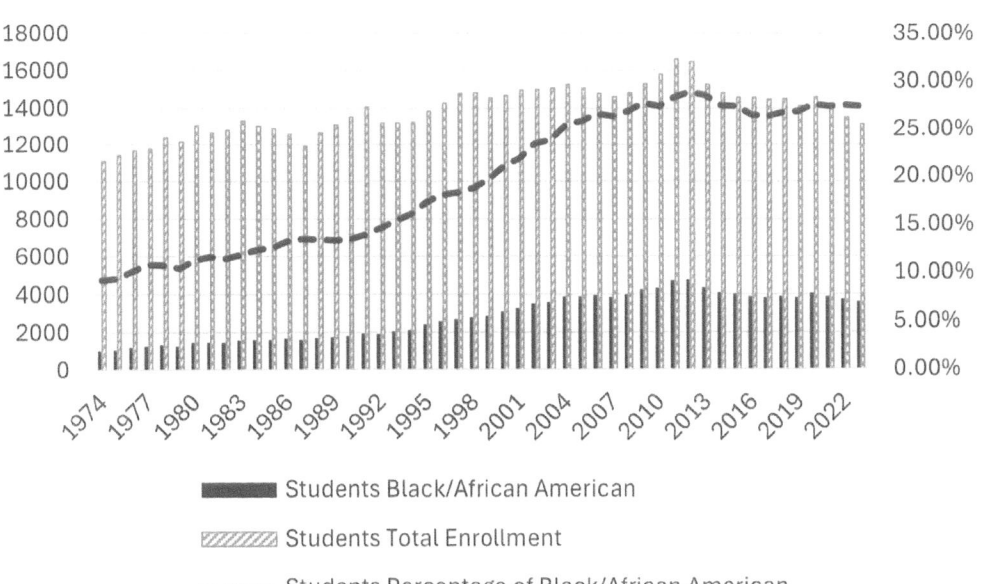

NOTES

INTRODUCTION

1. Clyde Kennard, "Mixing," *Hattiesburg American*, December 6, 1958.

2. See Myrlie Evers with William Peters, *For Us, the Living* (Doubleday, 1967), 215–25, especially 24–25; Jerry Mitchell, "Story of False Arrest Called Civil Rights Movement's Saddest," *The Clarion-Ledger*, December 31, 2005, 1A; and Timothy J. Minchin and John A. Salmond, "'The Saddest Story of the Whole Movement': The Clyde Kennard Case and the Search for Racial Reconciliation in Mississippi, 1955–2007," *Journal of Mississippi History* 81, no. 3 (2009): 191–234. Other works that discuss Kennard's martyrdom are John Dittmer, *Local People: The Struggle for Civil Rights in Mississippi* (University of Illinois Press, 1995), 79 (second quotation), and Joseph Crespino, *In Search of Another Country: Mississippi and the Conservative Counterrevolution* (Princeton University Press, 2007), 289.

3. Devery Anderson, *A Slow, Calculated Lynching: The Story of Clyde Kennard* (University Press of Mississippi, 2023), 4, 8, 10.

4. Zack J. VanLandingham to Governor J. P. Coleman, et al., Sovereignty Commission Report, December 17, 1958, 11–12, SCR ID # 1-27-0-6-1-1-1, Mississippi State Sovereignty Commission Records online (MSSCR), Mississippi Department of Archives and History, Jackson, MS, https://da.mdah.ms.gov/sovcom/result.php?image=images/png/cd01/001993.png&otherstuff=1|27|0|6|12|1|1|1944|, hereafter "VanLandingham December 17, 1958, report"; Minchin and Salmond, "Saddest Story," 199, 206–9; and Anderson, *A Slow, Calculated Lynching*, 11–16. Kennard received his GED in 1950 while enrolled at Wendell Phillips High School in Chicago.

5. Mississippi Southern College became a university in 1962 and was renamed University of Southern Mississippi.

6. Minchin and Salmond, "Saddest Story," 199, 206–9. Interestingly, McCain began serving as the fifth president of MSC on August 18, 1955, not long after Kennard's return home.

7. Ellie Dahmer, interview with Alyssia Steele, June 2017. On the notion that he was a "torchbearer" in the local fight for racial justice, see Minchin and Salmond, "Saddest Story," 210.

8. Though the dates of his initial application are unclear, news articles from December 1958, after Kennard's December 5 editorial, claim that Kennard had made a

first attempt three years prior. The VanLandingham December 17, 1958, report claims that Kennard had tried to apply three years prior but was blocked by his inability to furnish five letters of support from alumni. Kennard tried to apply again a few months later in 1956 and asked that the requirement of the letters be waived. See "McCain Expects to Confer Today with Kennard," *Hattiesburg American*, December 15, 1958, 1; and VanLandingham December 17, 1958, report, 6, 10; and Minchin and Salmond, "Saddest Story," 200–201. Anderson indicates that Kennard's first attempt was in November 1955 and "was rejected before the Christmas season began." Kennard then tried again "around mid-quarter" to inquire again about waiving the letter requirement but was rejected again. See Anderson, *A Slow, Calculated Lynching*, 24–25.

9. "Negro Hears: MSC's Admission Rules Explained," *Hattiesburg American*, December 16, 1958.

10. P. D. East, "East Side," *The Petal Paper* 6, no. 48 (October 8, 1959): 1–2, Chronicling America, Library of Congress.

11. VanLandingham December 17, 1958, report, 4, 18–19, 32; Zack J. VanLandingham to Governor J. P. Coleman, September 21, 1959, Mississippi Sovereignty Commission Records, SCR ID # 1-27-0-40-1-1-1, https://da.mdah.ms.gov/sovcom/result.php?image=images/png/cd01/002159.png&otherstuff=1|27|0|40|1|1|1|2104|, hereafter "VanLandingham September 21, 1959, report," 5; Minchin and Salmond, "Saddest Story," 203–4.

12. VanLandingham December 17, 1958, report, 28–31, 34–35; Minchin and Salmond, "Saddest Story," 204–5; and Anderson, *A Slow, Calculated Lynching*, 48–51.

13. Quote from Dr. M. W. Kenna, registrar during Kennard's first attempts to apply to MSC, VanLandingham December 17, 1958, report, 11. See also VanLandingham September 21, 1959, report, 1–3; Minchin and Salmond, "Saddest Story," 203.

14. VanLandingham September 21, 1959, report, 3–6; Salmond and Minchin, "Saddest Story," 211–12; and Anderson, *A Slow, Calculated Lynching*, 65, 69–70.

15. VanLandingham September 21, 1959, report, 5.

16. Minchin and Salmond, "Saddest Story," 211.

17. Minchin and Salmond, "Saddest Story," 213.

18. Minchin and Salmond, "Saddest Story," 214–15; Anderson, *A Slow, Calculated Lynching*, 121.

19. Editorial page: "Remember Clyde Kennard," *Mississippi Free Press*, December 29, 1962, 2, America's Historical Newspapers; Ronald A. Hollander, "One Mississippi Negro Who Didn't Go to College," November 8, 1962, *The Reporter* 27, no. 8 (1962): 30–34, Internet Archive; Ronald A. Hollander, "To the Editor," *The Reporter* 10 (December 6, 1962) Internet Archive; "Tougaloo Students Begin Petition to Aid Kennard," *Mississippi Free Press*, December 1, 1962, America's Historical Newspapers; "Petition to Free Clyde Kennard," to President John F. Kennedy and Attorney General Robert F. Kennedy, reprinted in *Mississippi Free Press*, December 22, 1962, 2; "Negro Sent to Prison Instead of College; Cancer-Stricken Miss. Prisoner," *Jet*, January 24, 1963, 20–24; Anderson, *A Slow, Calculated Lynching*, 163–68.

20. The Freedom50 Research Group was formed in the fall of 2015 as an initiative "to promote collaborative and integrative research" as prioritized by USM's College of Arts and Letters' strategic plan. Seed grants ($2,000) were provided for such faculty groups.

Led by Dr. Sherita L. Johnson, a select group of eight to twelve began meeting in a faculty seminar spring 2016. From that larger group, the authors of this edited volume remained steadfast in our collaborative research to organize a series of public lectures, present at conferences, and produce a short documentary film (in partnership with the Delta Jewels Support Foundation).

CHAPTER 1. "A LITTLE MAN WHO HAS DONE A LOT OF BIG THINGS": CLYDE KENNARD IN THE CIVIL RIGHTS MOVEMENT AND *JET* MAGAZINE

1. While Kennard was the first African American to attempt to enter a public institution of higher learning at the undergraduate level, Medgar Evers was the first to try to integrate the University of Mississippi Law School in 1954. Clennon King attempted to enter the history graduate program at the University of Mississippi in 1958. James Meredith applied and was admitted, under force, to the University of Mississippi as an undergraduate in 1962. See David G. Sansing, *Making Haste Slowly: The Troubled History of Higher Education in Mississippi* (University Press of Mississippi, 1990), for more on racial integration at colleges and universities in Mississippi.

2. John H. Johnson, "Why *Jet* Then? Why *Jet* Now?" *Jet*, November 11, 1976, 4; the publisher reprinted this statement with small revisions for other anniversary issues in 1991 and 1997.

3. Others have narrowed the scope by focusing on smaller media outlets and/or non-Black-owned publications. See, for example, Jason A. Peterson's "Forgotten and Ignored: Mississippi Newspaper Coverage of Clyde Kennard and His Efforts to Integrate Mississippi Southern College," presented at the Association for Education in Journalism and Mass Communication (AEJMC) in San Francisco, August 2006.

4. Accessible digital archives for these periodicals include the Black Abolitionist Archive (University of Detroit Mercy) and the Colored Conventions Project's exhibit *The Early Case for a National Press* (based on a course taught by Benjamin Fagan at Auburn University, fall 2016). In collaboration with teams of researchers, teachers, students, and tech specialists, the Colored Conventions Project contains the records for hundreds of Black conventions dating back to the 1830s, and it has created several exhibits to "bring 19th century Black organizing to digital life." Date of Access (DOA): October 29, 2022, https://coloredconventions.org/black-press/.

5. Statement issued by project directors Eurie Dahn and Brian Sweeney, who created the online accessible archive for the *Digital Colored American Magazine*, accessed October 29, 2022.

6. "Korean Veteran Arrested for Miss. College Integration Try," *Jet*, October 8, 1959, 20.

7. Jack Nelson, "The Civil Rights Movement: A Press Perspective," *Human Rights* 28, no. 4 (2001): 3–6, http://www.jstor.org/stable/27880281.

8. Shaila Dewan, "How Photos Became an Icon of the Civil Rights Movement," *New York Times*, August 28, 2005.

9. Brian Thornton, "The Murder of Emmett Till: Myth, Memory, and National Magazine Response," *Journalism History* 36, no. 2 (2010), 99–104. DOI: 10.1080/00947679.2010.12062820.

10. William Sturkey, *Hattiesburg: An American City in Black and White* (Harvard University Press, 2019): 168, 180, 218, 142; and "The Game Is Changing for Historians of Black America," *The Atlantic*, May 4, 2021, accessed July 2, 2021; Dr. Joyce Ann Ladner and Ms. Doris [sic] Ann Ladner interview, with Joseph Mosnier, PhD, September 20, 2011, transcript, 32, Southern Oral History Program, National Museum of African American History and Culture and Library of Congress.

11. Brian Thornton, "The Murder of Emmett Till: Myth, Memory, and National Magazine Response," *Journalism History* 36, no. 2 (2010), 96–104. DOI: 10.1080/00947679.2010.12062820.

12. Brent Staples, "How the White Press Wrote Off Black America." *The New York Times*. July 10, 2021, https://www.nytimes.com/2021/07/10/opinion/sunday/white-news papers-african-americans.html, accessed June 17, 2022.

13. One of the most popular pages of *Jet* is its Beauty of the Week, which showcases "one of the country's most beautiful, shapely and radiant Nubian princesses" in every issue of the magazine. For the forty-fifth anniversary issue, a full-length feature story reminiscences past beauties who achieved lasting fame, Black actresses such as Ja'net DuBois (*Good Times* sitcom) and Pam Grier (*Foxy Brown* and other action films of the 1970s); singers Marilyn McCoo and Florence LaRue (both of the Fifth Dimension group) and Cindy Herron (of En Vogue); also, Janet Langhart, broadcast journalist. See "From Beauty of the Week to Stardom," *Jet* (November 3, 1997), 38–42.

14. Lance Hill, *The Deacons for Defense: Armed Resistance and the Civil Rights Movement* (University of North Carolina Press, 2004), 148.

15. Simeon Booker, *Shocking the Conscience: A Reporter's Account of the Civil Rights Movement* (University Press of Mississippi, 2013), google play version, 13–15.

16. Nelson, "The Civil Rights Movement," 5.

17. William Sturkey, "The Game Is Changing for Historians of Black America," *The Atlantic*, May 4, 2021, accessed July 2, 2021.

18. Jacqueline Goldsby examines "lynching's cultural logic" in the Till case, considering Mamie Bradley's shrewd decision to "make the whole world see" what white terrorism does to Black bodies, even those not as mutilated by physical violence. Goldsby's analysis reveals how photographic and print journalism made possible the fuller expression of a nation's "moral outrage and to mount political action," especially for African Americans. See *A Spectacular Secret: Lynching in American Life and Literature* (University of Chicago Press, 2006), 294–303.

19. Dewan, "How Photos Became an Icon of the Civil Rights Movement."

20. Library of Congress, "The Murder of Emmett Till," Civil Rights History Project, accessed July 3, 2022; Dr. Joyce Ann Ladner and Ms. Doris [sic] Ann Ladner, interview with Joseph Mosnier, PhD, September 20, 2011, transcript, 39, Southern Oral History Program, National Museum of African American History and Culture and Library of Congress.

21. Thornton, "The Murder of Emmett Till," 99.

22. Thornton, "The Murder of Emmett Till," 100.

23. Mia Anderson, "'I Dig You, Chocolate City': *Ebony* and *Sepia* Magazines' Coverage of Black Political Progress, 1971–1977," *Journal of African American Studies* 19, no. 4 (December 2015): 398–409. DOI:10.1007/s12111-015-9309-x.

24. Cheryl Thompson-Morton, Emily Boardman Ndulue, and Christine McKenna, "Why Black Media Matters Now," Black Media Initiative at the Newmark J-School's Center for Community Media, City University of New York, 2021.

25. Brent Staples, "How the White Press Wrote Off Black America," *The New York Times*, July 10, 2021, https://www.nytimes.com/2021/07/10/opinion/sunday/white-news papers-african-americans.html, accessed June 17, 2022.

26. Minchin and Salmond, "Saddest Story," 195.

27. Sansing, *Making Haste Slowly*, chapter 9.

28. "Jail Miss. Man Who Lost Bid to Enter White School," *Jet*, October 1, 1959, 46, Google Books.

29. News on Kennard was mostly silent until his subsequent attempt, rejection for admission, and arrest on charges of reckless driving and possession of illegal liquor in September 1959. News of both his reapplication to Mississippi Southern College and subsequent arrest traveled around the country in dozens of newspapers. See "Negro Refused Admittance at MSC, Then Arrested," *Hattiesburg American*, September 15, 1959, 1. A UPI news story traveled around the country. See for instance, "Negro Arrested after Integration Try Fails," *The Delta Democrat-Times*, September 15, 1959; "Negro Denied Entrance to College," *Carlsbad Current*-Argus (Carlsbad, New Mexico), September 15, 1959, 9; "Negro, Barred by White School, Grabbed, Jailed," *The Courier-Journal* (Louisville, KY), September 16, 1959, 3. While President McCain, admissions director Aubrey Lucas, and arresting constables Lee Daniels and Charlie Ward are all quoted in the *Hattiesburg American*'s first story announcing the arrest, Kennard's voice is noticeably absent from the article. See "Negro Refused Admittance at MSC," 1. An article the next day in the *American* led with the statement that Kennard had been rejected because of "'deficiencies' in his scholastic record." While the *Hattiesburg American* article mentions that Kennard had no idea how the illegal whiskey got in his car, the article says nothing about his abstinence from alcohol. See "Negro Student's Trial Sept. 25," *Hattiesburg American*, September 16, 1959, 1 and 10. An account of Kennard's trial in the *Hattiesburg American* on September 29 continues to highlight only the perspective of arresting constables Daniels and Ward. "Negro Kennard Fined $600," *Hattiesburg American*, September 29, 1959, 1 and 6. Note that this article does include a compelling picture of Kennard by *Hattiesburg American* photographer Winfred Moncrief, who would go on to take compelling pictures of the civil rights movement in Hattiesburg.

30. "Former Rockville Centre Resident, Accomplished Journalist Ron Hollander Dies at 80," liherald.com, April 7, 2022, https://liherald.com/stories/former-rockville-centre-resident-accomplished-journalist-ron-hollander-dies-at-80,139903?; Ron Hollander, Clyde Kennard, speech to USM, October 23, 2010, Veterans of the Civil Rights Movement website, https://www.crmvet.org/comm/kennard.htm, accessed June 15, 2022. For more on Hollander's role in telling Kennard's story, see also Anderson, *A Slow, Calculated Lynching*, especially chapter 9.

31. "Editorial Page: Remember Clyde Kennard," December 29, 1962, *Mississippi Free Press*, 2, America's Historical Newspapers; Ronald A. Hollander, "One Mississippi Negro Who Didn't Go to College," November 8, 1962, *The Reporter* 27, no. 8 (1962): 30–34, Internet Archive; Ronald A. Hollander, "To the Editor," December 6, 1962, *The Reporter*, 10, Internet Archive.

32. "Tougaloo Students Begin Petition to Aid Kennard," *Mississippi Free Press*, December 1, 1962, America's Historical Newspapers.

33. "Petition to Free Clyde Kennard," to President John F. Kennedy and Attorney General Robert F. Kennedy, reprinted in *Mississippi Free Press*, December 22, 1962, 2.

34. *Student Voice* 3, no. 4 (December 1962): 1, 4; "Around the town with Lee Ivory," *The Detroit Tribune*, December 22, 1962, 5, *Chronicling America*.

35. "Remember Clyde Kennard," *Mississippi Free Press*, December 29, 1962, 2.

36. "Negro Sent to Prison Instead of College; Cancer-Stricken Miss. Prisoner," *Jet*, January 24, 1963, 20–24. Dick Gregory also claims that a white UPI reporter was so upset by the story that he traveled to Mississippi and learned that Kennard was dying of cancer. According to Gregory, Irv Kupcinet, *Chicago Sun-Times* columnist and tv personality, "broke the story." Gregory's "new researcher" then shared Kennard's medical records with the press. See Dick Gregory, *Nigger: An Autobiography* (Plume, 1964), 172.

37. Larry Still, "Governor Acts after Mother, Sister Plead to High Court," *Jet*, February 7, 1963, 14–15; Anderson, *A Slow, Calculated Lynching*, 139–43, 153–54.

38. Taylor Branch, *Pillar of Fire: America in the King Years, 1963–65* (Touchstone, 1999), 62. See also, Anderson, *A Slow, Calculated Lynching*, 164.

39. "Governor Acts," 14–15.

40. "Governor Acts," 14–15; Larry Still, "Clyde Kennard Leaves Final Message to All Mankind," *Jet*, July 25, 1963; "'Badly Ill' Kennard to Go to Hospital," *Clarion-Ledger*, January 25, 1963, 1; "Clyde Kennard Dying of Cancer; Charge Refusal of Medical Care," *Mississippi Free Press*, January 26, 1963, 1; "Kennard Is Free," *Mississippi Free Press*, February 2, 1963; and Branch, *Pillar of Fire*, 62–63. Also, the US Civil Rights Commission was created as a part of the 1957 Civil Rights Act and authorized federal appointees to hear and investigate instances of racial discrimination around matters of civil rights.

41. "Ark. Whites Aid Negro under Faubus 'Blood' Law; Woman Courts Death as Donors Ponder New Separate Blood Bill," *Jet*, April 23, 1959, 24–27.

42. Simeon Booker, *Shocking the Conscience: A Reporter's Account of the Civil Rights Movement* (University Press of Mississippi, 2013); "Larry Still, 78, News Reporter and Teacher, Dies in Washington," *Jet*, December 3, 2001, 62.

43. Dorie Ladner, "'I Just Had a Fire!': An Interview with Dorie Ann Ladner," *Southern Quarterly* (Fall 2014); phone conversation with Rebecca Tuuri, July 4, 2022.

44. King's diary entry dated Sunday, July 29, mentions that Larry Still had visited him in jail during the Albany campaign. See "The Albany Movement," the Martin Luther King, Jr. Research and Education Institute, Stanford University, https://kinginstitute.stanford.edu/publications/autobiography-martin-luther-king-jr/chapter-16-albany-movement, accessed July 15, 2025; 2007. Written testimony of Bob Moses to the US Senate Judiciary Committee mentions Larry Still as crucial to the fight to dismantle Jim Crow in the state. See p. 7 of Moses testimony, https://www.google.com/books/edition/The_50th_Anniversary_of_the_Civil_Rights/4NDNVQOadXoC?hl=en&gbpv=1&dq=Jet+Magazine+%22Larry+Still%22&pg=PA121&printsec=frontcover, accessed July 15, 2025; Wayne Dawkins, *Black Journalists: The NAJB Story* (August Press, 1997), 208.

45. Lance Hill, *The Deacons for Defense: Armed Resistance and the Civil Rights Movement* (University of North Carolina Press, 2004), 148, 162, 307 n. 65.

46. See *Jet* between January 24, 1963, and July 25, 1963.

47. See *Jet* between January 24, 1963, and July 25, 1963, and Anderson, *A Slow, Calculated Lynching*, 73.

48. "Negro Student Faces Death in Miss. Prison: Governor Acts after Mother, Sister Plead to High Court," 17.

49. 0 James Meredith, *Three Years in Mississippi* (University of Indianna Press, 1966), 78.

50. Evers with Peters, *For Us, the Living*.

51. James A. DeVinney, Julian Bond, Henry Hampton, *Eyes on the Prize* (Blackside, 1990).

52. Taylor Branch, *Parting the Waters: America in the King Years, 1954-63* (Simon & Schuster, 1988).

53. John Dittmer, *Local People: The Struggle for Civil Rights in Mississippi* (University of Illinois Press, 1994), 181–82, 79–83, 453–54.

54. Charles Payne, *I've Got the Light of Freedom* (University of California Press, 1995), 55, 64, 159, 451, 463.

55. Taylor Branch, *Pillar of Fire: America in the King Years, 1963-1965* (Simon & Schuster, 1998), 51; see also 51–53, 62–63.

56. Yasuhiro Katagiri, *The Mississippi Sovereignty Commission: Civil Rights and State's Rights* (University Press of Mississippi, 2001).

57. Patricia Boyett, *Right to Revolt: The Crusade for Racial Justice in Mississippi's Central Piney Woods* (University Press of Mississippi); William Sturkey, *Hattiesburg: An American City in Black and White* (Harvard University Press, 2019).

58. Derek R. King, *The Life and Times of Clyde Kennard* (LULU, 2018). King attempts to contextualize Kennard's experiences in broader civil rights struggles though with slight inaccuracies.

59. Anderson, *A Slow, Calculated Lynching*.

60. Brian Thornton examines how the public's reaction to the murder is not evident from the contemporary coverage of it beyond the extensive coverage in *Jet*; the "consensus myth" of how the public immediately condemned the white South (Roy Bryant and J. W. Milam, the excused) is unfounded, considering the reality of audience engagement in responding directly to publications in the form of letters, editorials, and so on. Thornton, "The Murder of Emmett Till: Myth, Memory, and National Magazine Response," *Journalism History* 36, no. 2 (Summer 2010): 96–104.

61. There are numerous examples of works—scholarship, literature, film, music, and other cultural forms—that verify how much Till is remembered and mourned. See Goldsby, *A Spectacular Secret*, 295, and 401 n. 32.

62. Wideman, "Looking at Emmett Till," *Creative Nonfiction*, no. 19, Diversity Dialogues (2002), 49–66.

63. Wideman, "Looking at Emmett Till," 49.

64. Wideman, "Looking at Emmett Till," 49. Wideman's perspective demonstrates the effectiveness of visual media, particularly in exploring the archive of lynching photography as evidence of white supremacy. With the open-casket ceremony attended by thousands on September 6, 1955, Mamie Till invited journalists to photograph her son's corpse "so all the world can see what they did to my boy." *Jet*, "Will Mississippi 'Whitewash'" 10. Till's "spectacle funeral" signaled a shift in how we witness racial terror

lynching from "the shaming of the black subject to a black-controlled" mourning ritual. Apel and Smith, 62–64. Wideman registers the shock as experienced also by those attending Till's funeral in a church on the South Side of Chicago. See also Jacqueline Goldsby, *A Spectacular Secret*, 294 n. 32.

65. There were other cases of racial violence as reported in *Jet* prior to Kennard but after Till; for instance, the lynching of Mack Charles Parker on April 25, 1959, is covered in *Jet* extensively.

66. "Jail: Miss Man Who Lost Bid to Enter White School," *Jet*, October 1, 1959, 46.

67. "Korean Veteran Arrested for Miss. College Integration Try," *Jet*, October 8, 1959, 20.

68. "Koren Veteran Arrested," 20.

69. Wideman, "Looking at Emmett Till," 54.

70. "Korean Veteran Arrested," 20; also, see chapter 2 in this volume for details about Kennard's enrollment at the University of Chicago.

71. "Kennard Plans to 'Devote Rest of My Life to Improving Mississippi,'" *Jet*, April 11, 1963, 21

72. "Korean Veteran Arrested," 21.

73. There are meticulous details for servicemen's uniforms in the US Army for different eras. The olive drab, serge, wool uniform Kennard wears dates to World War II, though he enlists shortly after, and many of the vintage supply was still being distributed into the 1950s as necessary to meet demands. There is no surviving image of Kennard in a Korean War–era uniform. The *Jet* portrait is most often used in biographies and typically appears in Google searches of Kennard. That there are two versions of this image illustrating slightly different angles of Kennard, which might suggest that it is not an official military portrait but instead one he might have taken while on leave. Also, this could explain his choice of uniform since the vintage-style peaked cap he wears was favored by soldiers even when it was no longer government issued. Soldiers would privately purchase such items to wear while on leave throughout the war years. See "United States Military Uniforms of World War II," http://www.usww2uniforms.com/8-31D.html#, accessed May 18, 2022; Olive-Drab.com, https://olive-drab.com/, accessed May 18, 2022.

74. The use of "embodied discourse," as it relates to reporting about Kennard in *Jet*, is drawn from studies of African American rhetorical traditions, especially among early Black women figured as "race women"; also, the field has expanded to include interdisciplinary considerations of embodiment as a rhetorical concept in communication studies: O. C. McSwite, "Reflections on the Role of Embodiment in Discourse"; Aliyyah I. Abdur-Rahman, "Black Grotesquerie"; Susan Kates, "The Embodied Rhetoric of Hallie Quinn Brown"; Brittney C. Cooper, *Beyond Respectability: The Intellectual Thought of Race Women*.

75. "Man Who Sought Integration Asks Jail Release," *Jet*, December 6, 1962, 53.

76. "Protest Jailing of Negro Who Tried to Go to College," *Jet*, January 10, 1963, 6; "Kennard Awaits New Verdict—Gregory Offers Help," January 17, 1963, 4.

77. As reported in *Jet*, Kennard supposedly had written a statement to congratulate Meredith, but his attorney, Jesse Brown, chose not to release it. Kennard understood his role in desegregating higher education in Mississippi "was just one of the prices [he] had to pay." "Cancer-Stricken Miss Prisoner Fights for Home State Education," *Jet*, January 24, 1963, 23–24.

78. Considering developments in a new interdisciplinary field, we can better understand "the Clyde Kennard story" viewed through the lens of disability studies. Lennard J. Davis, ed., *The Disabilities Studies Reader*, 4th ed. (Routledge, 2013).

79. "Cancer-Stricken," 20.

80. Aliyyah I. Abdur-Rahman, "Black Grotesquerie," *American Literary History* 29, no. 4 (Winter 2017): 682–703.

81. Though it is beyond the scope of this project, more research about Kennard's farm (acreage, tax records, etc.) could flesh out his story. Oral accounts suggest that the sale of the land once owned by Kennard's family may have not been profitable for them considering developments for new highways in the area under eminent domain.

82. Considering Sarah's travel, the story appears in the January 31 issue of *Jet*, and one can assume she had recently returned from her trip.

83. "Sister Visits Kennard for First Time since Miss Jailing," *Jet*, January 31, 1963, 50–51.

84. "Governor Acts," 15.

85. "Governor Acts," 16.

86. We learn in later reporting about the treatment Kennard received after his release from Parchman and transferal to the University of Chicago's Billings Hospital, as credited to *Jet*'s publicity campaign.

87. "Governor Acts," 17.

88. For more information about Coleman's administration as the 52nd governor of Mississippi: https://www.mshistorynow.mdah.ms.gov/issue/james-plemon-jp-coleman-fifty-second-governor-of-mississippi-1956-1960.

89. "Governor Acts," 18.

90. "Governor Acts," 19–20.

91. "Governor Acts," 20.

92. "Kennard Plans to 'Devote Rest of My Life to Improving Mississippi,'" *Jet*, April 11, 1963, 20–21.

93. Advocacy for "wounded warriors" today likely would've made a difference for Kennard's generation of veterans. There are local efforts, especially in Hattiesburg, to provide resources for Black veterans. Also, the city has been committed to recognizing "those who have served our Nation, returned home [to Hattiesburg] and continue to serve our community" as "Veterans of the Year" typically on the national celebration of Veterans Day. In 2020, Vernon Dahmer Jr. was honored as Veteran of the Year. The Disabled American Veterans (DAV) Hattiesburg Chapter also hosts VetFest annually.

94. "McNair, Warfield Start at Chicago NAACP Dinner," *Jet*, June 6, 1963, 27.

95. "Clyde Kennard, Mississippi School Victim, Dies of Cancer," *Jet*, July 18, 1963, 21.

96. As quoted in the article, the sermon delivered by Rev. A. J. Benns evokes the image of a Kennard as a soldier, a Christian soldier even: "Clyde was like a great warrior in battle. . . . He would not want us to stop now. Just as soldiers step over the dead bodies of their comrades to move forward, we must keep going ahead to complete the work he was trying to do." Drawing even more parallels with the imprint of Emmett Till on later generations, the minister reminds the congregation that "it is the youth of today who [are] revolutionizing the world. . . . The Bible says the dead shall rise again and I hope we can see Clyde rising again in some of you." Larry Still, "Clyde Kennard Leaves Final Message to All Mankind," *Jet*, July 25, 1963, 14–15.

97. Our understanding of visual media and print literacy in the Kennard case is drawn from Jacqueline Goldsby's analysis of Emmett Till's in the Black press. "Seeing" lynching photographs had to contend with other forms of "knowing" about racial terrorism, and the publication of images from Till's funeral in *Jet* and *The Chicago Defender* especially served to express moral outrage and incite political action. See Goldsby, *A Spectacular Secret: Lynching in American Life and Literature*, 294–301.

98. Consider how these professionals were likely influenced by the documentation of the Holocaust. See Barbie Zelizer, *Remembering to Forget: Holocaust Memory through the Camera's Eye* (University of Chicago Press, 2000), 61–63. Goldsby explains the use of photography to (re)construct reality by midcentury drawing from Bernice Abbot's 1951 essay "Photography at the Crossroads," as cited in Zelizer.

99. See Kathy Roberts Forde and Sid Bedingfield, eds., *Journalism and Jim Crow: White Supremacy and the Black Struggle for a New America* (University of Illinois Press, 2021).

100. The deaths and burials of other civil right martyrs include Vernon Dahmer Sr. and, most notably, Dr. Martin Luther King Jr.'s widely publicized funeral (see *Jet*'s special issue on May 2, 1968). Dahmer's hospitalization after the firebombing of his home first appears in the January 27, 1966, issue of *Jet*, alongside the image of Clyde Kennard arriving in Chicago with his sister Sarah. Dahmer's funeral was covered by local photographer Winfred Moncrief, with the *Hattiesburg American*. The Moncrief Photograph Collection is housed at the Mississippi Department of Archives and History (MDAH), and it is available online: https://da.mdah.ms.gov/moncrief/, accessed June 16, 2022.

101. We hesitate to include also institutional racism in the military, which Kennard likely experienced. More research is necessary to reveal, for instance, if Kennard received veteran benefits for his disabilities (from his injuries as a paratrooper) and/or subsequent healthcare as a cancer patient. With the Black Lives Matter movement, given its force following the uncensored murder of George Floyd in 2020, systemic racism is a radical reawakening of Americans' social consciousness to promote real, lasting political changes. Now, as during the civil rights movement, key concerns are to address inequalities in education as the basis of racial disparities in wealth, housing, employment, healthcare, and all other aspects of obtaining the benefits of full citizenship in the United States. The debates have generated much coverage in news media and academic scholarship, and we cite here just a few sources as conversation starters: James Baldwin, *The Fire Next Time* (1962); Joe R. Feagin, *Systemic Racism: A Theory of Oppression* (Routledge, 2006); Michelle Alexander, *The New Jim Crow: Mass Incarceration in the Age of Colorblindness* (New Press, 2010); Ta-Nehisi Coates, *Between the World and Me* (Spiegel & Grau, 2015); Robin DiAngelo, *White Fragility: Why It's So Hard for White People to Talk about Racism* (Beacon, 2018); Ibram X. Kendi, *How to Be an Antiracist* (One World, 2019); Nikole Hannah-Jones, *The 1619 Project: A New Origin Story* (One World / *The New York Times*, 2021); N'dea Yancey-Bragg, "What Is Systemic Racism? Here's What It Means and How You Can Help Dismantle It" (*USA Today*, June 15, 2020 / January 29, 2021), accessed June 16, 2022; Pierre-Antoine Louis, "Color of Change: Tackling Systemic Racism One Strategy at a Time" (*New York Times*, September 5, 2020), accessed June 16, 2022.

102. "U. Of So. Miss. Names Building for Black It Refused to Let Enroll," *Jet*, April 26, 1993, 24–25.

CHAPTER 2. LETTERS TO THE EDITOR:
CLYDE KENNARD'S PUBLIC APPEALS FOR JUSTICE AND EQUALITY

1. Kennard's tragic story is recounted in John Dittmer's *Local People* (79–83) based on reporting in the press and the recollections of Medgar and Myrlie Evers (see *For Us, the Living: The Widow of Civil Rights Leader Medgar Evers Tells the Story of Their Life Together and His Tragic Assassination*, 1967); also, Dittmer is quoted in Jerry Mitchell's "Story of False Arrest Called Civil Rights Movement's Saddest," *Clarion-Ledger*, December 31, 2005, 1A. Mitchell's article appears in "Exhibit B," appended to the pardon docket, "Memorandum in Support of Application for Clemency of Clyde Kennard," submitted to Mississippi governor Haley Barbour on behalf of petitioners, with the Center on Wrongful Convictions at Northwestern University. Hereafter, references to this source will appear as "Exhibit B, Pardon Docket." Barbour was governor of Mississippi from 2004 to 2012, when he refused to posthumously pardon Kennard, but Barbour joined the petitioners (and other supporters) to get the wrongful conviction of burglary charged Kennard in 1960 overturned by a judge in May 2006.

2. The records of the Mississippi State Sovereignty Commission have proven to be invaluable for research on civil rights struggles, including the Clyde Kennard case. As the agency was established in 1956 and resolved in 1977, it monitored the activities of leaders and "foot soldiers" of the movement by investigating them (and other citizens) as enemies of the state. The files were digitized and made available to the public years later and are housed at the Mississippi Department of Archives and History (MDAH) in its Sovereignty Commission online archive. Kennard's admission's letter isn't accessible in the online archive, but there is a copy of the letter in "Exhibit E" of the pardon docket (as labeled SCR ID# 1-27-0-29-1-1-1) from the MDAH catalog. See https://da.mdah.ms.gov/sovcom/, accessed November 9, 2022.

3. Subsequent references to each editorial in this chapter will appear by titles only. Archival and transcribed copies of Kennard's open letters / editorials appear in the appendix of this book.

4. C. G. Andrews Harmon served as editor of the *Hattiesburg American* until his retirement in June 1960. He succeeded his older brother Francis Harmon in 1932, who later became the international president of the YMCA. As editor, "Andy" Harmon was dedicated to the news department, and he was determined to make the *Hattiesburg American* the best "real newspaper" in Mississippi. See "Former American Editor Andy Harmon Dies at 78," *Hattiesburg American*, August 29, 1979, 2, https://www.newspapers.com/clip/16315930/obituary-c-g-andrews-harmon/.

5. Susan M. Weill examines the collective responses to *Brown v. Board of Education* by the daily presses throughout Mississippi, and she finds consistent, though not monolithic, coverage of this pivotal case from May to August 1954. See Weill's "Mississippi's Daily Press in Three Crisis," in *The Press and Race: Mississippi Journalists Confront the Movement*, ed. David R. Davies (University Press of Mississippi, 2001), 17–53, *ProQuest Ebook Central*, http://ebookcentral.proquest.com/lib/usmiss/detail.action?docID=1026893. Created from USMISS on 2022-12-19 22:01:00.

6. Quoted in Weill, "Mississippi's Daily Press," 28.

7. According to a former editorial-page editor, Ben Lee, under the Harmons and later owners of the *Hattiesburg American* (Robert, Zach, and Henry Hederman), "the paper's basic editorial tenet involved 'not opposing anything except forest fires and drownings, being in favor of everything else, making no one mad, rocking no boats, and endorsing no political candidates.'" Barton Spencer, "Hattiesburg American," *Mississippi Encyclopedia*, April 14, 2018, http://mississippiencyclopedia.org/entries/hattiesburg-american/.

8. Outspoken critics of the *Brown* decision included Mississippi governor Hugh Lawson White (1936–1940, 1952–1956), who vowed in the press "to resist by every legal means at our command." Senators James Eastland and John Stennis were also proponents of segregation and refused to uphold the ruling (Weill 21). Another segregationist, Governor James P. Coleman (1956–1960) was more actively involved in preventing Clyde Kennard's enrollment attempts. Under Coleman's administration, the Mississippi State Sovereignty Commission was created as an agency charged solely for monitoring race relations while maintaining the segregation status quo. For more on White's and Coleman's terms in office, see their profiles at the National Governors Association: https://www.nga.org/governor/hugh-lawson-white/ and https://www.nga.org/governor/james-plemon-coleman/, accessed April 17, 2024. Also, Anderson, *A Slow, Calculated Lynching*, 32, 35–37, 49–50, 58–59.

9. The *Hattiesburg American*'s circulation had increased to 14,795 by 1957 under the ownership of the Harmons (Spencer). Examples of the statewide news coverage of Kennard's case is found also in the *Jackson Advocate*, a Black-owned publication with majority African American readership. *The Advocate* published reports around the same time each of Kennard's letters appears in the *Hattiesburg American*: "State School Officials Ready Defense against Negro Student: Student Says He Will Try to Enter Mississippi Southern Next Month" *Jackson Advocate* (Jackson, Miss.), December 20, 1958; Chronicling America: Historic American Newspapers. Lib. of Congress, https://chroniclingamerica.loc.gov/lccn/sn79000083/1958-12-20/ed-1/seq-1/; "Prospective Student Is Arrested on Mississippi Southern Campus" and "Negro Student Renews Bid to Enter Mississippi Southern College," *Jackson Advocate* (Jackson, Miss.), September 19, 1959; Chronicling America: Historic American Newspapers, Lib. of Congress, https://chroniclingamerica.loc.gov/lccn/sn79000083/1959-09-19/ed-1/seq-1/. Also, *The Petal Paper*, published just outside of Hattiesburg by Percy Dale (P. D.) East, covered Kennard's case throughout his ordeal. East was noted for his more liberal stance on race problems compared to most other white editors in Mississippi. In his controversial editorial, East Side, East asks and answers for his audiences "Whatever Happened to Clyde Kennard?" following his arrest, and East reprints Kennard's last letter from January 26 as it appeared in the *Hattiesburg American*. *The Petal Paper* 7, no. 14 (Petal, Miss.) February 11, 1960; Chronicling America: Historic American Newspapers, Lib. of Congress, https://chroniclingamerica.loc.gov/lccn/sn85044791/1960-02-11/ed-1/seq-1/, accessed December 15, 2022.

10. It is not possible to weigh the full impact of Kennard's letters on his audience, but what is clear is that his epistolary essays were meant to persuade segregationists to consider various factors at stake if school integration was not upheld by the law. My analysis thus focuses on the structure of his arguments as persuasive discourse.

11. David R. Davies, "Introduction," in *The Press and Race: Mississippi Journalists Confront the Movement*, ed. David R. Davies (University Press of Mississippi, 2001), 10.

12. Assumably, Clyde Kennard would have been familiar with the apostle Paul's teachings considering Kennard's role as a Sunday School teacher at Mary Magdelene Church in Hattiesburg. One of his former students, Gloria Jean Pack, remembers Kennard leading her youth class at the church. Pack was interviewed for the documentary *Measure of Progress: The Clyde Kennard Story*, https://vimeo.com/287295452.

13. That Clyde Kennard structures his letters in a Pauline tradition is cause for a more in-depth study. I do find useful an abundance of sources that span centuries, and I cite scholarship that most influenced my analysis of Kennard's letters: Sam Tsang, "Are We 'Misreading' Paul? Oral Phenomena and Their Implication for the Exegesis of Paul's Letters," *Oral Tradition* 24, no. 1 (March 2009): 205–25; John L. White, "Saint Paul and the Apostolic Letter Tradition," *The Catholic Bible Quarterly* 45, no. 3 (July 1983): 433–44; John L. White, "Introductory Formulae in the Body of the Pauline Letter," *Journal of Biblical Literature* 90, no. 1 (March 1971): 91–97; Paul Schubert, "Form and Function of the Pauline Letters," *The Journal of Religion* 19, no. 4 (October 1939): 365–77; James A. Fischer, "Pauline Literary Forms and Thought Patterns," *The Catholic Biblical Quarterly* 39, no. 2 (April 1977): 209–23; C. Joachim Classen, "St. Paul's Epistles and Ancient Greek and Roman Rhetoric," *Rhetorica: A Journal of the History of Rhetoric* 10, no. 4 (Autumn 1992): 319–44; E. P. Gould, "The Literary Character of St. Paul's Letters I," *The Old and New Testament Student* 11, no. 2 (August 1890): 71–78; E. P. Gould, "The Literary Character of St. Paul's Letters II," *The Old and New Testament Student* 11, no. 3 (September 1890): 134–41.

14. Schubert, "Form and Function of the Pauline Letters," 376.

15. Kennard, "Mixing."

16. Kennard, "The Race Question."

17. Kennard, "School Mix."

18. Vincent Carretta, *Phillis Wheatley: Biography of a Genius in Bondage* (University of Georgia Press, 2014), 159–60. Samson Occom (1723–1792) had written an indictment of slave-holding Christian ministers, and the exchange of letters with Wheatley offers rare evidence of her activist sentiments. Wheatley's letter was published in *The Connecticut Gazette* on March 11, 1774.

19. The private exchange of letters between Banneker and Jefferson were made public to embarrass the statesman by his political foes, by claiming that Jefferson held abolitionist sentiments contrary to his beliefs about racial distinctions that categorized Blacks as inferior to whites. See the Jefferson-Banneker correspondences: "To Thomas Jefferson from Benjamin Banneker, 19 August 1791," *Founders Online*, National Archives, https://founders.archives.gov/documents/Jefferson/01-22-02-0049. [Original source: *The Papers of Thomas Jefferson*, vol. 22, 6 August 1791–31 December 1791, ed. Charles T. Cullen (Princeton University Press, 1986), 49–54.], accessed December 19, 2022.

20. Frederick Douglass, "To My Old Master, Thomas Auld" [1848], in *The Portable Frederick Douglass*, ed. John Stauffer and Henry Louis Gates, Jr. (Penguin, 2016), 413–20.

21. Douglass, "To My Old Master," 414.

22. Douglass, "To My Old Master," 418.

23. Kennard, "The Race Question."

24. Kennard, "Mixing."

25. Kennard, "School Mix."

26. Kennard, "School Mix."

27. Though I exclude it from the listing above, Alice Walker's *The Color Purple* (1982) is written as an epistolary novel and makes a significant contribution to the tradition of African American literature. This feminist work has appealed to audiences with its protagonist, Celie, surviving against the odds in protesting traditional patriarchal and racist denouncement of Black womanhood. Celie writes her letters to God initially for protection from her abusive husband before the novel develops with the exchange of letters between Celie and her sister (Nettie). Other notable examples of the epistolary form in the African American literary tradition include James Baldwin's *The Fire Next Time* (1963), a piercing critique of race relations in America (written in two letters), and Ta-Nehisi Coates's *Between the World and Me* (2015), which picks up where Baldwin ends, reflecting on the state of the nation with the struggles of African Americans at the forefront of our consciousness. Coates mimics Baldwin's form as both address their epistles to the next generation of vulnerable, young Black boys (Baldwin to his nephew and Coates to his son).

28. In describing Clyde Kennard as a Black public intellectual within a longer tradition, I do not place him among the ranks of individuals who emerge within the "crisis canon," who were called (at times, by other great thinkers) to represent the race by taking full responsibility of meeting whites' expectations of solving the race problem. Kennard does respond to the "crisis of the moment," segregation in higher education, but he does so as an activist-intellectual on his own terms given the outlet he chose to effect immediate change. Kennard operates outside of academia, applying his knowledge as a form civic engagement. Jonathan Scott Holloway, "The Black Intellectual and the 'Crisis Canon' in the Twentieth Century," *The Black Scholar* 31, no. 1 (Spring 2001): 2–13.

29. Charles Pete Banner-Haley, "Introduction: What Is an African American Intellectual?," in *From DuBois to Obama: African American Intellectuals in the Public Forum* (Southern Illinois University Press, 2010), 1–11.

30. "Mixing" was printed on p. 2A of the local news / entertainment section of the *Hattiesburg American*.

31. Minchin and Salmond, "Saddest Story," 191–234. The authors explain Kennard's attempts to seek white alumni endorsement (200–201).

32. Kennard, "Mixing."

33. Davies, *The Press and Race*, 9.

34. Comments about Harold Cruse are drawn from *The Crisis of the Negro Intellectual* (1967), as a controversial manifesto. Generations of thinkers have responded to Cruse, and the essays collected in *The Crisis of the Negro Intellectual Reconsidered: A Retrospective* (2004), ed. Jerry G. Watts, was most useful. Watts's "Cruse's Dismissal of African American Liberalism" (287–91) influenced my analysis of Kennard's intellectualism.

35. The Civil Rights Act (1964) and the Voting Rights Act (1965) both were goals touted by the leadership of the Black struggle for equal citizenship.

36. Kennard, "Mixing."

37. In response to the segregation struggles at the University of Mississippi, James W. Silver, historian, penned *Mississippi: The Closed Society* (1964). Silver recalls the campus riots on September 30, 1962, when white students clashed with federal armed forces responding to James Meredith's integration. Kennard understood the same racial dynamics to which Silver reacts and offers his reflections as a white Mississippian critical of white supremacists' control of the state's educational system. Silver publishes a series of correspondences—some private and a few as editorials—to reveal his political views in the book; such documents can serve a similar purpose as Kennard's, though the medium alters the effect (from an academic exercise for Silver to an activist stance for Kennard).

38. Kennard, "Mixing."

39. Martin Luther King Jr., "I Have a Dream, August 28, 1963," *Ripples of Hope: Great American Civil Rights Speeches*, ed. Josh Gottheimer, et al., Perseus, 1st edition, 2003. Credo Reference, https://lynx.lib.usm.edu/login?url=https://search.credoreference.com/content/entry/pershope/martin_luther_king_jr_i_have_a_dream_august_28_1963/0?institutionId=3440, accessed May 30, 2023.

40. Also, in their activism, both King and Kennard seem to take heed to the "great commission" of Jesus Christ (Matthew 28:16–20) as they would become civil rights martyrs to later generations.

41. A seventeen-year-old King was likely reacting to the unjustifiable lynchings of two African American couples—George Dorsey and Mae Murray Dorsey and Roger Malcolm and Dorothy Malcolm—in Georgia that summer. Published in the *Atlanta Constitution* on August 6, 1946, King's "Kick Up Dust" letter also appears online in the King Papers at Stanford University. Source: Martin Luther King, Jr. Research and Education Institute at Stanford University, https://kinginstitute.stanford.edu/king-papers/documents/kick-dust-letter-editor-atlanta-constitution, accessed May 30, 2023.

42. Rosalind Bentley, "Young MLK's Letter to the Editor Revealed the Man He Would Become," *The Atlanta-Journal Constitution*, January 15, 2019, https://www.ajc.com/news/local/young-mlk-letter-the-editor-revealed-the-man-would-become/errtQtc9wFejZFGhM9n4yO/, accessed May 31, 2023.

43. Between 1956 and 1962, King delivered versions of the "Paul's Letter to American Christians" sermon at least fifteen times, most notably on September 7, 1956, at the National Baptist Convention in Denver and at Dexter Avenue Baptist Church in Atlanta on November 4, 1956.

44. The transcript excerpt of King's speech is drawn from a version he delivered in Pittsburg, Pennsylvania, on June 3, 1958, to the Commission on Ecumenical Missions and Relations, Presbyterian Church, USA. Source: The Martin Luther King, Jr. Research and Education Institute at Stanford University, https://kinginstitute.stanford.edu/king-papers/documents/pauls-letter-american-christians-sermon-delivered-commission-ecumenical#fn1, accessed May 30, 2023.

45. For these reasons, I do not include references to the pastoral epistles Paul wrote to Timothy and Titus as models for understanding Kennard's letters.

46. King's "Letter from a Birmingham Jail," in *The Norton Anthology of African American Literature*, vol. 2, 3rd ed., ed. Henry Louis Gates Jr. (W. W. Norton, 2014), 592–607. King's letter was written "on scraps of paper" to address white clergymen who

questioned his activism as an "outside agitator," and the letter was later published in *The Atlantic Monthly* in 1963. See also Hortense J. Spillers, "Martin Luther King and the Style of the Black Sermon," *The Black Scholar* 3 no. 1 (1971): 14–37.

47. King, "Letter from a Birmingham Jail," 594. Scholars examining King's "Birmingham Jail" letter draw parallels with Paul's epistles in rhetorical composition, the crisis of the occasion, and the use of "type / antitype" in religious discourse. Malinda Snow, "Martin Luther King's 'Letter from Birmingham Jail' as Pauline Epistle," *Quarterly Journal of Speech* 71 (1985): 318–34. Richard Walsh, "Reading 'Letter from Birmingham Jail' as a New Testament Letter," *Proteus: A Journal of Ideas* 15, no. 1 (Spring 1998): 20–22.

48. King, "Letter from a Birmingham Jail," 596.

49. King is defined as an activist-intellectual similar to Frederick Douglass in the abolitionist movement. See Charles Pete Banner-Haley, *From DuBois to Obama*.

50. References to McCain appear in the archival files (see the Pardon Docket and/or MDAH collection). The letter to Lucas is found in "Exhibit E" of the Pardon Docket. Kennard contacts McCain on August 26, 1959, and writes to Lucas on September 8, 1959. McCain was USM's fifth president (1955–1975), and Lucas became the sixth president (1975–1996).

51. The following are philosophers Kennard may have studied while attending the University of Chicago, as I discuss later in the chapter:

John Locke (1632–1704), an English philosopher and physician known as the 'Father of Classical Liberalism,' was an empiricist who contributed to social contract theory. Locke's work was highly influential in both political philosophy and epistemology. He proposed that the mind is a *tabula rasa*, a 'blank slate,' and that knowledge is composed of experiences which have made impressions on the mind; John Stuart Mill (1806–1873), a British philosopher and political economist, was a proponent of utilitarianism. His work *On Liberty* (1859) explores individual freedom and its relation to others. Jean-Jacques Rousseau (1712–1778), a Swiss philosopher from Geneva, influenced the French Revolution and modern political, sociological, and educational thought. He viewed humans as born essentially good and developing to maturity in stages; moreover, since morality is innate, society is what creates unnatural desires and thereby degrades humans. McKeon 335, 336, 339

52. Kennard, "Race Question." Patrick Henry (1736–1799) considered as one of America's "Founding Fathers," served as governor of Virginia and as a member of the First Continental Congress; his famous quote is dated 1775 as he delivered the freedom statement during the Virginia Convention.

53. As an activist-intellectual, David Walker's *Appeal* is a hallmark text in the protest tradition of African Americans literature and political history. See Walker's *Appeal*, ed. Peter P. Hinks (Pennsylvania State University Press, 2000).

54. Kennard, "Race Question."

55. An earlier version of Kennard's third letter had been written months earlier (dated September 8, 1959) as it was directed then to the registrar, Aubrey Lucas, with Kennard making his final appeal for attending MSC. Kennard redirects his address appealing to the public when the letter appears in the *Hattiesburg American*. To Lucas, Kennard reminds him—"as you know"—about the circumstances of his inability to enroll (namely, not

having the backing of white alumni as requested initially by McCain), and this remains consistent throughout the letter. That Kennard removes the "you know" (for Lucas) to "a general point of view" for the newspaper shows his attention to audiences; in either case, the integrationist lecture remains the same to change the opinion of the reluctant reader. The closing leaves the impression that his attempts to persuade might be successive: "Thank you for whatever consideration you might give this matter" (here acknowledging Lucas's authority at the institution) and "Respectfully submitted" (humble stance to the white segregationist in public forum). I draw attention to the form and purpose of Kennard's third letter to demonstrate again his methodical strategies as an activist-intellectual, one who carefully crafts his treatises consciously aware of the rhetorical exercise in a public forum. As he might have anticipated, Kennard's letter to Lucas, after all, was never a private correspondence, but instead it was shared then with other officials (at MSC and the Sovereignty Commission). And, now it is available to the public as preserved in the archives at MDAH. I appreciate the observations of the anonymous reviewer of the manuscript who requested clarification about the use and revision of Kennard's third letter.

56. Medgar Evers explains similar feelings of belonging and displacement in an *Ebony* interview, "Why I Live in Mississippi," published in 1958. Also, in *School Clothes: A Collective Memoir of Black Student Witness* (Beacon, 2023), Jarvis R. Givens examines discriminating experiences of education and markings on Black bodies in US history.

57. Kennard, "School Mix." As he reveals in this letter, Kennard had been approached by local Black leaders (and perhaps others in the community), asking him to withdraw his request for enrollment at MSC.

58. Kennard, "School Mix."

59. King, "Letter from Birmingham Jail."

60. Kennard, "School Mix."

61. "Law Graduates, A Woman and a Negro" *Chicago Tribune* 24, July 9, 1870. *Chronicling America: Historic American Newspapers*, Library of Congress, https://chroniclingamerica.loc.gov/lccn/sn82014064/1870-07-09/ed-1/seq-2/, accessed February 3, 2023; also, Richard A. Dawson (1848–1906) is listed among others on the website Arkansas Black Lawyers, an archival record of African American lawyers "known to have practiced between 1865–1950" in the state. This list was compiled by Judith Kilpatrick, professor emerita, University of Arkansas, accessed February 14, 2023, https://arkansasblacklawyers.uark.edu/. Moreover, Dawson was active in the colored conventions movement, participating as an elected delegate from Arkansas in the South Carolina convention of 1871. Southern States Convention of Colored Men (1871, Columbia, SC), "Proceedings of the Southern States Convention of Colored Men, Held in Columbia, S.C., Commencing October 18, Ending October 25, 1871," Colored Conventions Project Digital Records, https://omeka.coloredconventions.org/items/show/543, accessed February 4, 2023.

62. Jarvis R. Givens, *Fugitive Pedagogy: Carter G. Woodson and the Art of Black Teaching* (Harvard University Press, 2021). Givens brings Woodson's life and legacy into focus as a pioneering Black public intellectual who influenced generations of teachers and students.

63. The listing of distinguished Black intellectuals / UC alumni is presented in an archival exhibit Integrating the Life of the Mind: African Americans at the University of Chicago, 1870–1940, curated by faculty member Danielle Allen. It was originally on view at the Special Collections Research Center in the University of Chicago's library, from September 2008 to February 2009. The online exhibit has helped me reconstruct the Chicago experience of Clyde Kennard by focusing on the years leading up to his admission (accessed February 3, 2023); see https://www.lib.uchicago.edu/collex/exhibits/integrating-life-mind/; Amy Braverman Puma's "Color Lines," *University of Chicago Magazine* (January–February 2009), https://magazine.uchicago.edu/0902/features/color_lines.shtml.

64. As the university's unofficial motto, the "life of the mind" has also become a taxing moniker of mental unwellness in the era of COVID. Students feeling the pressure of academic achievement and mental health advocates call for more introspective initiatives at the University. Rachel Ong, "The Danger of the Life of the Mind," *The Chicago Maroon*, March 4, 2021, https://chicagomaroon.com/28353/viewpoints/column/danger-life-mind/, accessed February 21, 2023. Another forum addressed experiences of the "underrepresented graduate student population," whose UC experiences may not be fully integrated into the life-of-the-mind ethos. See Transcending Boundaries for Research Symposium: "Life of the Mind . . . Body and Soul," May 1, 2020. Social media post: https://www.facebook.com/197899206192/posts/life-of-the-mind-is-one-of-the-university-of-chicagos-most-beloved-unofficial-mo/10156605584126193/ and the call for papers: https://transcendingboundariesconference.wordpress.com/, accessed February 21, 2023.

65. Robert Maynard Hutchins led the University of Chicago from 1929 through 1951—through the Great Depression, World War II, and into the early years of the "Red Scare" during the Cold War. His tumultuous administration reads like a dramatic epic considering the public trials he faced with alumni benefactors, the autonomous role he proclaimed often against the university's board of trustees, and the heated battles waged with faculty during his tenure. Hutchins was an outspoken advocate for academic freedom in the 1930s, which brought him public notoriety and acclaim. He was a reluctant war president in support of US intervention in global affairs. His failure to secure financial stability left the university worse off than when he first arrived given the optimism of his youthful idealism for the university's role as a beacon of high intellectualism. Nevertheless, Hutchins's institutional imprint of modernizing higher education remains. See John Boyer, "One Man Revolution," in *The University of Chicago: A History* (University of Chicago Press, 2015), 215–320.

66. Hutchins's plans for reorganizing the graduate programs at the University of Chicago were unsuccessful; he wanted to divide the degree programs between graduates interested in only teaching careers earning a PhD and those graduates earning research degrees to become "productive scholars." Boyer, "One Man Revolution," 231–32. Keeping "the College" separate from the professional studies remained a unique challenge for later administrators, who spent years undoing Hutchins's radical changes. Alumni remember Hutchins's administration with frustration in the chaotic curricula he enforced for undergraduates by the late 1940s and early 1950s.

67. Boyer, "One Man Revolution," 231–34.

68. Boyer, "One Man Revolution," 232.

69. Boyer, "One Man Revolution," 234.

70. I examine yearbooks that were created by students and published by the university as a closer reflection of campus life than what may be gleaned from official records. In the yearbooks, archival images of student life, narratives about faculty-student relations, faculty achievements, and administration have been invaluable for the purpose of reconstructing Kennard's experiences. I examined yearbooks from 1953 through 1955, the years of Kennard's enrollment.

71. *Cap and Gown*, 1953, 47.

72. *Cap and Gown*, 1953, 50.

73. Frank Hyneman Knight (1885–1972), Morton D. Hull Distinguished Service Professor in Social Sciences and Philosophy, author of *The Economic Organization* (1951) and *Freedom and Reform: Essays in Economics and Social Philosophy* (1947), and founding member of the Chicago School of Economics; Friedrich A. von Hayek (1899–1992), professor on the Committee on Social Thought at the University of Chicago, author of *The Road to Serfdom* (1944), and cowinner of the Sveriges Riksbank's Nobel Memorial Prize in Economic Sciences for 1974; Richard P. McKeon (1900–1985), professor of history and dean of the humanities division at the University of Chicago, author of several books including *Freedom and History* (1952); Joseph J. Schwab (1909–1988), the William Rainey Harper Professor of Natural Sciences in the College at the University of Chicago and a founding member of the Committee on Social Thought; David Riesman (1909–2002), Reuel Denney (1913–1995), and Nathan Glazer, published *The Lonely Crowd: A Study of the Changing American Character* (1950), which remains a benchmark sociological study of problems confronting individuals in the twentieth century and is still a bestselling book. See archival photograph of Riesman and Denney by Stephen Lewellyn (ca. 1950) and cover of Riesman's *The Lonely Crowd* (1st edition).

74. Now bearing the name of one founder, the John U. Nef Committee on Social Thought is an interdisciplinary department of scholars who work with graduate students in open-inquiry fields of study. Historian John Ulric Nef, economist Frank Knight, anthropologist Robert Redfield, and Robert M. Hutchins conceived of the committee's purpose as an extension of the experimental curricula under Hutchins's administration at the University of Chicago. For more information, see https://socialthought.uchicago.edu/about, accessed March 17, 2023. Records of the committee are archived at the University of Chicago's library (along with the John Nef Papers): https://www.lib.uchicago.edu/about/news/john-u-nef-committee-on-social-thought-records/, accessed April 24, 2024.

75. Boyer, "One Man Revolution," 257.

76. To reconstruct a typical program of study, I requested an archival copy of the course catalog from the early 1950s at the University of Chicago and received scanned pages from the 1951 through 1952 academic year. *Announcements: The College* 51, no. 9 (July 1951). The library does not have catalogs for 1953 through 1955; however, the research librarian confirmed that the course offerings should be consistent through the 1950s to include Kennard's enrollment at the university. Course catalogs provide details about subjects, faculty teaching schedules, and programs in general. See email correspondences with Catherine Uecker, head of research and instruction in the Hanna Holborn Gray

Special Collections Research Center at University of Chicago Library. Catherine Uecker, "Are Catalogs for Courses Offered in the College Available for 1953–1955? Online / digitized?" Received by Sherita L. Johnson, February 28–March 13, 2023.

77. With assistance from Andrew S. Hannah (sr. assoc. university registrar at Chicago), I examined Clyde Kennard's official transcripts for research purposes only. As described by Hannah, "Mr. Kennard attended the University at a time when its curriculum was considered by many other schools to be unique or experimental, which will be visible in the entries on the transcript, which does not conform to standard transcripts containing chronological listings of courses, credits, and grades." Email from Andrew S. Hannah, "Research: Clyde Kennard's Files." Received by Sherita L. Johnson, November 9, 2022.

78. *Announcements: The College* (1951–1952), 18.

79. *Announcements: The College* (1951–1952), 19.

80. Kennard, "Mixing."

81. The redesign of the curriculum with Milton Singer as chair of the social sciences staff between 1947 and 1952 emphasized this core theme: "Singer helped David Riesman and others refashion the Social Sciences 2 course into a broad interdisciplinary project whose principal theme became the comparative study of personality and culture." Boyer, "One Man Revolution," 260.

82. Kennard, "Mixing."

83. Watts, "Cruse's Dismissal of African American Liberalism" 287

84. Watts, "Cruse's Dismissal of African American Liberalism" 288–91.

85. Denney and Reisman are both listed in the 1951 through 1952 course catalog as instructors for the second year of social science classes. *Announcements: The College*, 19. I only then speculate about how their philosophical ideas would permeate the campus given Chicago's "life of the mind" ethos and their popularity. Reisman was featured on the cover of *Time* magazine on September 27, 1954, the only sociologist to gain such recognition. Considering the central claims of Reisman and Denney's work in *The Lonely Crowd*, the influences of modern culture and the increasing conformity to consumerism, students would have been introduced to the book's arguments prior to its publication, and it may have even been used as supplemental material. For all its acclaim, this tome does not anticipate social movements for civil rights and feminism in its wake, and I cite Reisman and Denney only as liberal intellectuals at the University of Chicago whose life and work produce rippling effects for generations. Nicolas Lemann, *The Lonely Crowd* (book review), *Social Research: An International Quarterly* 88, no. 3 (Fall 2021): 621–26; Randle W. Nelsen, "Remembering Reuel Denney: Sociology as Cultural Studies," *The American Sociologist* 34, no. 4 (Winter 2003): 25–39.

86. John F. Callahan, "Richard Peter McKeon, 1900–1985," *Journal of the History of Ideas* 47, no. 4 (October–December 1986): 653–62; quote from p. 653.

87. Richard P. McKeon, *On Knowing: The Social Sciences*, ed. David B. Owen and Joanne K. Olson (University of Chicago Press, 2017), xv.

88. McKeon, *On Knowing: The Social Sciences*, 1–14.

89. Kennard, "Race Question."

90. McKeon's lecture "Philosophic Problems in the Social Sciences" is cataloged in the collection *On Knowing: The Social Sciences*, from which I draw inspiration to

understand Kennard's philosophic postering in his letters better. McKeon introduced students to thinkers and readings by Thomas Hobbes (*Leviathan*), Benedict de Spinoza (*Ethics* and *Tractatus Theologicao-Politicus*), Immanuel Kant (*Fundamental Principles of the Metaphysics of Morals*), John Stuart Mill (*On Liberty*), and Niccolo Machiavelli (*The Prince* and *Discourses on Livy*). While I cannot directly place Kennard in McKeon's classes, their paths likely crossed, considering class scheduling from 1953 through 1955. The first Ideas and Methods 202: The Social Sciences course McKeon taught was in the winter quarter of 1953, when Kennard first enrolled, and it was available annually from 1954 through 1963. See McKeon, "Philosophic Problems in the Social Sciences," vx. McKeon is featured in the "Highlights of the Faculty" for the 1954 yearbook with the caption, "Richard P. McKeon, Professor of Philosophy and Classics, was elected Vice President of the International Federation of Philosophy." See *Cap and Gown*, 1954, 52. This 1954 image of McKeon does not appear cataloged in the University of Chicago's Photographic Archive, while several others of him are undated, and a few are from 1974.

91. McKeon, "Philosophic Problems in the Social Sciences," 8.

92. McKeon, "Philosophic Problems in the Social Sciences," 11.

93. Gandhi spoke this truth during his address on October 17, 1931, at Kingsley Hall in London.

94. Thanks to Paula Smithka (philosophy), a former colleague at the University of Southern Mississippi, for her careful review of how I analzye Clyde Kennard's experiences at Chicago. Her invaluable suggestions improved this critical perspective in the chapter, helping to explain and encourage my use of Richard McKeon's philosophical concepts to understand Kennard's writing. In a more in-depth study, I would examine more closely McKeon's frameworks as an imprint on Kennard's ideas and strategies for dissecting the race problem.

95. Boyer details the clash of presidential administrations as Kimpton appeared to launch a counterrevolution to Hutchins, whom he once admired and with whom had a close relationship. But the school had lost too much financial backing from alumni under Hutchins's tenure due to the radical curricula changes and other policies. Boyer, "One Man Revolution," 325–29. In February 1953, at the same time Kennard was enrolling, Kimpton tasked administrator Emery T. Filbey to review the BA degree. This assessment would generate more strife among faculty and students alike; it called for the reorganization of the College, with shared governance between the graduate divisions and the general education core of faculty (as had been implemented under Hutchins's administration). The "turf war" was waged in challenging the extent of general education and specialized training with students paying the ultimate price (literally, the cost of enrollment), considering the extension of an undergraduate career to possibly five years. Having experienced academic reorganization at USM in 2017, part of the "Vision 2020," I can attest to the challenges and frustrations of faculty unsure about the ultimate repercussions of strategic plans. Reading about Chicago's woes during the 1950s has been enlightening, learning about administrative measures that were not always transparent to faculty who were most affected by such radical changes in the workplace. USM's Vision 2020 plan appears under the Office of the Provost: https://www.usm.edu/provost/academic-reorganization-planning-0.php, accessed March 28, 2023.

96. Boyer, "One Man Revolution," 330.

97. Comprehensive exams were required to graduate, and only fourteen exams were required in the 1950s for a bachelor's degree, which Kennard would have needed by the end of spring of his last year (if he hadn't transferred in May 1955): three each in the humanities, social sciences, and natural sciences; "one each in history, foreign language, mathematics, English, and OII" ("Observation, Interpretation, and Integration"), the latter designed by Richard McKeon (Boyer, "One Man Revolution," 257). Comprehensive exams were all written rather than oral; this system was phased out by the late 1950s at the University of Chicago. In reviewing Kennard's transcripts, we decided not to bring attention to the course grades as a measure of his intelligence, as we believe, to do so would apply the same pressures he faced when tested by administrators of MSC to deny Kennard's application for enrollment. Also, some of his biographers offer reasons for Kennard's academic performance without documenting Kennard's testimony about his experiences at the University of Chicago. The conclusions I draw from institutional records are meant to provide as accurate an account as possible of the years Kennard spent there. See *Cap and Gown*, 204, http://pi.lib.uchicago.edu/1001/dig/campub/mvol-0001-0048-0000/210.

98. "Trustees Announced for County Schools," *Hattiesburg American*, Thursday, August 25, 1955, 7, https://www.newspapers.com/newspage/276942952/.

99. Andrew Feiler, *A Better Life for Their Children: Julius Rosenwald, Booker T. Washington, and the 4,978 Schools That Changed America* (University of Georgia Press, 2021); Stephanie Deutsch, *You Need a Schoolhouse: Booker T. Washington, Julius Rosenwald, and the Building of Schools for the Segregated South* (Northwestern University Press, 2015); Mary S. Hoffschwelle, *The Rosenwald Schools of the American South* (University Press of Florida, 2006).

100. William P. Hustwit, "Rosenwald Schools," *Mississippi Encyclopedia*, Center for Study of Southern Culture, July 11, 2017, accessed March 25, 2023: http://mississippiencyclopedia.org/entries/rosenwald-schools/.

101. Typically, the process of building Rosenwald schools began with the community's efforts to raise money or in-kind contributions of materials and labor before receiving about one-third of the cost for the buildings from philanthropic grants to match. According to oral accounts by locals, much of the materials used to build the Bay Springs School was donated by community members with direct access to lumber on the property and/or surrounding farms; even the land was donated by a wealthy white man.

102. Among the fourteen students graduating from the Bay Springs School in 1955 was one of Vernon Dahmer's sons, George W. Dahmer. Clarence Edward Bates was the school's principal, and Edward Tademy was the assistant principal. Archival photograph of the class of 1955 courtesy of Dennis Dahmer, owner / caretaker of the Bay Springs School and youngest son of Vernon Dahmer Sr. and Ellie J. Dahmer.

103. Jennifer Baughn, "Rosenwald Schools in Mississippi," *Mississippi History Now*, February 2010, https://mshistorynow.mdah.ms.gov/issue/rosenwald-schools-in-mississippi, accessed April 27, 2023.

104. It remained a useful site, however (once as a church), until succumbing to years of neglect and deterioration. The Bay Springs School was renovated in 2012 with grant funding by the Mississippi Department of Archives and History. "Bay Springs

School," Historic Resources Inventory Fact Sheet, Mississippi Department of Archives and History, https://www.apps.mdah.ms.gov/Public/prop.aspx?id=100446&view=facts&y=680, accessed March 25, 2023.

105. Archival copies of the *Daily Maroon* are an invaluable resource for our research as is *The Student Printz* from Mississippi Southern College / University of Southern Mississippi in reporting on Clyde Kennard over the years. Beginning as a weekly, independent student publication in 1892 (titled *University of Chicago Weekly* until 1899), the *Daily Maroon* was published from 1902 through 1987, and it continues as *The Chicago Maroon* today.

106. "Kennard Needs Blood," *Daily Maroon*, February 14, 1963, 1, http://pi.lib.uchicago.edu/1001/dig/campub/mvol-0004-1963-0214/1. An ad under the classified column was also published to request blood donations for Clyde Kennard on page 2 of the same issue. About a week later, another brief notice appears in the publication announcing that "Kennard Thanks Donors." It is addressed to UC students and employees at Billings, with Kennard expressing his "sincere gratitude" for the blood donations. An editor's annotation confirms that at least twenty-five people donated blood in response to the appeal from *The Daily Maroon*. This student publication, like other print publications discussed in our volume, played an important role in documenting the Clyde Kennard story. See "Kennard Thanks Donors," *Daily Maroon*, February 22, 1963, 2, http://pi.lib.uchicago.edu/1001/dig/campub/mvol-0004-1963-0222/2. Another report of "15 UC students" donating blood also was reported in the *University of Chicago Magazine* in March 1963.

107. "Kennard Needs Books," *Daily Maroon*, April 17, 1963, 2,
http://pi.lib.uchicago.edu/1001/dig/campub/mvol-0004-1963-0417/2. Also see "Kennard Returns Home; Needs Books," *Daily Maroon*, April 19, 1963, 8, http://pi.lib.uchicago.edu/1001/dig/campub/mvol-0004-1963-0419/8.

108. I like to think that Kennard received (hopefully) St. Clair Drake and Horace R. Cayton's *Black Metropolis: A Study of Negro Life in a Northern City* (1954). Drake was an activist anthropologist who worked to uncover racist perceptions of Black people traceable to environmental factors rather than biological elements. He collaborated with sociologist Cayton in studying the migration of Black Southerners to Chicago, pioneering the field of race and urban anthropology. Drake had completed his studies while attending the University of Chicago and earning his PhD in 1954. Working as a sociologist professor at Roosevelt University, Drake had returned to Chicago early in 1963 to deliver a series of lectures on "The American Dream and the Negro," as reported in the *Daily Maroon*: the first lecture on "Emancipation: The Triumph of Interracial Social Action" (January 30), the second about "the efforts of private initiative and the federal government to meet the continuing educational challenge" (February 6), and the last installment covered integration—"the unfinished business of emancipation" (February 13). So just as Kennard had also returned to the University of Chicago for medical care, Drake was delivering his last lecture on a subject all too familiar to Kennard. See "Negro in America Lecture Tonight," *Daily Maroon*, January 30, 1963, 3, http://pi.lib.uchicago.edu/1001/dig/campub/mvol-0004-1963-0130/3. See "Origins of the Black Metropolis Research Consortium," influenced by the work of Drake and Cayton, https://www.lib.uchicago.edu/collex/exhibits/black-metropolis-research-consortium

-fifteen-years-preserving-and-documenting-black-history-and-culture-chicago/origins-bmrc/.

For an image of St. Clair Drake at the UC, see Photographic Archive, "Reunion of University of Chicago Anthropology PhDs at the division of Social Sciences' 25th anniversary" (November 18, 1955), https://photoarchive.lib.uchicago.edu/db.xqy?one=apf1-05364.xml. For archival images of both Drake and Cayton, see the University of Chicago's exhibit *The Black Metropolis Research Consortium: Fifteen Years of Preserving and Documenting Black History and Culture in Chicago*, accessed May 1, 2024.

CHAPTER 3. *THE STUDENT PRINTZ* AND ARCHIVAL RECOVERY OF A SEGREGATED PAST

1. MSC became the University of Southern Mississippi (USM, Southern Miss) in 1962, and it was desegregated in 1965 when two Black female students enrolled as we discuss later in this chapter. It is important to consider gender dynamics in these cases of integrating higher education in Mississippi as distinct historical moments sensationalized (or not) in the press.

2. "Records: Would Be Student Framed," *Clarion-Ledger* (Jackson, MS), September 9, 1991.

3. Chris Atton and James F. Hamilton, *Alternative Journalism* (Sage, 2008), 9.

4. Stevie J Collins, "Levels of on-Campus Activities Predicts Student Paper Readership," *Newspaper Research Journal* 24, no. 4 (2003): 102–5, https://journals.sagepub.com/doi/pdf/10.1177/073953290302400409?casa_token=TwaLY2oHqdoAAAAA:7qiVGMhRGW189oMF-VVigaeYJFoFfDHAVs6A-YEEmdLTUYEf8OjKgGWrdNd8VgrXEaXjQcwGm-Y.

5. Hans C. Schmidt, "Student Newspapers Show Opinion Article Political Bias," *Newspaper Research Journal* 36, no. 1 (2015): 6–23, https://journals.sagepub.com/doi/pdf/10.1177/073953291503600102?casa_token=tvzg0-7ZFY4AAAAA:PIZQ8OXoW3d5G7vHOJGDxd544uANEBeO7VI3GT-H7-rrYIMaLnQDqZDmirGoakHhkDPaY3c4r-k.

6. Kaylene Dial Armstrong, "Telling Their Own Story: How Student Newspapers Reported Campus Unrest, 1962–1970" (PhD Dissertation, University of Southern Mississippi, 2013), 227, http://lynx.lib.usm.edu/dissertations-theses/telling-their-own-story-how-student-newspapers/docview/1461742774/se-2?accountid=13946.

7. Roger D. Kelley, "Decision Making at College Student Newspapers" (PhD Dissertation, Duquesne University, 2012), 13, http://lynx.lib.usm.edu/dissertations-theses/decision-making-at-college-student-newspapers/docview/1009056822/se-2?accountid=13946.

8. Kelley, "Decision Making at College Student Newspapers," 13.

9. Atton and Hamilton, *Alternative Journalism*, 45.

10. Linda Steiner, "Journalism Must Tackle Tough Local Issues," in *Foundations of Community Journalism*, ed. Bill Reader and John A. Hatcher (Sage, 2012), 22–24.

11. Walter R Fisher, "Narration as Human Communication Paradigm: The Case of Public Moral Argument," *Communication Monographs* 51, no. 1 (1984): 6.

12. Daniel Deslauriers, "Dimensions of Knowing: Narrative," *Paradigm, and Ritual, ReVision* 14, no. 4 (1992): 188.

13. Deslauriers, "Dimensions of Knowing," 188.
14. Fisher, "Narration as Human Communication Paradigm," 9–10.
15. Jack Lule, *Daily News, Eternal Stories: The Mythological Role of Journalism* (Guilford, 2001), 19.
16. Lule, *Daily News, Eternal Stories*, 15.
17. Lule, *Daily News, Eternal Stories*, 16.
18. Lule, *Daily News, Eternal Stories*, 21–25.
19. Lule, *Daily News, Eternal Stories*, 125–27.
20. Lule, *Daily News, Eternal Stories*, 130.
21. Lule, *Daily News, Eternal Stories*, 136.
22. Lule, *Daily News, Eternal Stories*, 143.
23. Stuart Hall, "Introduction," in *Paper Voices: The Popular Press and Social Change, 1935-1965*, ed. Anthony Charles H. Smith, Elizabeth Immirzi, and Trevor Blackwell (Rowman and Littlefield, 1975), 11.
24. Hall, "Introduction," 17.
25. Hall, "Introduction," 18.
26. David Paul Nord, *Communities of Journalism: A History of American Newspapers and Their Readers*, vol. 131 (University of Illinois Press, 2001), 10–11.
27. Nord, *Communities of Journalism*, 2.
28. Armstrong, "Telling Their Own Story," 3–4.
29. Hall, "Introduction," 15.
30. Hall, "Introduction," 15.
31. Riva Brown, "A Talk with Aubrey K. Lucas," *Unheard Word* (Hattiesburg, MS), October 1991.
32. Minchin and Salmond, "Saddest Story," 198.
33. "1st Negro Attempts to Enter School," *Student Printz* (Hattiesburg, MS), March 2, 1956, 1.
34. "1st Negro Attempts."
35. Donald Dana Jr., "'College for All' Present Critical Problem—McLemore," *Student Printz* (Hattiesburg, MS), December 7, 1956.
36. Dana, "College for All," 1.
37. Kelley, "Decision Making at College Student Newspapers," 6.
38. Kelley, "Decision Making at College Student Newspapers," 7.
39. Donald Dana Jr., "Negro Warns He Will Seek Admission to MSC," *Student Printz* (Hattiesburg, MS), December 12, 1958.
40. This news article appears roughly six days after Kennard's letter "Mixing" was published in the *Hattiesburg American*, as referenced in chapter 2 of this volume. Johnson also notes in chapter 2 details about Kennard's intellectual journey at the elite University of Chicago.
41. Dana, "Negro Warns He Will Seek Admission to MSC," 1.
42. Catherine Squires, *African Americans and the Media*, vol. 4 (Polity, 2009), 67.
43. "Negro Is Again Refused Entry," *Student Printz* (Hattiesburg, MS), Septtember 12, 1959.
44. Minchin and Salmond, "Saddest Story," 217. While his case was on appeal, Kennard spent more than a year in the county jail before being transferred to the notorious

Parchman prison in November 1961. He would spend a shortened sentence at Parchman thanks to the advocacy of his supporters concerned about his failing health. He was released in January 1963. See Anderson, *A Slow, Calculated Lynching*, 119, 128, 131–32, 177.

45. William D. McCain, "No title," *Student Printz* (Hattiesburg, MS), September 6, 1965.

46. Richard Boyd, "Dean Grantham Lauds Southern Miss Students for Sound Judgment in Ole Miss Crisis," *Student Printz* (Hattiesburg, MS), October 5, 1962.

47. Boyd, "Dean Grantham Lauds Southern Miss Students," 1.

48. "Dr. McCain's Report to Students," *Student Printz* (Hattiesburg, MS), May 10, 1963.

49. Armstrong, "Telling Their Own Story," 24.

50. "Frazier's Attempt to Matriculate Is Unsuccessful," *Student Printz* (Hattiesburg, MS), March 20, 1964, 1.

51. Daniel Mungai, "Discussion Brings Out USM Racial Problem," *Student Printz* (Hattiesburg, MS), October 24, 1991.

52. David Bernstein, "Black Conservatives Stress Diversity," *Student Printz* (Hattiesburg, MS), September 19, 1991.

53. Edward McLellan, "Lucas Appoints Committee for Memorial Proposal," *Student Printz* (Hattiesburg, MS), October 29, 1991.

54. The University of Southern Mississippi Office of Planning, Evaluation and Institutional Effectiveness Fiscal Year 1995. The University of Southern Mississippi *Fact Book*, 1994–1995.

55. Brown, "A Talk with Aubrey K. Lucas," *Unheard Word* (Hattiesburg, MS), October 1991.

56. Brown discussed the significance of the interview with Lucas during her presentation at the Freedom50 Research Group's Clyde Kennard lecture series, Can We Achieve This Togetherness in Our Time?, held March 30, 2017, at the Historic Eureka School in Hattiesburg, Mississippi. The series was supported by an external grant from the Mississippi Humanities Council. To learn more about the Freedom50 Research Group and the lecture series, visit USM's Center for Black Studies, https://www.usm.edu/black-studies/research.php.

57. Minchin and Salmond, "Saddest Story," 209–10.

58. Brown, "A Talk with Aubrey K. Lucas," 7.

59. Brown, "A Talk with Aubrey K. Lucas," 7.

60. Minchin and Salmond, "Saddest Story," 221.

61. Riva Brown, "University Considers Giving Honor," *Student Printz* (Hattiesburg, MS), September 24, 1991.

62. Mike Goff, "White Students Should Be Outraged at Kennard's Death Too," *Unheard Word* (Hattiesburg, MS), October 1991.

63. Fisher, "Narration as Human Communication Paradigm," 9–10.

64. "Almost No Blacks in the Student Newsrooms at the Nation's Highest-Ranked Universities," *The Journal of Blacks in Higher Education*, no. 42 (2003): 22–23. Doi:10.2307/3592422, accessed February 18, 2021.

65. Katherine Knott, "In Tense Times, Black Students Find Ways to Tell Their Own Stories," *Chronicle of Higher Education*, 2017, A22–A23.

66. Minchin and Salmond, "Saddest Story," 221–22.

67. Minchin and Salmond, "Saddest Story," 226.

CHAPTER 4. "MAKING SURE HIS LEGACY DID NOT DIE WITH HIM":
BLACK STUDENT ACTIVISM AND THE MEMORY OF CLYDE KENNARD

1. "Afro-American Cultural Society Banquet Saturday," *Hattiesburg American*, April 14, 1972, 6; "Afro-American Society Installs Officers at USM," *Hattiesburg American*, April 29, 1972, 9; "Afro-American Group at USM to Have Banquet," *Hattiesburg American*, April 13, 1973, 8; and "The Talon: Southern Miss Alumni Association" (Summer 2009), 55.

2. Quote is from Anthony Harris, interview with the author, January 28, 2017, Jackson, Mississippi, Center for Oral History and Cultural Heritage, University of Southern Mississippi, Hattiesburg, Mississippi (hereafter, USM-COHCH). For more on Harris, see also Anthony J. Harris Facebook post, July 6, 2025, https://www.facebook.com/anthony.j.harris.96, DOA July 7, 2025; Anthony Harris, *Ain't Gonna Let Nobody Turn Me 'Round: A Coming-of-Age Story and Personal Account of the Civil Rights Movement in Hattiesburg, Mississippi* (CreateSpace Independent Publishing Platform, 2013), 185.

3. Quote is from Harris, *Ain't Gonna Let Nobody Turn Me 'Round*, 186. See also Harris interview.

4. Timothy Minchin and John A. Salmond, in "'The Saddest Story of the Whole Movement': The Clyde Kennard Case and the Search for Racial Reconciliation in Mississippi, 1955–2007," *Journal of Mississippi History* 71, no. 3 (2009), 220, point out that there was "little broader awareness" of the Kennard case, but his memory certainly lived on at the local level at USM and in Hattiesburg.

5. Monte Piliawsky, *Exit 13: Oppression and Racism in Academia* (South End, 1991), 27.

6. As discussed in chapter 1, two of the most significant treatments of Kennard's story have been Salmond and Minchin's article and Devery Anderson's recent *A Slow, Calculated Lynching*.

7. Works that examine Black students at PWIs in the Deep South have been increasing as of late. One of the most significant studies for this chapter is Kinchen, *Black Power in the Bluff City*, especially chapter 5. For more on PWIs, see Stefan M. Bradley, *Lessons from the Past: Unearthing African American Student (or "Black Ivy Leaguer") Activism during the Black Power Era* (New York University Press, 2018) and *Harlem vs. Columbia University Black Student Power in the Late 1960s* (University of Illinois Press, 2009); Robert Cohen and David J. Snyder, *Rebellion in Black & White: Southern Student Activism in the 1960s* (John Hopkins University Press, 2013); Jeffrey Turner, *Sitting in and Speaking Out: Student Movements in the American South, 1960–1975* (University of Georgia Press, 2010); Charles Eagles, *The Price of Defiance: James Meredith and the Integration of Ole Miss* (University of North Carolina Press, 2009); Robert A. Pratt, *We Shall Not Be Moved: The Desegregation of the University of Georgia* (University of Georgia Press, 2005); and Joy Ann Williamson, *Black Power on Campus: The University of Illinois, 1965–75* (University of Illinois Press, 2003). For more on the Black student protest at HBCUs in the South, see Bristow, *Steeped in the Blood of Racism*; Jelani M. Favors, *Shelter in a Time of Storm: How Black Colleges Fostered Generations of Leadership and Activism* (University of North Carolina Press, 2019); Joy Ann Williamson, *Radicalizing the Ebony Tower: Black Colleges and the Black Freedom Struggle in Mississippi* (Teachers College, 2008); Tim Spofford, *Lynch Street: The May 1970 Slayings at Jackson State College* (Kent State University Press, 1988).

8. For more on the Black campus movement in the North and West, see Richard P. McCormick, *The Black Student Protest Movement at Rutgers* (Rutgers University Press, 1990); Martha Biondi, *The Black Revolution on Campus* (University of California Press, 2012); Ibram H. Rogers, *The Black Campus Movement: Black Students and the Racial Reconstitution of Higher Education, 1965–1972* (Palgrave Macmillan, 2012); and Joy Ann Williamson, *Black Power on Campus: the University of Illinois, 1965–75* (University of Illinois Press, 2003).

9. See Turner, *Sitting In and Speaking Out*, 113.

10. For more on how memory is divided by race, see Karen Cox, *No Common Ground: Confederate Monuments and the Ongoing Fight for Racial Justice* (University of North Carolina Press, 2021); Dell Upton, *What Can and Can't Be Said: Race, Uplift, and Monument Building in the Contemporary South* (Yale University Press, 2015); Ari Kelman, *Misplaced Massacre: Struggling over the Memory of Sand Creek* (Cambridge: Harvard University Press, 2013); David Fort Godshalk, *Veiled Visions: The 1906 Atlanta Race Riot and the Reshaping of American Race Relations* (University of North Carolina Press, 2005). For more on how the civil rights movement has been (mis)remembered, see Jeanne Theoharis, *A More Beautiful and Terrible History: The Uses and Misuses of Civil Rights History* (Beacon, 2018) and Renee C. Romano and Leigh Raiford, eds., *The Civil Rights Movement in American Memory* (University of Georgia Press, 2006).

11. Shirletta J. Kinchen, *Black Power in the Bluff City: African American Youth and Student Activism* (University of Tennessee Press, 2016), 7.

12. Raylawni Branch has stated that when she and Gwendolyn Elaine Armstrong came to campus, "We needed no welcome. We only wanted to be able to attend, make our grades, and participate in whatever we wanted." Raylawni Branch, phone conversation with author, July 6, 2024, and written comments to author, July 7, 2024, in possession of the author. Jacqueline Heath Leggett Hayes, who transferred to USM in fall 1967 and graduated in May 1969, also indicated that she just wanted to take classes and complete her degree in these early years of integration. Jacqueline Heath Leggett Hayes, interview with the author, June 14, 2024, USM-COHCH.

13. Branch and Smith interview; Mallett, "USM's First Black Student Doesn't Regret Historic Role."

14. Betty Mallett, "USM's First Black Student Doesn't Regret Historic Role," *Hattiesburg American*, February 17, 1985, 1B, 2B. See also Riva Brown, "Kennard's Legacy Enables First Two African American Students to Enroll," *Student Printz*, February 16, 1993.

15. Raylawni G. Branch and Jeannette Smith, interview with Emilye Crosby, December 1, 2016, 18, Civil Rights History Project, Southern Oral History Project, NMAAHC and LOC, https://www.crmvet.org/nars/branch-smith.pdf, accessed January 15, 2023. See also Rachel Leifer, "Pioneer's Struggle Not Forgotten," *Hattiesburg American*, March 30, 2006, 1A and 2A.

16. Turner, *Sitting In and Speaking Out*, 106–7, 201–2.

17. The "maid of cotton" is on p. 182 in the 1966 *Southerner*, and Elaine Armstrong is on p. 97 of the 1967 *Southerner*.

18. See *Student Printz* issues throughout both years.

19. Turner, *Sitting In and Speaking Out*, 201–2.

20. Debbie Elliott, "A Half-Century Later, Students at the University of Mississippi Reckon with the Past," *NPR*, February 28, 2024, https://www.npr.org/2024/02/28/1233239700/university-of-mississippi-ole-miss-racial-reckoning, accessed June 1, 2024; Rosalind Early, "The Sit-In at Delta State, 40 Years Later," *Humanities* 43, no. 1 (Winter 2022), https://www.neh.gov/article/sit-delta-state-40-years-later, accessed June 1, 2024. See also Turner, *Sitting In and Speaking Out*, 113.

21. Mallett, "USM's First Black Student Doesn't Regret Historic Role."

22. Mallett, "USM's First Black Student Doesn't Regret Historic Role."

23. Branch and Smith interview, 16; Raylawni Branch, phone interview with author, July 6, 2024, and written comments to author, July 7, 2024, in possession of the author.

24. Hayes interview.

25. Melvin Miller, interview with the author, January 7, 2023, USM-COHCH. Miller has said that while he learned about Kennard, he and other students never felt that it was a priority to spread the story publicly. Alvin Williams (BS 1974) also said that while there was some conversation about Kennard, it was not extensive. Instead, he said that he learned more about Kennard's story in the 1990s while helping to set up the Kennard Scholars program to assist Black and other minority undergraduates. See Alvin Williams, interview with the author, March 6, 2019, USM-COHCH.

26. Deborah Gambrell, interview with the author, January 19, 2022, USM-COHCH, 18.

27. Melvin Miller interview.

28. Eddie Holloway, "He Was Bigger than One Man," USM Center for Black Studies webpage, https://www.usm.edu/black-studies/clyde-kennard.php, accessed January 15, 2023. See also Eddie Holloway, interview with the author, February 22, 2017, USM Center for Oral History and Cultural Heritage.

29. For the example of his father escorting Kennard home, see Harris, *Ain't Gonna Let Nobody Turn Me 'Round*, 141. See also his Facebook post from September 5, 2021 (PDF in possession of author). See also "Kennard Is Free," *Mississippi Free Press*, February 2, 1963, 1, 4. For more on Harris and his mother's civil rights activism, see Harris, *Ain't Gonna Let Nobody Turn Me 'Round*, introduction, chapters 5 and 6, 9, and p. 111. For more on his desegregation of Thames Elementary and Blair High School, see chapter 11. See also Harris interview.

30. Melvin Miller interview; many other students to be the first to integrate were equally impressive, including Charlayne Hunter and Hamilton Holmes, who were the best and brightest in their communities. See Pratt, *We Shall Not Be Moved*, 72–73.

31. In 1974, both Alcorn and Jackson State became universities. See Alcorn, History, https://www.alcorn.edu/discover-alcorn/history/, accessed May 22, 2024, and Jackson State University, Our History, https://www.jsums.edu/about-jsu/, accessed May 22, 2024.

32. Miller interview. See also 1967 *Southerner*.

33. Harris interview.

34. Gambrell interview, 14.

35. Miller interview.

36. Harris, *Ain't Gonna Let Nobody Turn Me 'Round*, 188.

37. Jack Hurst, *Nathan Bedford Forrest: A Biography*, reprint ed. (Vintage, 1994); History, Forrest County MS, https://forrestcountyms.us/?page_id=83, accessed May 22, 2024.

38. Quote is from Harris interview. See also Harris, *Ain't Gonna Let Nobody Turn Me 'Round*, 188–89, and Melvin Miller interview.

39. Colonel Reb Foundation, "About Us," https://www.colonelreb.org/saving-colonel-reb, accessed May 22, 2024; the Colonel Reb Facebook page, https://www.facebook.com/TheColonelReb, accessed May 22, 2024; Colonel Reb Foundation Facebook Page, https://www.facebook.com/groups/2200176798, accessed May 22, 2024.

40. Harris, *Ain't Gonna Let Nobody Turn Me 'Round*, 186–87; Harris Interview. Harris and Armstrong's treatment was echoed by the experiences of other Black students in the first generation. See Elliott, "A Half-Century Later, Students at the University of Mississippi Reckon with the Past"; Early, "The Sit-In at Delta State, 40 Years Later"; Mimi, "Black History Month: The Memphis State Eight," *Exponent II* blog, February 25, 2023, https://exponentii.org/blog/black-history-month-the-memphis-state-eight/, accessed June 1, 2024.

41. Miller interview.

42. Williams interview. Other accounts from the first generation of Black students at PWIs echo this idea that some white faculty were very supportive of integration broadly and Black students on campus. James Silver was kicked off of the faculty at Ole Miss in 1964 for calling the state a "Closed Society." Later, the Department of English at Ole Miss was criticized for bringing students from Tougaloo on campus. Other liberal faculty around the state tangled with more conservative Board of Trustees of the Institutions of Higher Learning in Mississippi. See Sansing, *Making Haste Slowly*, 200–202, 207. Other faculty tried to shift the thinking of their white students toward integration through course assignments that prodded them to reflect on their segregationist stances. See Turner, *Sitting In and Speaking Out*, 113–14.

43. Holloway interview.

44. Harris interview.

45. Miller interview and Williams interview.

46. This name differed from the more prominent choice among Black student groups at HWCU of *Black Student Union*. See Rogers (Kendi), *Black Campus Movement*, 108–9.

47. Melvin Miller estimated that there were about sixty students on campus at this time. See Miller interview.

48. Turner, *Sitting in and Speaking Out*, 204–5.

49. Harris interview. Shirletta Kinchen highlights the importance of Black cultural spaces, especially "beauty spaces," as sites of Black Power at the PWI Memphis State. See Kinchen, "Beauty and the Black Student Revolt: Black Student Activism at Memphis State and the Politics of Campus 'Beauty Spaces,'" in *An Unseen Light: Black Struggles for Freedom in Memphis, Tennessee*, ed. Aram Goudsouzian (University Press of Kentucky, 2018), 330–47.

50. WORV was created by Vernon Floyd, Robert Floyd, and Ruben Hughes as Hattiesburg's first Black-owned station in 1969. See "Radio," *Mississippi Encyclopedia*, April 14, 2018, https://mississippiencyclopedia.org/entries/radio/, accessed June 9, 2024.

51. Quote comes from Harris interview. The number of students comes from Harris, *Ain't Gonna Let Nobody Turn Me 'Round*, 193. For more on the Afro-American Cultural Society cultural and social events, see 185–86, 193. According to Kendi, social support to

raise black consciousness and combat the oppressive racial environment at HWCU were two of the eight functions of BSUs in the late 1960s. See Rogers (Kendi), *Black Campus Movement*, 109–11. Other functions that the AACS embraced were to effect change on campus for Black students and fight for Black students to win positions of power in mainstream organizations and campus-wide competitions.

52. See the 1969 *Southerner* yearbook, especially senior biographies for Joshua E. Lee, 346; Delores McGruder, 347; Gloria Anne McLeod, 347; and Robert Makeba Thompson, 351.

53. Turner, *Sitting In and Speaking Out*, chapters 6 and 7, especially 204; Ibram Rogers, *The Black Campus Movement*, chapters 5 through 8; and Biondi, *The Black Revolution on Campus*.

54. Compared to demands at other PWIs around the country, USM's demands for Black courses and faculty were very mild. See Kendi, *Black Campus Movement*, 113–17.

55. Melvin Miller claimed in his interview that USM did not have a Black faculty member at the time of the May 1970 protest in the wake of the murders at Jackson State University. However, according to a report in *The Student Printz*, McCain claimed there was a Black faculty member then. See Jack Elliot, "Bond Cancellation Spurs Demonstration," *Student Printz*, Tuesday, May 19, 1970, 1, McCain Library and Archives, USM. However, McCain's claim in *Printz* seems to be untrue as later commemorations identified Dr. John Berry, of the College of Education and Psychology, as the first Black faculty member in fall 1970. This was highlighted both in *The Student Printz* and on a plaque currently in the Kennard Washington Hall. See "2:30 Classes Cancelled for Dedication as Part of 'Celebration of Diversity,'" *Student Printz*, February 16, 1993, and photograph of Kennard Washington Building, March 31, 2017, in possession of author.

56. Melvin Miller interview.

57. Nancy K. Bristow, *Steeped in the Blood of Racism: Black Power, Law and Order, and the 1970 Shootings at Jackson State College* (Oxford University Press, 2020), 1–4; James Downey, "Two Students Killed at Jackson State College," *Hattiesburg American*, May 15, 1970, 1, 12.

58. Melvin Miller interview.

59. Jack Elliot, "Bond Cancellation Spurs Demonstration," *Student Printz*, Tuesday, May 19, 1970, 1, McCain Library and Archives, USM. Note that the president's home used to be at the Ogletree House on campus. Also, for more on the Augusta rebellion, see John Hayes, "Augusta Riot," *New Georgia Encyclopedia*, May 19, 2023, https://www.georgiaencyclopedia.org/articles/history-archaeology/augusta-riot/, accessed May 31, 2024.

60. Elliot, "Bond Cancellation Spurs Demonstration"; and Melvin Miller interview.

61. Elliot, "Bond Cancellation Spurs Demonstration"; and Melvin Miller interview.

62. Deborah Gambrell interview, 15.

63. Deborah Gambrell and Melvin Miller interviews; Edgar C. Fortenberry, "Weekly Activity Report," 5/18–5/22/70, SCR ID # 3-87-0-68-1-1-1, Mississippi Sovereignty Commission Files (MSCF).

64. "Board Acts against Students," *Student Printz*, Thursday, June 11, 1970, 1; Fortenberry, "Weekly Activity Report," 5/18-5/22/70.

65. "Court Suspends Students," *Student Printz*, Tuesday, September 29, 1970, 1.

66. Arlene Sanders, Carrie Freshour, and Sykina Butts, "Student Protest at Delta State in March 1969," *Mississippi History Now*, October 2022, https://mshistorynow.mdah.ms.gov/issue/delta-state-protest, accessed June 1, 2024; Early, "The Sit-In at Delta State, 40 Years Later."

67. "Black Power at Ole Miss: Remembrance, Reckoning and Repair at 50 years," Conferences and Events webpage, University of Mississippi, https://egrove.olemiss.edu/blkpower/, accessed June 1, 2024; Elliott, "A half-century later, students at the University of Mississippi reckon with the past"; Turner, *Sitting In and Speaking Out*, 222.

68. Kinchen points out how Black students were the ones who pushed Memphis State to "transform the campus," and this was also the case for USM. See *Black Power in the Bluff City*, 14, and chapter 5.

69. See the appendix for more institutional research data about Black student enrollment at USM. This is the earliest year that USM has institutional data that lists race in enrollment records.

70. See Melvin Miller, Eddie Holloway, and Alvin Williams interviews.

71. Jean Hendershot, "Council Invites Delta Sigma Theta," *Student Printz*, December 3, 1970, 2.

72. *Southerner*, "New Sorority at USM," *Hattiesburg American*, January 15, 1975, 3; "In New Fraternity at USM," *Hattiesburg American*, April 16, 1975, 32. Delta Sigma Theta's Mu Nu Chapter charter members were inducted in fall 1975; see "Mu Nu Chapter Charter Members," *Hattiesburg American*, August 26, 1975, 3, and "A Day of Fun and Food," *Hattiesburg American*, August 5, 1975, 7. By fall 1976, Kappa Alpha Psi was on campus; see Jerry Parson, "Rush Week: A Colorful Pageant on Today's College Campuses," *Hattiesburg American*, September 5, 1976, 35.

73. *Southerner*, 1973; Deborah Gambrell interview.

74. See *The Southerner* from 1972, 1973, and 1975

75. *Southerner*, 1974, 122–23, 127, 186, 190, 199.

76. Harris, *Ain't Gonna Let Nobody Turn Me 'Round*, 194; Harris interview.

77. Mickey Edwards, "They Say," *Hattiesburg American*, April 26, 1971, 13; "Ready for a Home Game," *Hattiesburg American*, October 23, 1971; "USM Homecoming," *Hattiesburg American*, November 14, 1972, 9.

78. Harris interview.

79. For Delta Sigma Theta data, see "Mu Nu Chapter Charter Members," *Hattiesburg American*, August 26, 1975, 3, and "A Day of Fun and Food," *Hattiesburg American*, August 5, 1975, 7. For Kappa Alpha Psi, see Jerry Parson, "Rush Week: A Colorful Pageant on Today's College Campuses," *Hattiesburg American*, September 5, 1976, 35.

80. Betty Mallett, "Greek Organizations Serve Community," *Hattiesburg American*, February 19, 1984, 1B, 3B.

81. Mallett, "Greek Organizations Serve Community"; Henry E. Naylor, "Black History Week events slated Feb. 7–13 at USM," *Hattiesburg American*, February 6, 1977, 10.

82. Holloway has indicated two different dates for the initial meeting to raise money for the Kennard scholarship. In his interview, he indicated this happened in the late 1970s, but in a later written publication, he indicated this happened in 1989. See Holloway interview and "Clyde Kennard: He Was Bigger than One Man," and "Paving the Pathway:

Honoring the Life and Legacy of Clyde Kennard," Center for Black Studies webpage, https://www.usm.edu/black-studies/clyde-kennard.php, accessed January 15, 2023.

83. Holloway interview; Holloway, "Clyde Kennard: He Was Bigger than One Man"; Holloway, "Paving the Pathway."

84. "They Celebrate Black History," *Hattiesburg American*, February 13, 1979, 10; "Stokely Carmichael to Speak at USM," February 15, 1980, 6.

85. Bolton, *Hardest Deal of All*, 212–16; Gambrell interview.

86. By 1991, President Aubrey Lucas claimed that there were 1,702 Black students on campus. They were 14.3 percent of the total student body at the time. See Jerry Mitchell, "Plaque Sought at USM for Black Who Tried to Enroll," *Clarion-Ledger*, September 9, 1991, 5A. According to later University of Southern Mississippi Institutional Research data, there were 1,955 Black students, or 13.91 percent enrolled in fall 1991. In fall 1989, there were 17 Black faculty out of 676, or 2.51 percent of the total faculty. Racial data on staff members was not available until fall 1993, when there were 238 Black staff members out of 1,124 total staff members or 21.17 percent. There were only two Black administrative staff members out of 54 total, or 3.7 percent. In fall 2023 faculty comprised 7.83 percent of all faculty, Black staff comprised 18.39 percent, and Black administrative staff were only 3.85 percent of all administrative staff. See Req_3508, Institutional Research data request for the author, January 31, 2024, in possession of the author.

87. See yearbooks from the 1980s for strengthened presence of Black Greek Life and other groups.

88. Isaac Bishop, interview with the author, February 10, 2017. The yearbooks between 1985 and 1988 do not include a page for the Afro-American Cultural Society. However, a very small number of students or organizations continued to list the Afro-American Cultural Society as a club in which they participated. Starting in 1989, the Afro-American Student Organization included a dedicated page in the yearbook.

89. Isaac Bishop interview; *Southerner*, 1989, 266; "Odom Wins Homecoming Crown," *Hattiesburg American*, October 26, 1988, 10A.

90. *Southerner*, 1989, 303.

91. "The Unheard Word," Center for Black Studies, https://www.usm.edu/black-studies/unheard-word.php, accessed July 26, 2024; Robert Taylor, interview with the author, February 3, 2017.

92. Bishop interview;"Chantel Foretich, "Area Incidents Viewed Differently," *Hattiesburg American*, July 8, 1990, 1, 12.

93. Taylor interview.

94. Crystal R. Sanders, *Ayers v. Fordice*, *Mississippi Encyclopedia*, May 23, 2018, https://mississippiencyclopedia.org/entries/ayers-v-fordice/; Molly Minta, "The Settlement That Aimed to Desegregate Higher Education in Mississippi, Explained," *Mississippi Today*, December 28, 2021, https://mississippitoday.org/2021/12/28/settlement-to-desegregate-higher-education-explained/, accessed May 22, 2024.

95. Yasuhiro Katagiri, *The Mississippi State Sovereignty Commission: Civil Rights and States' Rights* (University Press of Mississippi, 2001), 227–37, 239–40.

96. Jerry Mitchell,"Records: Would Be Student Framed," *Clarion-Ledger*, September 9, 1991, 1, 10A. See also Salmond and Minchin, "Saddest Story," 221. Anderson has also shown

that Mitchell first learned about Kennard's case in late 1989 but had to drop the story until 1991 due to other commitments. See Anderson, *A Slow, Calculated Lynching*, 186.

97. Riva Brown, "A Talk with Aubrey K. Lucas," *Unheard Word*, October 1991.

98. Mitchell, "Plaque Sought at USM for Black Who Tried to Enroll"; Minchin and Salmond, "Saddest Story."

99. Riva Brown, "University Considers Giving Honor," *Student Printz*, September 24, 1991.

100. Steve Baylot, "Kennard Day Activities Set," *Student Printz*, October 15, 1991, 1; Riva Brown, "Students Honor Kennard Legacy," *Student Printz*, October 17, 1991, 1.

101. Alvin J. Williams to the Clyde Kennard Memorial/Tribute Committee, November 25, 1991, and "Ideas for a Memorial/Tribute to Clyde Kennard," in Robert Taylor's personal collection. See also Robert Taylor to the author, email correspondence, April 5, 2017. Eventually, in 2023, the Clyde Kennard lecture series was created by Dr. Sherita L. Johnson, as the director of the USM's Center for Black Studies, with the widespread support of the campus and local community.

102. Riva Brown, "USM to Honor African American Firsts," *Student Printz*, February 11, 1993; Riva Brown, "Webb's Hard Work Was Not in Vain," *Student Printz*, February 16, 1993; Riva Brown, "Kennard's Legacy Enables First Two African American Students to Enroll," February 16, 1993; Christa Clark, "Celebration Heals, Honors 'Firsts,'" *Student Printz*, February 18, 1993; Janet Braswell, "USM Celebrates Diversity With Special Dedication," *Hattiesburg American*, February 15, 1993, 5A; Janet Braswell, "Dedication Acknowledges Mistakes, Accomplishments," and "Columnist Page Speaks on Unity," *Hattiesburg American*, February 17, 1993, 7A.

103. Riva Brown, "Kennard Remembered," *Student Printz*, February 25, 1993, 2.

104. Jerry Mitchell, "Farmer Innocent in 1960 Burglary, Witness Declares," *Clarion-Ledger*, December 31, 2005, 1A, 4A. See also Minchin and Salmond, "Saddest Story," 225; Anderson, *A Slow, Calculated Lynching*, 200–202.

105. Johnny Lee Roberts, affidavit before Vanessa J. Jones, Notary Public, January 27, 2006, as found in mskennardexhibits.pdf, Northwestern Center on Wrongful Convictions online exhibits, https://wwws.law.northwestern.edu/legalclinic/wrongfulconvictions/exonerations/documents/mskennardexhibits.pdf, accessed January 30, 2023.

106. Mitchell, "Farmer Innocent in 1960 Burglary, Witness Declares," 4A.

107. Jerry Mitchell, "He Was Railroaded," *Clarion-Ledger*, January 12, 2006, 1B, 3B; Jerry Mitchell, "Action Would Clear Name," *Clarion-Ledger*, January 17, 2006, 1B, 3B.

108. Rachel Leafier, "Students Demand Kennard Pardon," *Hattiesburg American*, February 16, 2006; "Speak Out to Clear Kennard," *Hattiesburg American*, 7A; February 24, 2006, 1A, 3A; Rachel Leifer, "High Court Rejects Attempt to Clear Kennard"; Jerry Mitchell, "Diverse Group Calls for Pardon," *Clarion-Ledger*, March 19, 2006.

109. Quotes from Rachel Leifer, "Mississippi Honors Kennard," *Hattiesburg American*, March 31, 2006, 1A, 6A. See also Rachel Leifer, "USM Students to Honor Kennard at State Capitol," *Hattiesburg American*, March 30, 2006, 1A, 3A.

110. Rachel Leifer, "Fight for Kennard Pardon Continues at Meeting," *Hattiesburg American*, April 23, 2006, 2C.

111. Rachel Leifer, "Justice for Kennard: Helfrich Decision Clears Civil Rights Pioneer," *Hattiesburg American*, May 18, 2006, 1A, 9A.

112. Minchin and Salmond, "Saddest Story," 226; M. Daniel Gibbard, "Civil Rights-Era Case Moves Teens to Take Action," *Chicago Tribune*, sec. 2, p. 2.

113. Leifer, "Justice for Kennard", 1A, 9A; Barry Bradford, "Book Excerpt: Clyde Kennard and Judge Pickering," July 3, 2013, https://barrybradford.com/book-excerpt-clyde-kennard-and-judge-pickering/, accessed February 3, 2023; Anderson, *Saddest Story*, 219–20.

114. Text transcribed in Anderson, *A Slow, Calculated Lynching*, 222–23. See also Minchin and Salmond, "Saddest Story," 230; Leifer, "Justice for Kennard," 1A, 9A; "Kennard Chronology," *Hattiesburg American*, May 18, 2006, 9A.

EPILOGUE

1. The film premiered on February 21, 2018, in Hattiesburg at the Convention Center, and it was screened again on March 20, 2018, at the University of Mississippi. To learn more about the Freedom50 Research Group and to view the film online, visit USM's Center for Black Studies, https://www.usm.edu/black-studies/research.php. It is also available on Vimeo: https://vimeo.com/287295452.

2. Devery Anderson, *A Slow, Calculated Lynching*, 190–91.

3. For more information about the dedication ceremony for the historic marker, see https://www.usm.edu/KennardMarker, accessed July 1, 2023.

4. Jarvis R. Givens specializes in the history of African American education. See Givens, *Fugitive Pedagogy: Carter G. Woodson and the Art of Black Teaching* (Harvard University Press, 2021); Givens, *School Clothes: A Collective Memoir of Black Student Witness* (Beacon, 2023); David Tisdale, "Givens Stresses Importance of Black Educators' Role in Quest for Racial, Social Justice in America during Kennard Lecture," October 18, 2023, DOA, July 14, 2025, https://www.usm.edu/news/2023/release/jarvis-givens-kennard-lecture.php.

5. Lici Beveridge and Laurel Thrailkill, "Clyde Kennard Memorial Highway: Section of US 49 Dedicated to Civil Rights Activist," *Hattiesburg American*, May 28, 2021, accessed July 15, 2025, https://www.hattiesburgamerican.com/story/news/local/2021/05/28/clyde-kennard-memorial-highway-dedication-civil-rights-activist-usm-hattiesburg/7465145002/.

6. The Generations Strong Wall commemorates inspiring African Americans of Hattiesburg as a permanant exhibit at the Historic Eureka School, https://hattiesburgeureka.com/generations/.

INDEX

Advocate, 5
Afro-American Cultural Society (AACS), 67, 69, 71, 75–76, 79–82, 85, 88, 151n
Afro-American Student Organization (AASO), 84–85, 86–87, 88
Ain't Gonna Let Nobody Turn Me 'Round (Harris), 68
Alcorn Agricultural and Mechanical College, 73
American Civil Liberties Union (ACLU), 83
Anderson, Devery S., x, 15
Appeal (Walker), 37, 136n
Armstrong, Gwendolyn Elaine, viii, 56–57, 64, 67, 69–71, 73, 85, 148n, 150n
Ayers, Jake, Sr., 58, 83, 88

Banneker, Benjamin, 29, 133n
Barbour, Governor Haley, 87, 131n
Barnett, Governor Ross, xiii, 10, 12, 72
Bay Springs School, 46–47, 93, 142n
Billings Hospital, 22, 47, 110, 112, 114, 116, 129n
Bishop, Isaac, viii, 82–83, 153n
"Black Conservative Stresses Diversity" (Bernstein), 59
Black History Month, 39, 81
Black Hurricane, 64
Black Power movement, 12, 68, 69, 75, 88, 150n
Bond, Julian, 76
Booker, Simeon, 6
Boyz N' the Hood (Singleton), 58
Bradford, Barry, 87

Branch, Raylawni, 56, 64, 67, 69–70, 71, 73, 85, 86, 148n
Branch, Taylor, 11, 13, 14
Brown, R. Jess, xiii, 11–12, 17–18, 23, 128n
Brown, Riva, 58, 59, 60, 63, 82, 84, 85, 88, 146n
Brown v. Board of Education, xiii, xvi, 6–7, 26, 30, 32, 47, 54, 55, 131n, 132n
Bryant, LaKeisha, 86–87
Bush, President George, 58–59

Carmichael, Stokely, 81
Carter, Tangee, viii, 87
Cathey, Marcus, viii, 84
Center for Community Media (CUNY), 8
Chicago Defender, 6, 10, 130n
Chronicle of Higher Education, The (Knott), 64
Citizens Council, xi
Clarion-Ledger, 50, 59, 83–84, 86
Coleman, Governor J. P., xi, 21, 132n
Collins, Stevie, 51
Colored American Magazine, 4
Colored Conventions Project, 123n
Crisis of the Negro Intellectual, The (Cruse), 43, 134n
Cruse, Harold, 33, 43, 134n

Dabbs, Daniel W., xii
Dahmer, Betty, vii, x, 80
Dahmer, Dennis, vii, 142n
Dahmer, Ellie J., vii, x, 86, 87, 121n, 142n
Dahmer, Vernon, Sr., x, 9, 14, 22–23, 46, 47, 86, 130n

Daily Maroon, 47–48, 143n
Daniels, Lee, xii, 84, 125n
Dawson, Richard A., 38, 137n
Deacons for Defense, 12
Delta Leader, 5
Delta Sigma Theta, 79, 80, 152n
Delta State University, 70; Black student activism at, 78
Denney, Reuel, 41, 43, 140n
Different World, A, 64
Diggs, Charles, 7
"Discussion Brings Out USM Racial Problems" (Mungai), 59
Dittmer, John, ix, 13–14, 121n, 131n
Douglass, Anna Murray, 29
Douglass, Frederick, 4, 29–30, 33
DOWN Magazine, 64
Drizin, Professor Steve, 87
Dunham, Albert, 39
Dunham, Katherine, 39

East, P. D., xi, 132n
Eastland, Senator James, 132n
Ebony, 6, 8, 137n
Ebony and Ivy: Race, Slavery, and the Troubled History of America's Universities (Wilder), xiii
Evers, Charles, 23
Evers, Medgar, 9, 10, 13, 14, 24, 86, 123n, 131n, 137n
Evers, Myrlie, 13, 22, 131n
Ewing, James, 78
Exit 13 (Piliawsky), 68
Eyes on the Prize, 7, 13

Fairley, J. C., 11
Fish, Dr. Geoffrey, 71
For Us, the Living (Evers), 13, 14
Forrest, Nathan Bedford, 68–69, 73
Forrest County Board of Education, 46
Forte, Milton W., 77, 79
Fortune, Porter, 78
Frazier, John, 58
Frederick Douglass Paper, 4
Freedom Rides, 12

Freedom's Journal, 4
Freedom50 Research Group, xii, xvii, 91, 122n, 146n, 155n

Gambrell, Deborah Jones, xiii, 71, 73, 77, 84
Gandhi, Mahatma, 45
Generations Strong Commemorative Wall, 92, 155n
Gibbs, Phillip Lafayette, 76
Giovanni, Nikki, 81
Givens, Jarvis R., 92
Green, James Earl, 76
Gregory, Dick, xiii, 11, 14, 18, 23–24, 69, 75, 126n
Gregory, Ernest E., 77

Hall, Judge Stanton, xii, 86
Harmon, Charles Green Andrews, 26, 131n
Harris, Anthony, 67–68, 72, 73
Harris, James, Sr., 72
Hattiesburg: An American City in Black and White (Sturkey), 14–15
Hattiesburg American, xi, xii, xv, 26–27, 31, 35, 36, 37, 40, 43, 44, 46, 87, 92, 95, 99, 103, 108, 125n, 131n, 132n
Hayek, F. A., 41
Hayes, Curtis, 14
Hayes, Jacqueline, 71, 148n
Helfrich, Judge Robert, 87
Higher Learning (Singleton), 63
Hill, Lance, 6, 12
Hilliard, Elbert R., 83
Hobby, T. C., xii
Hollander, Ronald A., 10, 13–14
Holloway, Dr. Eddie A., 72, 74–75, 81, 91, 152n
Hood, Jim, 87
Horhn, Senator John, 86–87
Howard University, 17, 112
Hutchins, Robert Maynard, 39–40, 41, 45, 138n, 139n, 141n

I've Got the Light of Freedom (Payne), 14

Jackson, David, 7
Jackson Advocate, 84, 132n

Jackson Daily News, 13
Jackson State College, 73; murder at, 76
Jefferson, Thomas, 29, 133n
Jet, xiii, xiv, 3, 6, 7, 15, 128n; Beauty of the Week in, 124n; and Emmett Till coverage, 7–8, 11, 15–16, 130n; as historical account, 4, 15; humanization of Black life in, 8, 9–10; Kennard coverage in, 9–10, 11–12, 13–14, 15, 16–24, 130n
Johnson, John H., 6
Jones, Charlie, 75
Journal of Negro History, 39
Just, Ernest Everett, 39

Kelly Settlement, vii, 46
Kennard, Clyde: activism through writing, x, xiii, xv, 9, 26–29, 31; African American liberalism and, 33, 43; arrests and framing of, xii, xvi, 9–10, 13–14, 16–17, 56, 62, 79, 84, 86, 88, 125n; attempts to enroll at MSC (USM), x–xi, 8, 9, 16, 21, 26, 30, 32, 42, 47, 50, 54–56, 60, 62, 63, 71, 92, 103–7, 112, 114, 132n, 136n, 142n; on character, 33–34; early life, x; exoneration of, 15, 60–61, 64, 86–88; funeral of, 23; humanization of, 9, 12, 16, 28; as integrationist, ix, xiv, 16–17, 28, 31, 32–34, 36–37, 42–44, 88, 95–98, 99–101, 137n; letters to the editor as epistolary essays, 27–28, 30; as martyr, xiii, 9, 23, 121n, 135n; medical treatment, lack of adequate, 10, 11, 12, 18–19, 20–21; military service, x, 3, 16, 17, 18, 19, 21, 22, 130n; and prison reform, 21; victim narrative of, xiii, xv, 13, 14–15, 17, 19–20, 23–24, 26, 31, 38, 53, 88
Kennedy, James, 78
Kennedy, President John F., 10–11
Kennedy, Robert, 11, 18
"Kick Up the Dust" (King), 34–35, 135n
Kimpton, Lawrence, 45–46, 141n
King, Clennon, 13, 123n
King, Derek R., 15, 127n
King, Ed, 83

King, Dr. Martin Luther, Jr., 12, 34–36, 38, 126n, 130n, 135n; open format letters of, 34–35
Knight, Frank H., 41, 139n

Ladner, Dorie, 8, 11, 12, 14, 22
Ladner, Heber, 83
Ladner, Joyce, 8, 14
"Letter from a Birmingham Jail" (King), 35–36
Liddell, Colia, 5
Life, 8
Local People (Dittmer), 13
Locke, John, 36, 37, 101, 136n
Lonely Crowd, The (Denney and Resman), 41, 139n, 140n
Look, 8
Lucas, Aubrey, 25–26, 36, 54, 59, 60, 63, 82–83, 84, 85, 87, 125n, 136n, 137n, 146n, 153n
Lynching of Emmett Till, The (Metress), 7–8

Malcolm X, 69, 75
Malone, Maurice, 55
Mantinband, Rabbi Charles, xi
Mays, Benjamin E., 39
McArthur, Charles, 75, 85
McCain, William D., x–xi, 21, 25, 36, 54, 57–58, 60, 62, 77, 79–80, 84, 108, 121n, 125n, 136n, 151n
McKeon, Richard P., 41, 43–45, 140n, 142n
McLemore, Dr. Leslie, 92
Measure of Progress: The Clyde Kennard Story (Steele), 91, 133n
Meredith, James, xiv, 3, 10, 12, 13, 18, 19, 30, 49, 57, 68, 84, 123n, 128n, 135n
Metress, Chris, 7
Mill, John Stuart, 36, 37, 101, 136n
Miller, Melvin, 71–72, 73, 74, 76, 77, 78–79, 149n, 150n, 151n
Minchin, Timothy, ix, xii, 9, 14, 145n
Mississippi Department of Archives and History, 14, 83, 131n, 141n
Mississippi Enterprise, 5
Mississippi Free Press, 10–11

Mississippi Freedom Democratic Party Newsletter, 5
Mississippi Freedom Trail, xvii, 12
Mississippi Southern College (MSC), x, xii–xiv, 3, 9, 24, 25–26, 49, 54, 60, 70, 72, 95, 103–6, 108, 121n, 125n. *See also* University of Southern Mississippi
Mississippi State Sovereignty Commission, xi–xii, 14–15, 26, 55–56, 62, 77, 83–84, 86, 88, 131n, 132n, 137n
Mississippi State Sovereignty Commission, The (Katagiri), 13
Mitchell, Jerry, ix–x, 83–84, 86
"Mixing" (Kennard), 26–27, 32, 45, 95–98
Mobile-Bouie neighborhood, 72, 74, 93
Moses, Bob, 10, 12, 14, 126n
Mt. Carmel Missionary Baptist Church, 74–75
Mungai, Daniel, 59

National Association for the Advancement of Colored People (NAACP), xi, xiii, 5, 7, 9–10, 11, 12, 13, 14, 18, 22, 33, 55, 70, 80, 86, 112
Negro History Bulletin, 39
Nelson, Jack, 6–7
Nixon, President Richard, 80
Nixon, Judge Walter, Jr., 77–78
North Jackson Action, 5
North Star, 4, 29
Northwestern University Law School's Center on Wrongful Convictions, 87
Notes on the State of Virginia (Banneker), 29

Occom, Samson, 28–29, 133n
Omega Psi Phi, 79
Order of the Eastern Star, 13
Oubre, Willie V., 77
Oxford, Mississippi, 10, 49, 57, 58. *See also* University of Mississippi

Parting the Waters: America in the King Years, 1954-63 (Branch), 13
"Paul's Letter to American Christians" (King), 35, 135n

Peters, Richard A., 77
Pickering, Charles, 87
Piliawsky, Monte, 68
Pillar of Fire (Branch), 11, 14
Piney Woods School, 72
Pittsburgh Courier, 6, 17
Posey, Roderick, 80
Prairie View A & M University, 68, 72
Price, John Ellis, 67, 79
Pullman porters, 6
Purdue University, 64

"Race Question, The" (Kennard), 26, 36–37, 45, 99–102
Redd, Jacqueline Kay, 81
Reisman, David, 41, 43, 140n
Reiter, John, xi, xii
Right to Revolt, The (Boyett), 14–15
Roberts, Johnny Lee, xii–xiii, 20, 86–87
Rosenwald, Julius, 46–47, 142n
Rousseau, Jean, 36, 37, 101, 136n
Rowan High School, 70
Roy, C. E., xi
Ruffin, Susie B., 5

Salmond, John, xi, xii, 9, 14, 147n
Salter, John, 83
School Daze (Lee), 63
"School Mix" (Kennard), 26, 37, 45, 103–7
Schwab, Joseph J., 41
Sellers, Cleveland, 8
Selma to Montgomery March, 12
Simpson, Georgiana, 39
Sims, Juanita, 79
Slow, Calculated Lynching, A: The Story of Clyde Kennard (Anderson), x, 15
Somalia, 59
Southerner, 70, 75, 151n
Speake, Phillip R., 77
Starlight Missionary Baptist Church, 74–75
Stennis, Senator John, 132n
Still, Larry, xiii, 11–13, 18–19, 22, 44
Student Nonviolent Coordinating Committee (SNCC), xiii, 10, 11, 14, 18

Student Printz, vii, xv, xvi, 49–65, 70, 82, 84, 151n
Sturkey, William, 6, 7, 14

Tarpley, Sarah, 11, 12–13, 18, 20, 112
Thames, Shelby, 87
Thames Middle School, 72
Thomas, Dr. Andrew, 22, 112n
Thompson-Morton, Cheryl, 8
Three Years in Mississippi (Meredith), 13
Till, Emmett, xv, 6, 7–8, 11–12, 15–16, 17, 19, 20, 23, 124n, 127n, 129n, 130n
Till, Mamie Bradley, 7, 23, 124n, 127n
Tisdale, Charles, 84
"To My Old Master, Thomas Auld," (Douglass), 29–30
Tougaloo College, 12, 18, 73
Towne, Celia, 47–48, 110
Turner, Charles H., 39
Turner, Lorenzo Dow, 39
Tuskegee Institute, 39

Unheard Word, xvi, 49–50, 51–52, 53–54, 56, 59, 60–61, 63, 64, 82, 84–85; Aubrey Lucas interview in, 49–50, 60–61. *See also* Brown, Riva
University of Chicago, x, xii, 16–17, 31, 38–40, 45, 47–48, 55, 62, 110, 116, 136n, 138n, 139n, 142n, 143n; and the New Plan, 40–42
University of Mississippi, xiii–xiv, 10–11, 12, 13, 18, 20, 30, 49, 57–58, 70, 74, 78, 84, 91, 123n, 135n, 155n; Black student activism at, 78. *See also* Meredith, James
University of Southern Mississippi (USM), xiii–xvii, 24, 49, 60; Black cultural spaces at, 71–73; Black Greek organizations at, 79; Black student activism at, 76, 77, 82–83; Celebration of Diversity at, 85; Center for Black Studies, 92; Clyde Kennard Day at, 84–85; and "Dixie," 80; and General Nat mascot, 73–74, 80; integration of, 56–57, 69–70; Kennard building dedication, 92. *See also* Mississippi Southern College (MSC)

Wade, Daisy Harris, 72, 75
Ward, Charlie, xii, 125n
Washington, Booker T., 39, 46–47
Washington, Walter, 85, 92
Watkins, Hollis, 14
Weathers, Jon Mark, 87
Webb, Reverend John, 84
Wheatley, Phillis, 28–30
White, Governor Hugh Lawson, 132n
Wideman, John Edgard, 15–16
Williams, Alvin J., 74, 80
Winter, William, 83
Woodson, Carter G., 38–39
Work, Monroe Nathan, 39

ABOUT THE AUTHORS

Photo by Kate Kenealy, Penn State College of the Liberal Arts

Sherita L. Johnson is director of the College of Liberal Arts' Africana Research Center and associate professor of English at Pennsylvania State University. She is author of *Black Women in New South Literature and Culture*.

Photo by Talladega College Office of Communications & Marketing

Cheryl D. Jenkins is chair of the Mass Media Studies Department and associate professor in the School of Humanities and Fine Arts at Talladega College. She is coauthor of *Race and News: Critical Perspectives*.

Photo courtesy of the author

Loren Saxton Coleman is assistant professor and director of graduate studies in the Communication, Culture, and Media Studies Department in the Cathy Hughes School of Communications at Howard University. She is coeditor of *Media, Myth, and Millennials: Critical Perspectives on Race and Culture*.

Photo by Kelly Dunn

Rebecca A. Tuuri is associate professor of history and associate dean of the Honors College at the University of Southern Mississippi. She is author of *Strategic Sisterhood: The National Council of Negro Women in the Black Freedom Struggle*, which won the Julia Cherry Spruill Prize from the Southern Association of Women Historians.

www.ingramcontent.com/pod-product-compliance
Lightning Source LLC
Chambersburg PA
CBHW030236240426
43663CB00037B/1169